T0301757

Lecture Notes in
International
Trade Theory
Classical Trade and Applications

World Scientific Lecture Notes in Economics and Policy

ISSN: 2630-4872

Series Editor: Ariel Dinar *(University of California, Riverside, USA)*

The World Scientific Lecture Notes in Economics and Policy series is aimed to produce lecture note texts for a wide range of economics disciplines, both theoretical and applied at the undergraduate and graduate levels. Contributors to the series are highly ranked and experienced professors of economics who see in publication of their lectures a mission to disseminate the teaching of economics in an affordable manner to students and other readers interested in enriching their knowledge of economic topics. The series was formerly titled World Scientific Lecture Notes in Economics.

Published:

Vol. 10: *Lecture Notes in International Trade Theory: Classical Trade and Applications*
by Larry S. Karp

Vol. 9: *Lecture Notes in International Trade: An Undergraduate Course*
by Priyaranjan Jha

Vol. 8: *Lecture Notes in State and Local Public Finance: (Parts I and II)*
by John Yinger

Vol. 7: *Economics, Game Theory and International Environmental Agreements: The Ca' Foscari Lectures*
by Henry Tulkens

Vol. 6: *Modeling Strategic Behavior: A Graduate Introduction to Game Theory and Mechanism Design*
by George J. Mailath

Vol. 5: *Lecture Notes in Public Budgeting and Financial Management*
by William Duncombe

Vol. 4: *Lecture Notes in Urban Economics and Urban Policy*
by John Yinger

Vol. 3: *Econometric Models for Industrial Organization*
by Matthew Shum

For the complete list of volumes in this series, please visit
www.worldscientific.com/series/wslnep

World Scientific Lecture Notes in Economics and Policy – Vol. 10

Lecture Notes in International Trade Theory

Classical Trade and Applications

Larry S Karp
University of California, Berkeley, USA

W World Scientific

NEW JERSEY · LONDON · SINGAPORE · BEIJING · SHANGHAI · HONG KONG · TAIPEI · CHENNAI · TOKYO

Published by

World Scientific Publishing Co. Pte. Ltd.

5 Toh Tuck Link, Singapore 596224

USA office: 27 Warren Street, Suite 401-402, Hackensack, NJ 07601

UK office: 57 Shelton Street, Covent Garden, London WC2H 9HE

Library of Congress Control Number: 2021949595

British Library Cataloguing-in-Publication Data
A catalogue record for this book is available from the British Library.

World Scientific Lecture Notes in Economics and Policy — Vol. 10
LECTURE NOTES IN INTERNATIONAL TRADE THEORY
Classical Trade and Applications

Copyright © 2022 by World Scientific Publishing Co. Pte. Ltd.

ISBN 978-981-124-986-0 (hardcover)
ISBN 978-981-124-987-7 (ebook for institutions)
ISBN 978-981-124-988-4 (ebook for individuals)

For any available supplementary material, please visit
https://www.worldscientific.com/worldscibooks/10.1142/12658#t=suppl

Desk Editors: Aanand Jayaraman/Sylvia Koh

Typeset by Stallion Press
Email: enquiries@stallionpress.com

Printed in Singapore

To the students for whom this book was written, and to my teachers (many of whom I have never met) for making it possible.

Preface

I developed these lecture notes in International Trade for an introductory PhD class and for a MSc class. Both courses contained about 22 hours of lectures. The notes cover major results in classical trade theory (the Ricardian, Ricardo–Viner and Heckscher–Ohlin–Samuelson model); they do not include later work that emphasizes monopolistic competition and intra-industry trade. The material in these notes should put students in a good position to take an advanced course in International Trade, but the notes are not a substitute for such a course.

Classical trade theory provides a good foundation for understanding the linkages between factor and commodity markets, i.e. general equilibrium relations. A basic knowledge of those relations, particularly in an open economy setting, equips students with a better chance of making sense of economic events.

Themes associated with the Theory of the Second Best figure prominently in these notes. This choice reflects my view that most interesting policy questions, across many fields of economics, involve a second-best setting. I also found that most students had at best a rudimentary understanding of this theory. I hoped that students leaving this course would instinctively look for a second-best angle when confronting policy questions, avoiding the temptation to reflexively apply intuition based on the assumption that markets are efficient — intuition that students worked so hard to acquire as undergraduates.

This is a course in applied microeconomics. Its two main objectives, providing a basic understanding of general equilibrium linkages and of second-best analysis, are closely related. Many of the most interesting and subtle second-best problems arise from the links between commodity and factor markets.

The material considers a number of applications related to resource and environmental economics, reflecting my interests and those of many of my students. Environmental and resource economics is a particularly fertile ground for second-best problems. In a few places I digress from both international trade and general equilibrium issues to address gaps that were evident, over a period of years, in students' knowledge base. For example, there is a short section on taxes in an autarchic partial equilibrium setting. I emphasize the relation between comparative statics exercises in optimization problems — which most students have a command of — and comparative statics in equilibrium problems — which many students have not seen.

To emphasize intuition rather than technicalities, I rely on two commodity, two country, two factor models $(2 \times 2 \times 2)$. The notes lean heavily on graphical methods, but most of the material also provides formal arguments using calculus. By focusing on the two-country two-commodity setting, the calculations remain straightforward, although in some cases they become lengthy. This material is important for PhD students, where an ancillary goal is to improve their modelling skills.

I developed these notes over a decade without intending to make them available as a book. Therefore, the notes do not include the citations that one expects from a textbook. Given that time is finite and my memory imperfect, I have not attempted to go back and insert citations. Instead, I will use this opportunity to indicate my major intellectual debts, with apologies to all of the people who I learned from but forget at this time to mention. My primary intellectual debt in this field is to J. Bhagwati, A. Panagariya, and T.N. Srinivasan. I cut my teeth on international trade, and especially on the role of the Theory of the Second Best, from a series of papers by combinations of those authors, culminating in their textbook *Lectures on International Trade*. I also appreciated and learned from N. Vousden's brief and informative survey *The Economics of Trade Protection*. I have drawn on insights about trade and natural resources and the environment contained in a series of papers involving a combination of J. Brander, B. Copeland and M.S. Taylor, and especially from Copeland and Taylor's *Trade and the Environment*. I have also drawn heavily from individual articles by G. Chichilniski and by L. Hotte, N. van Long, and H. Tian. I have used many of D. Newbery's sole and coauthored papers as a source of examples in these notes. I have also benefitted from a series of papers by A. Dixit, although the topics of those papers remains largely in the background in these notes. Finally, I thank A. McCalla for my first course in international trade as a second year graduate student, and in particular for introducing me to the theory of the second best, when the scales fell from my eyes.

About the Author

Larry Karp is a professor of Agricultural and Resource Economics at the University of California, Berkeley. He has also taught at Texas A&M and at Southampton University. His research interests include international trade policy, natural resource economics, industrial organization, and game theory. His recent research focuses on climate economics. His previous books are *Natural Resources as Capital* (MIT Press 2017) and (with J. Perloff and A. Golan) *Estimating Market Power and Strategies* (Cambridge University Press, 2007).

About the Book

These notes cover the fundamental models and results in classical trade, using both graphical and analytic methods. The material emphasizes second-best settings. The goal is to equip students with a good enough understanding of general equilibrium relations that they see how distortions ripple across different markets, e.g. commodity and factor markets.

Contents

Chapter 1

Introduction

These lectures present and apply the basic models and theorems of classical trade theory. However, a broader and more important objective is to improve students' ability to understand general equilibrium relations in both open and closed economies. Commodity markets and factor (e.g. capital and labor) markets are inextricably linked; the neck bone is connected to the toe bone. General equilibrium analysis explains these connections. By linking commodity markets across countries, international trade also links the countries' factor markets.

Basic theory at both the graduate and undergraduate level frequently emphasizes how markets work when they work well. These notes emphasize the consequence of market failures in a general equilibrium setting. Basic theory equips students with intuition about the effects of changes in, for example, technology or policy. By the end of this course, I hope that students have the tools to know when they should be skeptical of that intuition, and more significantly have an idea of how to modify it.

After describing the content of these lecture notes, I address a number of questions that frequently arose during the years that I taught the material.

Chapter 2 discusses the Ricardian model, relying primarily on an example. The chapter explains the meaning of comparative advantage, emphasizing the difference between comparative and absolute advantage. It presents a general equilibrium model that shows the relation between commodity prices and the price of labor, the sole factor of production. It then introduces the concept of the real wage, as distinct from the nominal wage, and shows how changes in commodity prices alter the real wage.

Using (primarily) graphical methods, I ask and answer comparative statics questions, showing how changes in technology or a move from autarchy (= no trade) to free trade changes welfare. I use the general equilibrium relations to construct a country's export supply and import demand functions, emphasizing the differences between these and familiar partial equilibrium demand and supply functions. The chapter also reviews intermediate tools, including the indirect utility function, differentials of functions, and the envelope theorem.

The assumptions about technology are central to the Ricardian model. Chapter 3 leaves technology in the background, assuming only that the production possibility frontier is strictly concave. In this setting, graphical methods make it easy to describe the equilibrium, and to determine how it changes with a change in policy. I illustrate the procedure by showing how different taxes (including tariffs), and different types of redistribution of tax revenue, change production, consumption, trade, and welfare. I then use these graphical tools to obtain the import demand and supply functions under trade. The intersection(s) of these curves give the equilibrium world price(s).

I introduce the concept of stability, imbedding the static model in a dynamic framework using the fiction of a Walrasian auctioneer. In an equilibrium problem, the assumption that an equilibrium is stable plays essentially the same role in conducting comparative static experiments, as does the second order condition in an optimization problem. Chapter 3 contains a section that collects technical details, and also a section that reviews taxes in a partial equilibrium setting.

The next chapter contains three applications of the model described in Chapter 3. I chose these examples for their intrinsic interest and for their value in illustrating methods. The first application shows a possible pitfall of using trade openness (defined as the value of imports over the value of national output) as a proxy for the liberality of trade policy. Many empirical studies have used this proxy to estimate whether liberal trade policies promote economic growth.

The problem is that openness might be either positively or negatively correlated with the liberality of a trade policy, making its use as a proxy for trade policy problematic.

The second application considers a famous economic question known as the Transfer Problem: how does a transfer (e.g. war reparations) from one country to another affect the terms of trade between these two countries? The answer to this question depends on the magnitude of the trading partners' marginal propensities to consume their respective import goods. We obtain this answer using comparative statics and the assumption that the pre-transfer equilibrium is stable. This application therefore illustrates the role of the stability assumption.

The third application compares a partial and a general equilibrium model of leakage, defined as the increase in pollution in a group of countries due to a decrease in pollution elsewhere. In the partial equilibrium model, pollution reductions in a group of countries are at least partly undone by increased pollution elsewhere: leakage is positive. However, in the general equilibrium setting, where income effects can be important, leakage might be either positive or negative.

Chapter 5 explains and illustrates the Theory of the Second Best (TOSB). This emphasis, which is unusual in a short course in applied microeconomics, reflects my view of the TOSB's importance, relative to (most) students' level of exposure to the ideas underlying it. This chapter makes extensive use of the graphical approach developed in Chapter 3 and the mathematical tools presented in several chapters.

The first general equilibrium example shows that trade liberalization in the presence of fixed distortionary domestic taxes can raise or lower welfare. The second example concerns missing markets: the creation of an international market (opening up to trade) might raise or lower welfare when insurance markets are missing. I then use a rather non-standard definition of "distortion" to discuss the possibility that growth can be immizerizing. This stretched definition shows the power of the TOSB to provide a unified framework for studying a range of economic issues. The final example shows that achieving an exogenous constraint suboptimally constitutes a distortion, thereby creating another setting in which the TOSB is relevant. This application also provides an opportunity to introduce the Principle of Targeting.

Chapter 6 presents the Ricardo–Viner model with one mobile factor, labor, and other factors that are fixed in the two sectors. I show the relation between output, labor allocation, and factor prices as a function of the relative commodity price. As the economy moves from autarchy to trade, or as the price at which it trade changes, it is easy to map out the changes in labor allocation and factor prices. This material therefore provides practice in working through a simple general equilibrium model with more structure than the model studied in Chapter 3.

Chapter 6 contains two applications, involving imperfect property rights and a minimum wage constraint, both discussed through the lens of the TOSB. I show how the autarchic equilibrium depends on the level of property rights and level of the minimum wage in the two settings, and the effect of opening up to trade in both scenarios. A final section extends the minimum wage model by considering the effect of adjustment of the specific factors, holding the trade regime fixed. As the (erstwhile) sector-specific capital flows to the sector with higher private returns, social welfare might either increase or decrease — yet another example of the TOSB.

Chapter 7 presents and explains the four theorems of the Heckscher–Ohlin–Samuelson (HOS) model. The Factor Price Equalization Theorem provides conditions under which trade in commodities results in international equality of factor prices. When these conditions hold, trade in commodities is a perfect substitute for trade in factors. The Stolper–Samuelson Theorem establishes the relation between relative commodity prices and real factor returns. This theorem provides a clear illustration of the fact that trade harms some factor owners even when it increases national income. The Rybczynski Theorem shows how a change in factor endowments changes output at a given commodity price. The HOS Theorem establishes the relation between countries' relative factor endowments and their comparative advantage.

This chapter provides the final example of immizerizing growth. It also shows that when a country imposes both a restriction on commodity trade and on trade in factors, liberalization of one of those two markets has ambiguous welfare effects. This possibility is another example of the TOSB, which by this point students should find natural. To the extent that the course is successful, students have a strong enough command of general equilibrium analysis to determine the forces that determine the direction of welfare effect of liberalizing capital markets under a fixed commodity tariff.

Appendix B collects problem sets and Appendix C provides most of the answers. Most of the problems are based on the general equilibrium material presented in the text, and provide practice using the methods developed there. However, several problems use partial equilibrium models. The partial equilibrium models (some of which are challenging) illustrate the possibility that partial and general equilibrium models can produce different answers to apparently similar questions. These differences illustrate the importance of channels of causation (e.g. income effects) that are present in the general equilibrium setting, but absent in the partial equilibrium setting.

I also take this opportunity to address some issues that frequently arose during the years I taught this material. Many students are unclear about the distinction between a partial and general equilibrium model. The former treats all prices except for the price of the good under consideration as exogenous. For example, the level of income and the prices of substitutes and complements, which affect the demand function, are taken as exogenous; and the prices of inputs which affect the supply function are taken as exogenous. Changes in the exogenous variables (prices, income, tastes) change the location of the partial equilibrium supply and/or demand function, changing the equilibrium price of the commodity in question. A general equilibrium model has at least two endogenous prices. In most of the models in this course, the prices of factors of production, such as capital and labor, and thus the level of income, are jointly determined with the relative price of commodities.

The choice to use a partial or a general equilibrium model seems arbitrary to some students. Because partial equilibrium models are usually simpler, they provide a good place to start most analyses.

But sometimes indirect effects, such as those operating through changes in factor prices or changes in income, can be important and can qualify or even reverse the conclusions from partial equilibrium models. You do not know until you look. For example, Section 4.4 of Chapter 4 shows that although environmental "leakage" (defined above) is always greater than or equal to zero in a partial equilibrium model, it might be negative once we take into account general equilibrium effects, e.g. those related to changes in income.

Many students are sensitive to the lack of realism in the models presented here. I try to persuade them that a model can be revealing even if it is not accurate. I like Jorge Luis Borges' short story "On exactitude in science" and Alfred Korzybski's aphorism "the map is not the territory" for this purpose. The Ricardian model is absurdly unrealistic, or wonderfully elegant, depending on your point of view. After Chapter 2, students should ask themselves whether they have a better understanding of: comparative advantage; the relation between commodity and factor prices; and how to determine the welfare-effect of an exogenous change. If the answer to any of these questions is "yes" it is probably because of model simplicity, not realism.

The models discussed here use a representative agent. In contexts where there is a single type of agent, this assumption is innocuous. In the Ricardian model, labor is the only factor of production. With nothing to distinguish one worker from another, it seems innocuous to assume that they all have the same preferences and income and face the same prices: any worker is literally the representative worker. In even slightly more complicated models, it is not reasonable to assume that everyone in the economy has the same income. Often I assume that agents have identical homothetic preferences, so that differences in income do not preclude aggregation. I also invoke a social planner who somehow aggregates the preferences of agents in the economy.

These lectures — with only a few digressions — consist of applied theory; they rely on graphical and mathematical methods. As a matter of personal preference, I try to avoid using extended math in oral lectures: that leads to a race to see who goes to sleep first. However, the written material provides extensive mathematical derivations; these help students understand the concepts and the results. The graphs play a much larger part in the oral lectures. The written material contains most of the graphs; but as soon as a figure contains more than two or three curves, it becomes difficult to read. For that reason, it is essential that students gain command of the construction presented in Chapter 3, where I explain the use of three curves: the production possibility frontier, the income expansion path, and the balance of payments constraint. If students understand exactly what these curves mean, and what causes them to shift, the ensuing material is much more digestible.

Even with this solid background, students should "think with their fingers", rebuilding the figures shown. In some places I drop an important curve, simply because a figure becomes incomprehensibly cluttered it the curve is included. There, I provide a verbal description of the missing curve and explain its role. Students who master the construction presented in Chapter 3 will be able to supply the missing curve. Even though the resulting figure will be cluttered, the fact that the student has created the clutter means that it is comprehensible.

Chapter 2

Ricardian Model

2.1 Introduction

The Ricardian model provides the simplest general equilibrium setting to illustrate comparative advantage and the gains from trade. This chapter uses a two-country two-commodity version of the Ricardian model. It has the following objectives:

- Introduce the concept of comparative advantage: A country has a comparative advantage a commodity if the ratio between its pre-trade marginal costs of producing that commodity and of the other commodity is lower than its trading partner's corresponding ratio.
- Illustrate the use of equilibrium conditions (here, zero profit conditions) to determine endogenous variables (here, relative prices).
- Provide a simple setting in which to understand the relation between commodity prices and factor prices.
- Explain the meaning of "real returns to a factor" and show how trade affects this "real return".
- Combine these tools to conduct comparative statics experiments, e.g. to show how a change in technology affects equilibrium welfare.

The example used to explain the Ricardian model involves two countries, Canada and the US, who both produce two commodities, corn and umbrellas. The alliteration is a mnemonic device. It may become tiresome to read about corn and umbrellas, but not more so than reading about commodities 1 and 2. It is easier to refer to "corn" than "commodity 1", and it is easier to refer to "Canada" than to "the country with the comparative advantage in commodity 1". In some places, e.g. as variable indices, it is convenient to use the numbers 1 and 2 instead of the names.

2.2 Technology and Markets

The Ricardian model assumes that production uses only 1 input, called labor, with constant returns to scale. This assumption means that the technology in each country and each sector is entirely determined by that sector's labor requirement per unit of output. The other assumptions are that (a) labor moves freely between sectors within a country, but (b) labor cannot move between countries. Assumption (a) implies that in a particular country, the wage must be the same in both sectors when both have positive production; assumption (b) means that the wage need not be the same (and typically is not the same) in the two countries. In addition, we assume that all agents are price takers, i.e. there is perfect competition, and there are no externalities (spillovers).

Table 2.1 summarizes our numerical example. The entries give the unit labor requirements for corn (good 1) and umbrellas (good 2). Subscripts indicate commodity, superscripts indicate country. The example states that in the US both goods require one unit of labor

Table 2.1. Labor requirements.

	Unit labor requirement	
	Corn (Good 1)	Umbrellas (Good 2)
US	$a_1^u = 1$	$a_2^u = 1$
Canada	$a_1^c = 3$	$a_2^c = 6$

to produce one unit of output. This assumption is without loss of generality; it amounts to a choice of units.[1]

Production of both goods require less labor in the US than in Canada. In this example, the US has an absolute advantage in the production of both goods. This assumption does not reflect anti-Canadian bias, but helps to emphasize that comparative and absolute advantage are distinct concepts. The gains from trade are *not related* to absolute advantage. In this and in more general models, a "country" benefits from trade if and only if the relative prices at which it can trade differ from the equilibrium autarchic relative prices. In this example, Canada needs more labor to produce either commodity, so it is less productive than the US; but both countries have a comparative advantage in one of the two commodities. At least one country gains from trade, and both countries gain if the equilibrium relative price differs from both autarchic relative prices.

We speak of a "country" as benefiting from trade. In this model with a single homogenous factor of production, there is no distinction between the benefit to individuals and the "benefit to the country". We return to this issue later, where it is important to recognize that trade liberalization, as with many other policy changes, has different effects for different types of agents.

In the numerical example above, the relative production costs in the two countries are different. This fact means that the efficient pattern of production requires at least one country to specialize. To convince yourself of this conclusion, suppose to the contrary that both countries produce both goods. How should a social planner reallocate labor to (weakly) increase output of both goods?[2] To answer that question, suppose that we increase production of corn by one unit in the US and decrease production of corn by one unit in

---

[1]For example, if it takes half an hour to produce 10 bushels of corn, we can choose a "unit" of labor time to be half an hour, and a "unit" of corn to be 10 bushels. With this choice of units, it takes one unit of labor to produce one unit of corn.
[2]The statement that aggregate production of both commodities "weakly" increases means that the production of at least one commodity strictly increases, and the production of neither commodity decreases.

Canada, so that aggregate corn production remains the same. Given full employment, the additional unit of labor required in the US corn sector results in a loss of one umbrella; the three units of labor released from Canada's corn sector produce half an umbrella, for a net loss of half an umbrella, with no change in corn production. This reallocation does not (weakly) increase production of both commodities.

Now try the opposite experiment: decrease the production of corn by one unit in the US and increase the production of corn by one unit in Canada. Using the same reasoning as above, we see that this change results in a net increase of half an umbrella, with no change in corn production: aggregate production of both commodities weakly increases. The example illustrates the fact that if we begin in a situation where both countries produce both commodities, we can weakly increase aggregate production by reallocating labor so that Canada produces more corn and the US produces more umbrellas.

The *opportunity cost* of producing corn, for example, is the number of umbrellas that need to be sacrificed to obtain an additional unit of corn.

$$\text{US corn opportunity cost} = \frac{a_1^u}{a_2^u} = \frac{1}{1} > \text{Canadian corn opportunity cost} = \frac{a_1^c}{a_2^c} = \frac{3}{6}.$$

In Canada, the opportunity cost of producing one unit of corn is the loss of $1/2$ umbrella. The extra unit of corn requires three units of labor, leading to the loss of $1/2$ unit of umbrella. In the US, the opportunity cost of producing 1 unit of corn is the loss of 1 umbrella. Canada has a lower opportunity cost of producing corn.

The statement that Canada has a lower opportunity cost of corn (something that is determined by only the relation between relative — as distinct from absolute — input requirements) is equivalent to the statement that Canada has a comparative advantage in corn.

Denote the wage in Canada as w^c and the wage in the US as w^u. The marginal cost of producing corn in Canada is $w^c a_1^c$ and the marginal cost of producing umbrellas is $w^c a_2^c$. The ratio of these marginal costs depends only on the technological parameters, the labor input requirements — not on the wage. Therefore, the technology in the two countries determines the pattern of comparative advantage. In more general models discussed in later chapters, technology is one of several factors that determine the pattern of comparative advantage.

In the Ricardian model, by knowing the labor input coefficients and of the total stock of labor we can graph the production possibility frontier. Suppose that the amount of labor in Canada is $L^c = 120$ and the amount of labor in the US is $L^u = 200$. Denoting the amount of corn and umbrella production as c and u, the full employment condition in Canada is $3c + 6u = 120$, and the full employment condition in the US is $c + u = 200$. Figures 2.1 and 2.2 graph these equations, showing the production possibility frontiers (PPFs) for the two countries. The figures are not to scale. A wavy curve indicates the slope of a line.

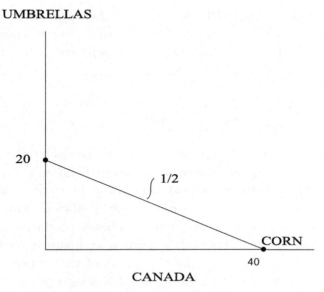

Figure 2.1. Production possibility frontier for Canada.

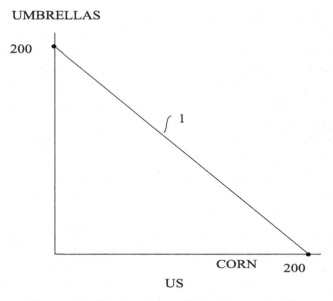

Figure 2.2. Production possibility frontier for US.

The slope of the PPF depends on the ratio of labor input requirements, not the absolute amounts of the requirements. The marginal rate of transformation of umbrellas for corn is $\frac{a_1}{a_2}$. The units of this ratio are

$$\text{units}\left(\frac{a_1}{a_2}\right) = \frac{\frac{\text{labor}}{\text{corn}}}{\frac{\text{labor}}{\text{umbrella}}} = \frac{\text{umbrella}}{\text{corn}}. \qquad (2.1)$$

The trapezoid in Figure 2.3 shows the combinations of world output that result in full employment. At any point on the trapezoid, labor is fully employed in both countries. The outer part gives the world PPF, the set where production is efficient. On the PPF Canada always produces corn and US always produces umbrellas, the commodities for which they have a comparative advantage. Production is inefficient on the inner part of the trapezoid, where Canada always produces umbrellas and US always produces corn.

The full employment conditions lead to the trapezoid shape because of the assumption that the ratio of input requirements $\frac{a_1}{a_2}$ is

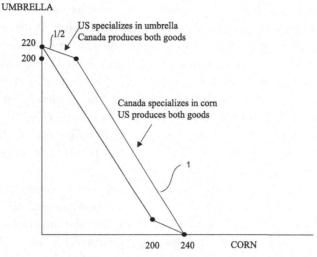

Figure 2.3. Locus of production points that involve full employment in both countries. The outer sides of the trapezoid comprise the production possibility frontier; points on the inner sides comprise the least efficient full employment allocation of inputs across counties.

different in the two countries. If this ratio was the same in the two countries, the trapezoid would collapse to a line.

2.2.1 *Commodity prices*

Economic modeling uses equilibrium conditions to determine endogenous variables. The discussion above uses the full employment condition to construct the production possibility frontier. Next, we consider the determination of prices, where the relevant equilibrium conditions are the requirements that there are zero-profits in every sector. In this simple example, it is easy to see how these conditions determine equilibrium relative prices. In some cases, neither the relevant equilibrium condition nor the way it which it is used is so obvious. The current exercise provides an example of how to proceed. Students need to understand what they are looking for (here, the equilibrium relative prices), what the equilibrium conditions are (here, the zero profit conditions) and how to use them (here, simple algebra).

In the Ricardian model, autarchic relative prices depend on technology, but not on preferences, provided that both goods are produced in equilibrium. ("autarchic" means "no trade".) Here-after we will assume that in equilibrium both commodities are consumed. Because national production equals national consumption under autarchy, both countries are incompletely specialized in autarchy. (A country is said to be "incompletely specialized" if it produces all goods — in the present example, both goods.) Trade breaks the equality between national production and national consumption.

Let p_1 be the price of corn and p_2 the price of umbrellas. The wage is w^c, w^u in Canada and the US. (Remember, labor is the only input in the Ricardian model.) What are the autarchic prices in Canada? Suppose that both goods are produced in autarchy. With perfect competition and constant returns to scale, profits (rents) must be 0. We use the 0-profit conditions to find the equilibrium prices in Canada.

$$p_1^c - w^c a_1^c = 0 \quad \text{and} \quad p_2^c - w^c a_2^c = 0. \tag{2.2}$$

Denote p^c as the relative price of corn (the price of corn relative to the price of umbrellas) in autarchy in Canada. Taking the ratio of these 0-profit conditions gives

$$p^c = \frac{p_1^c}{p_2^c} = \frac{a_1^c}{a_2^c} = \frac{1}{2}. \tag{2.3}$$

Here, as in most economic models, only relative prices matter. For example, if we double all commodity prices and also double the wage, all relative prices remain the same; nothing of substance has changed. We have one degree of freedom, so we can set one price equal to 1 without loss of generality. It does not matter which commodity or factor we chose as the numeraire. In autarchy there is only one factor, but with trade there are two factors, labor in the US and labor in Canada. These are distinct factors because of the assumption that there is no international labor mobility.

The units of the relative price are (using equation (2.1))

$$\text{units} \left(\frac{p_1^c}{p_2^c} \right) = \frac{\frac{\text{dollars}}{\text{corn}}}{\frac{\text{dollars}}{\text{umbrella}}} = \frac{\text{umbrellas}}{\text{corn}} = \text{units} \left(\frac{a_1^c}{a_2^c} \right). \qquad (2.4)$$

There are (at least) three reasons it is useful to identify the units of a ratio. First, it is easy to get confused about whether we are talking about a ratio like $\frac{p_1}{p_2}$ or its inverse. If you check the units you can usually figure it out. Second, checking the units provides a "consistency check" for computations. Third, equation (2.4) shows that the units of relative prices are the same as the units of the marginal rate of transformation (MRT, the slope of the production possibility frontier). We know that this relation has to hold, because in equilibrium the relative price has to equal the MRT.

Given incomplete specialization, *the autarchic relative price is determined by technology in the Ricardian model*; this result is due to Ricardian production technology, and does not hold more generally.

The autarchic relative price in the US is

$$p^u = \frac{p_1^u}{p_2^u} = \frac{a_1^u}{a_2^u} = \frac{1}{1}.$$

Canada has a comparative advantage in corn if and only if the Canadian autarchic relative price of corn (equal to Canada's ratio of marginal costs) is lower than the US autarchic relative price. This inequality holds in the numerical example.

2.3 Relative Prices Under Free Trade

The equilibrium relative price under trade is the price that actually arises when the two countries trade. With trade, the equilibrium relative price depends not only on technology (as is the case under autarchy), but also on demand. Demand depends on taste, i.e. on preferences, as well as on prices and income. Section 2.11 shows how the equilibrium price is determined. For the time being, we take this price as given. Depending on the equilibrium price, world production could occur on regions A or C or at point B, on the production possibility frontier shown in Figure 2.4. We now describe the pattern

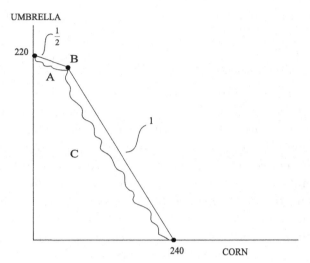

Figure 2.4. World production possibility frontier with three regions: in A US is specialized; in C Canada is specialized; and at B both are specialized.

of production and trade, and the change in welfare relative to the autarchic level, in these three regions.

Assume that there are 0 transportation costs and no government interventions in the market, e.g. no commodity taxes or trade restrictions. These assumptions imply that under trade, the relative price *is the same in both countries.* The inequality in relative autarchic prices is the motivation for trade, and is also the reason that there exist gains from trade. The equality of relative prices under trade is a *consequence* of trade. If, under free trade, the relative prices within the two countries were different, then there would be further opportunities for arbitrage. People could make money by buying a commodity where it is cheap and selling it where it is expensive. Free trade eliminates these opportunities for arbitrage.

This distinction between the "reason for trade" and the "consequence of trade" is quite obvious here, but a similar distinction crops up elsewhere in equilibrium problems where it is less obvious, e.g. in a model in Chapter 4. Students who understand this distinction would not ask "Why is there trade, given that the (relative) prices in the two countries are the same?" They know that the (relative) prices in the two countries are the same precisely because there is trade (and of course because of the assumptions that there are no transport costs or government intervention).

The *levels* of the two commodity prices (as distinct from their ratios) are related by the exchange rate, e, defined as the number of units of Foreign currency that exchanges for a unit of Home currency (e.g. the number of pesos per dollar). The Home and Foreign price of commodity i are related by $p_i = e p_i^*$. (A convention uses the "*" to denote Foreign variables.) Equality of relative prices implies equality of price *levels* if and only if the exchange rate is $e = 1$. There is no loss in generality in assuming that the exchange rate is 1. For example, suppose that initially $e = 0.1$, so 1 dollar equals 10 pesos; invent a new unit of currency, say the peseta, where one peseta equals 10 pesos. With this invention, one dollar equals one peseta, and the exchange rate with this new unit of currency is equal to 1. Therefore, there is no loss in generality in speaking as if the *levels* of commodity prices are also equal when the relative prices are equal; it is nothing more than a "normalization", i.e. a choice of units. Hereafter we use this normalization.

We will be interested in determining the actual levels of production in the two countries. For the time being, we put that question aside and merely ask what must be true under the assumption that in equilibrium production occurs on regions A or C or at point B. We consider these possibilities in turn. In region A, Canada is incompletely specialized and the US produces only umbrellas. In region C, Canada produces only corn and the US is incompletely specialized. At point B both countries are completely specialized.

Above we wrote the 0-profit condition using the equation "price = average cost". Profits in a sector are also zero if the sector shuts down. Thus, the complete description of the 0-profit condition is "price = marginal cost if production is positive, and price is less than or equal to marginal cost when production is 0". This kind of relation is sometimes described as a "complementary slackness" condition. The only possibility excluded by the 0-profit condition is that price is strictly greater than average costs.

Now confirm, as an exercise, that the ("full") 0-profit conditions (i.e., those including the inequality constraints) hold at each point on the world production possibility frontier. Consider a free trade equilibrium in region A. In this region, Canada is incompletely specialized. As we saw above, the 0 profit conditions requires that if Canada is incompletely specialized, then the relative price of corn in Canada must be $\frac{1}{2}$ (see equation (2.3)). Under free trade (given the assumptions above about 0 transport costs and the absence of government tax intervention) relative prices are equal in the two countries. Therefore, if equilibrium production occurs in region A, the world relative price of corn must be $\frac{1}{2}$ in both countries.

To confirm that this relative price "supports" production in region A, we need to verify that at this price it is an equilibrium for the US to be completely specialized. Recall that we can choose any good or factor as the numeraire; pick the US wage as numeraire, i.e. set $w^u = 1$. In Region A, where the US produces umbrellas, 0 profits in the umbrella sector requires

$$p_2 = w^u a_2^u = 1 \Rightarrow p_2 = 1. \tag{2.5}$$

Equation (2.5) and the fact that in region A the relative price of corn is 1/2 imply $p_1 = \frac{1}{2}$. In region A, corn production in the US would generate negative profit: $p_1 = \frac{1}{2} < w^u a_1^u = 1$. The US corn sector therefore shuts down.

The same logic shows that in region C, where the US is incompletely specialized, the equilibrium world relative price of corn is 1: the only relative price at which 0 profits in the US are consistent with production of both commodities. At this price, 0 profits in Canada require that the umbrella sector shuts down. At point B the relative world price of corn is between 1 and $\frac{1}{2}$ so both countries are specialized. (We ignore the knife-edge cases where production occurs at point B and the world price equals 1 or $\frac{1}{2}$; both of these prices are also consistent with complete specialization in both countries.) Thus, there is a simple relation between the equilibrium world price (or the set of prices) and the "type" of production equilibrium, i.e. whether production occurs on regions A or C or at point B.

2.4   Wages in the Two Countries

We want to know the relation between US and Canadian wage
under trade. This relation depends on the equilibrium world price,
which we saw above is related to the equilibrium levels of production
under trade. Again, we take as given the equilibrium world price
for this exercise, asking how the relation between the wages in the
two countries varies with the price. As above, use the normalization
$w^u = 1$. In region A, we saw that this normalization implies
$p_2 = 1$ (equation (2.5)). The zero profit condition for Canada,
equation (2.2), implies $w^c = \frac{1}{6}$. Thus, the Canadian wage is 1/6th
the US wage if production occurs in region A. Both countries
produce umbrellas (in region A), which under free trade (with
zero transport costs) sells for the same price. Because the US is
six times as productive as Canada in the umbrella sector, the
US equilibrium wage must be six times as large as the Canadian
wage. The equilibrium prices in region A, using the normalization
$w^u = 1$, are

$$p_1 = \frac{1}{2}, \quad p_2 = 1, \quad w^c = \frac{1}{6}, \quad w^u = 1. \tag{2.6}$$

Similarly, if production occurs in region C, the US wage is three
times as large as the Canadian wage. If production occurs at point B,
the US wage is between three and six times as large as the Canadian
wage, depending on the exact equilibrium price (which depends on
tastes).

The fact that the US wage is always higher than the Canadian
wage is due to the assumption that the US has an absolute advantage
in both commodities — it can produce either commodity using
less labor, compared to Canada. By changing the technological
coefficients in this example so that each country has an absolute
advantage in one commodity, either country might have the higher
wage. For example, replacing $a_1^c = 3$ with $a_1^c = 0.5$ in Table 2.1,
students should be able to identify the range of world prices over
which each country has the higher wage.

2.5   Trade

Recall that we assumed that in equilibrium both countries consume a positive amount of each good. This assumption implies (for this example) that in equilibrium Canada exports corn and the US exports umbrellas. More generally, countries export the commodity for which they have the comparative advantage. This conclusion does not depend on the world equilibrium price, i.e. it does not depend on whether production is on A, B or C. For example, in region A, the US is specialized in umbrellas, so it must import Corn, which Canada must export. To pay for its imports, the US must export umbrellas.

The Ricardian model demonstrates a very simple but profound point: Providing that two countries have different *relative* labor input requirements (i.e., providing that the ratio $\frac{a_1}{a_2}$ differs in the two countries), each country has a comparative advantage in one good. This fact does not depend on whether a country as an *absolute* advantage in either good. In equilibrium the wage adjusts so that the *production cost* (i.e., the cost in dollars) of a commodity is lower (more precisely: "not higher") in the country that has the lower *opportunity cost* for that commodity.

For example, consider again region A, and use the normalization $w^u = 1$ and the resulting equilibrium prices summarized in equation (2.6). In Canada it costs $\$\frac{3}{6} = \$0.5$ to produce a unit of corn. In region A, the US does not produce corn, but if it were to do so at the prevailing US wage, it would cost $1. Corn is cheaper to produce in Canada. Because (in region A) both countries produce umbrellas, the dollar cost of production of umbrellas must be the same in the two countries. Similarly, in region C, the dollar cost of producing umbrellas is lower in the US than in Canada (despite the fact that the US wage is three times higher); the dollar cost of producing corn is the same in the two countries. At point B, where both countries are completely specialized, the dollar cost of producing corn is lower in Canada, and the dollar cost of producing umbrellas is lower in the US.

2.6 National Income

In a competitive equilibrium, profits are 0. Because of the assumption of constant returns to scale, all revenue from the sale of products is returned to the factors of production. Here, where labor is the only factor of production, national income equals labor income. National income in a country is wL, where L is the stock of labor.

We hold the aggregate amount of labor in each country fixed in all of the comparative static experiments considered here. "Real" income is a measure of the amount that the country is able to consume. Thus, real income depends both on nominal income (the number of dollars that the country earns) and the commodity prices. In the Ricardian model, because labor income is equal to national income, real income is equal to the real wage times the amount of labor. Therefore, to know how an exogenous change (e.g. liberalization of trade or a change in technology or market structure) affects real income, we need to know how the change alters the real wage.

2.7 The Real Wage

Suppose that each worker sells one unit of labor, and assume that agents consume both goods. The *nominal income* of this worker equals the *nominal wage*, e.g. the salary per month (the object we denote as w). The worker's *real income* (or equivalently the *real wage*)[3] provides a measure of the agent's welfare. The real wage depends on the quantity of commodities that the worker can buy, which depends on both the nominal wage and the commodity prices.

Rather than looking for the direct welfare effect of an exogenous change (e.g. in technology or trade policy), we determine the effect of the change on the price ratios $\frac{w}{p_i}, i = 1, 2$. Using two approaches,

---

[3]The real wage and the real income are equivalent because we chose units so that each worker has one unit of labor to sell. If some workers have more labor to sell than others, their real wage is the same but their real income differs. If a worker sells ten units of labor then her nominal income is 10 times the nominal wage.

we show that the real wage is an increasing function of these two ratios. Therefore, if the exogenous change weakly increases the two ratios, we conclude that the change increases the agent's real wage (welfare); if the change weakly reduces both ratios, the change lowers the real wage. If the change increases one ratio and decreases the other ratio, then we need additional information to determine the change in welfare.

As a special case of a more general result, the analysis here also shows that a movement from autarchy to trade increases the real wage if and only if the relative commodity price under trade is *different* than the autarchic relative commodity price. The conclusion does not depend of the direction of the change in relative commodity price.

One method of relating prices to welfare defines the real wage as the number of "consumption bundles" that an agent can purchase by selling one unit of labor. A consumption bundle in the two-commodity setting can be written as (a, b) where a, b are positive numbers; one bundle consists of a units of commodity 1 and b units of commodity 2.[4] Therefore, n consumption bundles consist of an units of commodity 1 and bn units of commodity 2. The real wage *unambiguously* increases if and only if the number of consumption bundles that an agent can purchase by selling one unit of labor increases. "Unambiguously" here means that the conclusion does not depend on the specific consumption bundle, i.e. on the values of a and b.

The second method defines the real wage as the amount of utility that an individual can obtain by selling one unit of labor. The real wage increases if and only if utility increases. In this case, the statement that a particular change *unambiguously* increases

---

[4]The assumption that a and b are strictly positive, i.e. that both goods are consumed, leads to a succinct statement of the two remarks in the text. If for, example, we had $a > 0 = b$ then if $\frac{w}{p_1}$ remains constant and $\frac{w}{p_2}$ increases, the real wage is unchanged. Thus, without strictly positive values of a and b, an increase in only one of the ratios $\frac{w}{p_1}$ and $\frac{w}{p_2}$ is not sufficient for an increase in the real wage.

(or decreases) the real wage means that the sign change does not depend on the precise utility function or its parameters — any concave utility function will do.

The two approaches — using a consumption bundle or a utility function — produce, respectively.

Remark 2.1. A necessary and sufficient condition for the real wage to unambiguously increase, for any consumption bundle (i.e. for all positive values of a and b) is that $\frac{w}{p_i}$ strictly increases for at least one i, and does not fall for either i.

Remark 2.2. A necessary and sufficient condition for the real wage to unambiguously increase, for any concave utility function is that $\frac{w}{p_i}$ strictly increases for at least one i, and does not fall for either i.

These remarks mean that regardless of the approach used to construct the real wage, determining unambiguously the change in the real wage requires knowing that both $\frac{w}{p_i}$ (weakly) decrease or both (weakly) increase.

Problem Set 1 asks students to confirm these two remarks. These exercises provide practice in totally differentiating equilibrium conditions to obtain comparative statics results. Proving Remark 2.2 also provides a review of the definition of and the properties of the indirect utility function (Section 2.8), and a reminder of the Envelope Theorem. Recall that the Envelope Theorem states that the total derivative of a maximized or minimized function, with respect to a parameter, equals the *partial* derivative of that function with respect to the parameter. For example, let x be a decision variable and α a parameter, and define $\pi(\alpha) \equiv \max_x F(x, \alpha)$ as the maximized value of $F(x, \alpha)$, with and $x^*(\alpha) = \arg\max_x F(x, \alpha)$, the optimal decision as a function of α. The Envelope Theorem states

$$\frac{d\pi(\alpha)}{d\alpha} = \frac{\partial F(x^*(\alpha), \alpha)}{\partial \alpha} \tag{2.7}$$
$$\left(\text{not } \frac{\partial F(x^*(\alpha), \alpha)}{\partial \alpha} + \frac{\partial F(x^*(\alpha), \alpha)}{\partial x}\frac{dx^*(\alpha)}{d\alpha}\right).$$

In taking the derivative of $\pi(\alpha)$ we do not need to consider how a change in α changes $x^*(\alpha)$, because x has been "concentrated out" by the maximization.

To repeat the main point: Whichever approach we use to define the real wage, we can conclude that it unambiguously increases following an exogenous change if and only if $\frac{w}{p_i}$ increases for one i and does not decrease for the other i. The real wage unambiguously decreases following an exogenous change if and only if $\frac{w}{p_i}$ decreases for one i and does not increase for the other i. If the two ratios change in different directions (one strictly decreases and the other strictly increases) the change in the real wage is ambiguous. In that case, we would need to make additional assumptions about the relative magnitudes of a and b, or about parameters in the utility function, in order to determine the effect of the exogenous change on the real wage.

Recall that this model assumes perfect competition and constant returns to scale. Therefore profits (or rent) are zero, and the firm's revenue equals its payments to factors. Because there is only one factor in this model (labor), workers receive all revenue. Therefore in this model *social welfare increases if and only if the real wage increases*. (Spend a moment to consider how this conclusion would change if there were pure rents, or more than one factor of production, or another source of revenue such as a revenue from tariffs.)

In the Ricardian model a nation gains from trade if and only if the relative commodity price at which it trades is *different* from its autarchic relative price. If the relative price at which it trades is the same as its autarchic relative price, welfare is the same under autarchy and free trade. We illustrate this claim by considering region A, where equation (2.6) gives equilibrium prices and wages under trade. For Canada, the zero profit conditions in equation (2.2) must still hold, because Canada produces both commodities. Therefore, the ratio

$$\frac{w^c}{p_i} = \frac{1}{a_i^c},$$

is independent of the nominal price and wage. A movement from autarchy to free trade does not alter the technological parameters a_i^c. Consequently, the Canadian real wage (and thus, social welfare) is the same under autarchy and under free trade when production occurs on A.

For the US, the autarchic ratios are

$$\frac{w^{u,\text{autarchy}}}{p_i} = \frac{1}{a_i^u}.$$

Under trade, when production occurs in region A, the ratios are

$$\frac{w^{u,\text{trade}}}{p_1} = \frac{1}{1/2} = 2 > 1 = \frac{w^{u,\text{autarchy}}}{p_1},$$

$$\frac{w^{u,\text{trade}}}{p_2} = \frac{1}{a_2^u} = \frac{w^{u,\text{autarchy}}}{p_2}. \tag{2.8}$$

The first line of equation (2.8) implies that the movement from autarchy to trade increase $\frac{w^u}{p_1}$; the second line implies that the movement leaves $\frac{w^u}{p_2}$ unchanged. Therefore, the US real wage is higher under trade (when production is at A) than under autarchy. Here, we compare a country's real wage under autarchy and under trade. Section 2.4, in contrast, compares the US and the Canadian nominal wages.

2.8 Review of Indirect Utility Function

The indirect utility function $\tilde{V}(p_1, p_2, y)$ is defined as

$$\tilde{V}(p_1, p_2, y) = \max U(x_1, x_2)$$

$$\text{subject to } p_1 x_1 + p_2 x_2 \leq y,$$

where y is the individual's income (e.g. measured in dollars) and U is the utility function. The Lagrangian is

$$\mathcal{L} = U(x_1, x_2) + \lambda \left(y - p_1 x_1 - p_2 x_2 \right),$$

where the constraint multiplier λ equals the increase in utility for a unit increase in income. In this context, λ is often called the shadow value of income. The indirect utility function is

$$\tilde{V}(p_1, p_2, y) = \mathcal{L}^*(p_1, p_2, y) = \max_{x_i} \min_{\lambda} \mathcal{L}.$$

Here, the superscript ∗ denotes the value of a function evaluated at the optimum; in other contexts, this superscript denotes the foreign country.

The indirect utility function is homogenous of degree 0 in prices and income, i.e. doubling all prices and income leaves the individual no better or worse off. This fact enables us to write the indirect utility function in different ways.

If an individual's entire income derives from labor, and she sells one unit of labor, then $y = w$, the wage per unit time. In this case, we can write the indirect utility function as

$$\tilde{V}(p_1, p_2, y) = \tilde{V}(p_1, p_2, w) = \tilde{V}\left(\frac{p_1}{w}, \frac{p_2}{w}, \frac{w}{w}\right) \equiv \hat{V}\left(\frac{p_1}{w}, \frac{p_2}{w}\right). \quad (2.9)$$

The first equality replaces y with w. The second equality uses the homogeneity of the indirect utility function: we divide prices and income by w. The final relation is a definition; we suppress the third argument, $\frac{w}{w}$, and give the function a new name (replacing $\tilde{V}$ with $\hat{V}$). Equation (2.9) shows that the indirect utility depends on the ratios between output price and the nominal wage. Taking the derivative of the last expression with respect to these relative prices, establishes Remark 2.2.

If commodity 1 is the numeraire then the relative price $p = \frac{p_2}{p_1}$ gives the number of units of commodity 1 that can be exchanged for one unit of commodity 2 in the market; this ratio therefore gives the price of commodity 2 in units of commodity 1. The ratio $Y = \frac{y}{p_1} = \frac{w}{p_1}$ gives the number of units of commodity 1 that can be bought with y dollars. With income, y, measured in dollars and p_1 measured in dollars per kilo of commodity 1, the units of Y are

$$\frac{\text{dollars}}{\frac{\text{dollars}}{\text{kilo of commodity 1}}} = \text{kilos of commodity 1}.$$

This fact suggests an alternative expression for the indirect utility function. Instead of dividing by w as in equation (2.9), we can divide by p_1 to write the indirect utility function as

$$\tilde{V}(p_1, p_2, y) = \tilde{V}\left(\frac{p_1}{p_1}, \frac{p_2}{p_1}, \frac{y}{p_1}\right) = \tilde{V}(1, p, Y) \equiv V(p, Y). \quad (2.10)$$

Comparison of equations (2.9) and (2.10) shows that $\hat{V}\left(\frac{p_1}{w}, \frac{p_2}{w}\right) = V\left(\frac{p_2}{p_1}, Y\right)$. The left side assumes that agents have one unit of labor, which they exchange for w, so $y = w$.

2.8.1 *The differential of a function*

Recall the meaning of the "differential" of a function. If $F = F(x, y, z)$ is a differentiable function, its differential (or "total change") is

$$dF = F_x dx + F_y dy + F_z dz, \tag{2.11}$$

where the subscripts indicate partial differentiation. The total change of F equals the sum of changes due to the changes in x, y and z. For example, the change in F per unit change in x is F_x, so dx units of change in x creates $F_x dx$ change in F.

We can manipulate these operators (e.g. dx or F_x) as if they were ordinary variables. For example, the arguments x and y may depend on z. In that case, an exogenous change in z, dz, changes x and y, and thus has both a direct effect on F and indirect effects, through the changes in x and y. We can divide both sides of equation (2.11) by dz to write the total derivative of F as

$$\frac{dF}{dz} = F_x \frac{dx}{dz} + F_y \frac{dy}{dz} + F_z.$$

We could also divide both sides of equation (2.11) by (for example) F_z to write

$$\frac{dF}{F_z} = \frac{F_x}{F_z} dx + \frac{F_y}{F_z} dy + dz. \tag{2.12}$$

To interpret this equation, it helps to have in mind the units. Suppose that F is measured in kilos and z is measured in dollars. The right-hand side of equation (2.12) contains dz, which is in dollars. Consequently every other term in the equation must also be measured in units of dollars: we can only add up and compare like quantities (apples and apples, not apples and oranges). The units of dF are kilos, and the units of F_z are $\frac{\text{kilos}}{\text{dollars}}$, so the units of $\frac{dF}{F_z}$ are kilos$/(\frac{\text{kilos}}{\text{dollars}})$ = dollars, as must be the case. Thus, the left side is the change in the dollar value of kilos.

2.8.2 *Using the differential with the indirect utility function*

We now apply this machinery to the indirect utility function $V(p, Y)$ to write

$$dV = V_p dp + V_Y dY.$$

Dividing by V_Y we obtain

$$\frac{dV}{V_Y} = \frac{V_p}{V_Y} dp + dY = -C_2 dp + dY, \qquad (2.13)$$

where the last equality uses Roy's equality (also known as Roy's identity) which states that $-\frac{V_p}{V_Y}$ equals consumption of good 2, denoted C_2. If we measure income, Y, in dollars, then dY has units of dollars; all terms in the equation are in units of dollars.

The ratio $\frac{dV}{V_Y}$ measures the change in real income in units of dollars. Utility is measured in utils, so dV is the change in utils. Therefore the units of V_Y are $\frac{\text{utils}}{\text{dollars}}$, so the units of the ratio $\frac{dV}{V_Y}$ are dollars (because the units of the ratio $\text{utils}/\frac{\text{utils}}{\text{dollars}}$ are dollars, for the same reason that $a/\frac{a}{b} = b$).

Dividing a change in utility (dV) *by the marginal utility of money* (V_Y) *gives a change in utility expressed as a change in income, expressed in dollars; that is, the ratio gives a dollar value of the change.*

2.9 Gains from Trade: Another View

Above we saw that the welfare effect of moving from autarchy to trade can be determined by considering the effect of trade on the real wage. In a more general setting (with more factors and/or government transfers), it is useful to examine the effect of trade on real national income. Real national income is defined analogously to the real wage. It is the number of "consumption bundles" (defined above) that a country can purchase with total income. Alternatively, it is the amount of utility that the representative citizen can obtain.

In the Ricardian model (with free trade) all income accrues to labor, so there is no difference between the wage bill and national income; there is consequently no difference between the real wage and real national income. Keep in mind that the modifier "real" means that we deflate a nominal wage or income, either by using a consumption bundle or by using the marginal utility of income, based on a utility function.

If there were two or more factors (and free trade) payments to factors other than wages would also be part of national income. If there were trade restrictions such as tariffs, the tariff revenues would also be part of national income.

In general, the gains from trade arise because of the possibility of separating consumption from production. The production point has to lie on the PPF, and the consumption point has to lie on a budget constraint. Under autarchy, the market clearing constraint requires that consumption equals production for each good. Under trade, the market clearing constraint requires that world production equals world consumption for each good. The market clearing constraint under trade is therefore weaker than the market clearing constraint under autarchy: the latter implies the former, but the former does not imply the latter. Trade relaxes a binding constraint, and therefore leads to the possibility of welfare gains.

An individual country (just like an individual consumer) does not concern itself with the requirement that markets clear. However, the country, just like the consumer, has to live within its means. If we exclude the possibility of borrowing or saving (because we are working with a static model), then the value of domestic consumption must equal the value of national income. But national income equals the value of domestic production. In the Ricardian model, but not in more general models, the value of national income equals the wage bill.

Let S_i and D_i equal domestic supply and demand of commodity i. The value of national income is

$$y = p_1 S_1 + p_2 S_2$$

and the value of consumption is

$$p_1 D_1 + p_2 D_2$$

when the country faces prices p_i. Here we assume that domestic consumer and producer prices are the same; they both equal the world prices. There are no taxes or trade restrictions. When we relax this assumption it will be important to distinguish among world prices, domestic consumer prices, and domestic producer prices.

The national income accounting constraint, i.e. the requirement that the value of consumption equals the value of production is

$$p_1 S_1 + p_2 S_2 = p_1 D_1 + p_2 D_2. \tag{2.14}$$

We can rearrange this equation to obtain

$$p_1 (S_1 - D_1) = p_2 (D_2 - S_2) \tag{2.15}$$

or

$$p_1 X_1 = p_2 M_2,$$

with $X_1 \equiv S_1 - D_1$ exports of commodity 1,

and $M_2 \equiv D_2 - S_2$ imports of commodity 2.

Equation (2.14) states that the value of consumption equals the value of national income; equation (2.15) states that the value of imports equals the value of exports, i.e., trade balances. These two conditions are equivalent. Future lectures refer to the constraint (2.15) as the "Balance of payments constraint".

Now we see how a change in the budget constraint changes a country's welfare level. Suppose that Canada is able to trade at a relative price of corn $p > 1/2$, i.e. at a price greater than its autarchic price. In this case, we have seen that Canada specializes in corn. Given the assumptions above, Canada produces 40 units of corn. ($S_1 = 40$ and $S_2 = 0$ using the notation above.) By choosing umbrellas as the numeraire, i.e. setting the $p_2 = 1$, $p = \frac{p_1}{p_2} = p_1$; with this normalization, p equals both the relative price of corn (the price of corn relative to the price of umbrellas) and the nominal price of corn. Canada's national income is $40p$. The balance of payments (BOP) constraint (equivalently, the national income accounting

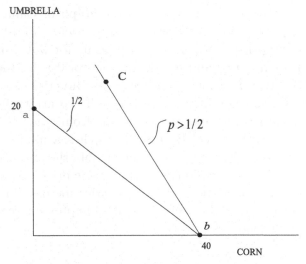

Figure 2.5. Production possibility frontier for Canada (flatter line) and budget or balance of payments constraint when world relative price of corn exceeds Canada's autarchic price (steeper line). The slope of steep line is the world relative price of corn facing Canada.

identity) in this case is

$$p(40 - D_1) = D_2. \tag{2.16}$$

Figure 2.5 graphs Canada's PPF from Figure 2.1, and adds the graph of the balance of payments constraint, the line through points b and c. This BOP constraint is analogous to the budget constraint in a consumer's utility maximization problem. The ability to trade at prices different than the autarchic price means that the BOP constraint lies strictly above the PPF except at the corners. An increase in p causes the BOP to rotate upwards (clockwise), making it possible to achieve higher levels of consumption. Absent other distortions (as we assume), an increase in p raises national welfare. Here an increase in p means that the price of exports rises, i.e. Canada's terms of trade improve.

Canada also benefits from trade if it faces world prices $p < 1/2$. In that case, Canada imports corn. Lowering p means that the price of imports falls, again leading to an improvement in its terms of

trade, and an increase in its welfare. The graph of Canada's gains
from trade, as a function of the world price, reaches a minimum of 0
at the autarchic price. The graph is decreasing for world price lower
than the autarchic price and increasing for world price higher than
the autarchic price. Provided that the utility function is continuous
in the consumption goods, so that the indirect utility function is
continuous in prices and income, the gains from trade is a smooth
function of the world price. Because it reaches a minimum at the
autarchic price, it must be convex in the neighborhood of that price.[5]

Thus, if the world price equals the autarchic price, a small change
in the world price causes only a second order increase in the gains
from trade. This fact will be useful in a later chapter where we discuss
environment externalities.

2.10   Some Comparative Statics Experiments

In answering the following comparative statics questions, assume that
the exogenous change is small enough that it does not change the
"nature" of the equilibrium. For example, if the initial equilibrium is
on region A, then it remains on that region after the change.

(i) What is the effect on trade and welfare (in both countries)
of a small improvement in US corn technology, i.e. a small reduction
in a_1^u? Using Figure 2.4, this change causes the line segment labeled
"C" to rotate counter-clockwise (become flatter) at point B. If the
equilibrium is in region A or at point B nothing happens in either
country under trade, because the US corn sector does not operate.
In the absence of trade, the technological improvement increases the
real wage in the US, and of course has no effect on the Canadian
economy.

If the equilibrium is initially on the segment C, then the
improvement in US technology reduces the world equilibrium price

---

[5]Students should make sure that they understand this paragraph by sketching
the U-shaped curve described, with gains from trade on the vertical axis and the
world relative price on the horizontal axis. The gains from trade are zero at the
world price equal to the autarchic price, and positive for all other relative prices.

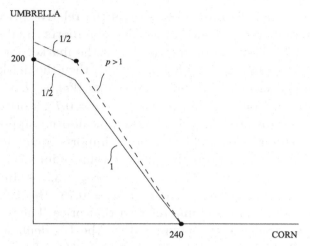

Figure 2.6. World production possibility frontier before (solid curve) and after (dashed curve) the improvement in umbrella technology.

of corn. Because Canada exports corn, the change lowers the price of Canadian exports and therefore lowers Canadian welfare. The price of US imports falls, so US welfare increases.

(ii) What is the effect on trade and welfare in both countries of a technical improvement in US umbrella production, i.e. a small reduction in a_2^u? This change causes the world PPF in Figure 2.4 to shift to the dotted lines shown in Figure 2.6. This question, which is a bit more subtle, is part of a problem set.

2.11   Equilibrium with Trade

This section shows how to use information about a country's technology and preferences to obtain its supply of exports and demand for imports at an arbitrary price. With this information for both countries, we can determine supply and demand curves and use these to determine the equilibrium commodity price.

In a partial equilibrium model, the equilibrium price is the price at which the supply and demand functions intersect. In the general equilibrium model here, with two commodities and two countries, we are interested in the equilibrium *relative* price under free trade.

Here the numeraire is umbrellas, so p is the relative price of corn. We assume that trade balances: the value of imports equals the value of exports. This assumption means that if the market for one good clears (supply equals demand for that good) then the market for the other good also clears. This fact is known as *Walras' Law*.

For example, consider the relative price $p = 0.75$, a price at which both countries are specialized in the example above. Suppose that at this price, Canada's demand for umbrella imports equals 10 units. In order for the value of exports to equal the value of imports, Canada's exports, x, must satisfy $0.75x = 10$, i.e. $x = 13.333$. In order for the market for umbrellas to clear at $p = 0.75$, the US must be willing to export 10 units of umbrellas at that price. The requirement that US trade balance then implies that the US demand for corn equals 13.333. The assumption that one market (e.g. for corn) clears, together with the assumption that trade is balanced, then implies that the other market also clears. Consequently, we need only find the price that clears one of the markets. In a general setting with n commodities, the assumption that $n-1$ markets clear, together with the assumption that trade is balanced, implies that the n'th market clears.

We consider the market for corn. Figure 2.7 shows the production possibility frontier for Canada for the example above, together with an indifference curve for society. With a single type of agent, the worker, and all workers assumed identical, there is no difficulty in aggregating their preferences into a single welfare function. In a more general setting, we need additional assumptions to achieve this aggregation. The figure shows that in autarchy, where $p = 0.5$, Canada consumes 25 units of corn and 7.5 units of umbrellas.

Figure 2.8 shows Canada's import demand and export supply functions. The vertical axis shows the relative price. The positive quadrant corresponds to Canada's positive imports. The curve in this quadrant is the graph Canada's import demand function. The negative quadrant corresponds to Canada's negative corn imports; negative imports are the same as positive exports. Therefore, the curve in the left quadrant corresponds to Canada's export supply function. The curve has a flat portion at $p = 0.5$, Canada's autarchic

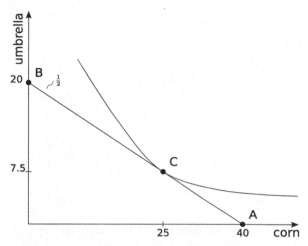

Figure 2.7. Indifference curve locating autarchic production point and level of welfare.

relative price. For lower prices, the import demand function decreases monotonically, as the right panel shows. For prices slightly above $p = 0.5$, the export supply function increases, but outside of this neighborhood the import supply function might continue to increase with the price, or it might bend backwards, as shown by the grey area with a question mark. We now discuss the different parts of the curve in Figure 2.8.

The import demand function is simply Canada's excess demand function, the difference between Canada's demand and supply, as a function of the relative price. At $p = 0.5$ Canada's import demand and export supply is a flat line. At $p = 0.5$, any production point on Canada's production possibility frontier is an equilibrium production level, i.e. a level that results in full employment and zero profits in both sectors. However, holding $p = 0.5$, the production point might change, but national income remains constant, and therefore consumption also remains constant at $(25, 7.5)$. As production changes and consumption remains constant, exports or imports change to exactly offset the change in production. For example, if the price remains at $p = 0.5$ and production moves to point A in Figure 2.7, where Canada is specialized in corn, then export supply equals

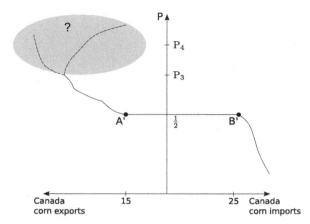

Figure 2.8. Canada's import demand (right panel) and export supply (left panel).

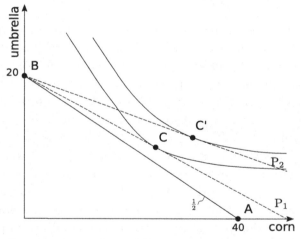

Figure 2.9. Consumption and production points for prices below Canada's autarchy price.

$40 - 25 - 15$, shown as point A' in Figure 2.8. This reasoning explains the flat portion of the import demand/export supply curve in the figure.

Next, we determine the shape of this curve for prices other than $p = 0.5$. Consider two price $p_2 < p_1 < 0.5$ shown in Figure 2.9.

Previous analysis shows that at these prices Canada is specialized in umbrellas. If the price were p_1, consumption would occur at point such as C in Figure 2.9. (Point C in Figure 2.9 is not related to point C in Figure 2.7.) This point lies on Canada's balance of payments constraint, which is strictly above Canada's PPF except at the corner. Because Canada is specialized in umbrellas at this price, all of its corn consumption must be met through imports. If the price falls to $p_2 < p_1$ then the relative price of Canada's imports have fallen: Canada's terms of trade have improved, resulting in higher national income.

The fall in p creates both an income and a substitution effect. The substitution effect (lower relative corn price) increases the demand for corn, thus increasing corn imports. Throughout these lectures we maintain the assumption that both goods are "normal", not "inferior": holding price constant, an increase in income increases the demand for both commodities. As p falls national income rises. Therefore, both the substitution and the income effects work in the same direction, increasing demand for corn. The point C' lies to the right of point C. Because this reasoning holds at arbitrary $p_2 < p_1 < 0.5$, Canada's import demand for corn must be a decreasing function of price. Thus, the right panel of Figure 2.8 shows the import demand function as negatively sloped for $p < 0.5$.

Figure 2.10 shows Canada's consumption point at a price $p_3 > 0.5$, point D. At this price, Canada is specialized in corn, so it must export corn; for $p > 0.5$ the left panel of Figure 2.8 (showing exports of corn, rather than imports) is relevant. For price increases above the autarchic prices there is again an income and a substitution effect, but here the two effects counteract rather than reinforce each other, resulting in the ambiguous slope of the export supply function. For example, as the relative price increases from p_3 to p_4, Canada remains specialized in corn, so it's production does not change. But the country becomes richer, creating an income effect, and the price of corn increases, creating a substitution effect. The income effect makes Canada want to consume more corn, and thus export less, but the substitution tends to lower domestic demand for corn, thereby increasing exports.

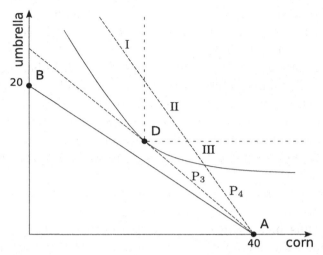

Figure 2.10. Consumption and production points for prices above Canada's autarchy price.

Figure 2.10 shows axes drawn through point D, the equilibrium consumption point at p_3. These axes intersect the higher budget constraint (the line with slope p_4), creating three regions labeled I, II and III. If the new consumption point lies on the budget constraint in region I, then the higher corn price causes Canada to reduce consumption of corn, thus increasing its exports. In this region, the substitution effect is stronger than the income effect, and the export supply increases with the price, as with a standard supply function. If the new consumption point lies in region II, the higher price causes Canada to increase consumption of corn, thus reducing its corn exports. In this region, the income effect is stronger than the substitution effect; here, the supply function bends backward. If the new consumption point were to lie in region III, Canada would be consuming fewer umbrellas when the relative price of umbrellas falls (i.e. as the relative price of corn increases). In that case, umbrellas would be an inferior good. By assumption, neither good is inferior, so we exclude the possibility that the new consumption point is in region III.

In summary, if the substitution effect is stronger than the income effect, export supply increases with the price of exports. But if the income effect dominates the substitution effect, the country's level of exports decreases with the price, i.e. the supply curve bends backward. To reflect this ambiguity, the export supply curve in Figure 2.8 shows two possibilities, with a circle drawn around them and a question mark.

We can obtain a similar graph of export supply/import demand for the US. For the example in this chapter, in equilibrium Canada exports corn and the US imports corn. We can rotate Canada's export supply function around the vertical axis, shown in Figure 2.8, to draw it as shown in Figure 2.11. This figure shows Canada's export supply function as upwardly sloping, i.e. it assumes that the substitution effect dominates the income effect. We have seen that the US import demand function must be downward sloping, because as the price of corn falls, both the income effect and the substitution effect make the US want to consume more corn, and

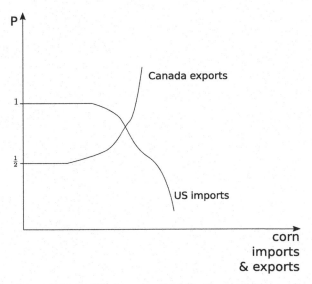

Figure 2.11. A possible equilibrium, in which both countries are diversified. The intersection of the two curves is off the flat portion of both curves.

therefore import more corn. Figure 2.11 illustrates the situation where there is a unique equilibrium at which both countries are completely specialized. Students should experiment by showing that there are many other possibilities, including multiple equilibria, a topic in Chapter 3.

Chapter 3

Comparative Statics:
Taxes and Stability

3.1 Introduction

This chapter uses graphical constructions to describe a two-commodity general equilibrium model. When discussing trade, we use a two-country setting. We examine the effect of taxes in the open economy and introduce the meaning of stability in an equilibrium framework. The next chapter contains two applications that rely on the definition of stability.

The model here, unlike the models in Chapters 2, 6, and 7, leave the technology in the background. Here we assume only that the technology is convex, i.e. the production possibility frontier (PPF) is concave. The lack of structure on technology limits our ability to show how changes (e.g. in prices) alter real factor returns. Therefore, in discussing welfare we need to posit a social welfare function.

We use the open economy model to examine the effect of taxes or subsidies that target production, consumption or trade. These different types of policies drive wedges between the relative prices for different agents. The policies' welfare effects depend on how the subsidy is financed or what is done with the tax revenue. We also show how a change in the relative price at which the country is able to trade changes consumption and production, thus changing imports and exports. We use this information to construct import demand and export supply curves. These curves are analogous to standard demand and supply curves, except that with they are general equilibrium relations, in that they allow income (and, implicitly, factor prices) to change as the relative price changes. With these curves we can determine the equilibrium world price. Section 2.11 of Chapter 2 introduced those curves in the Ricardian setting.

We then discuss the meaning of "stability" and explain the role of stability in comparative statics. In the trade setting, an equilibrium is stable if and only if the Marshall–Lerner condition, introduced below, is satisfied.

One section collects the technical foundation for the graphical approach. A final section reviews more basic material, using a partial equilibrium model of the closed economy to discuss the meaning and measurement of tax incidence.

3.2 Equilibrium Conditions in the Open Economy

We repeatedly use a simple construction that relates an exogenous world price to levels of production, consumption and trade. *For the time being we assume that the country does not impose any taxes or subsidies or tariffs. Therefore, the world relative commodity price equals the relative price faced by consumers and the relative price faced by producers.* In this context, there is no need to distinguish between the relative world price and the relative price faced by consumers and producers: those prices are all the same in the absence of taxes, subsidies and trade restrictions.

However, once we introduce taxes it is important to keep in mind that an agent's behavior depends on the tax-inclusive prices she faces. Producers' decisions depend on producers' tax-inclusive prices; consumers' decisions depend on the tax-inclusive prices that consumers face. Forgetting this obvious point leads to a great deal of confusion. The introduction of taxes or tariffs breaks the equality among the relative prices.

Exports equal domestic production minus consumption; imports equal domestic consumption minus production. We can identify these levels geometrically, under the assumption of convex technology, price-taking behavior and utility maximization.

First consider the level of production under the following assumptions:

- Producers take as given factor and commodity prices.
- Producers in all sectors face the same relative factor prices.
- The technology is convex: if two points are feasible, then any convex combination of these two points is also feasible.
- There are no taxes or externalities, e.g. spillovers across firms or sectors.

Under these assumptions, a competitive equilibrium is efficient; it maximizes the value of production given the relative producer prices. Figure 3.1 shows the equilibrium production point A when producers face the relative price of corn p.[1] Under these

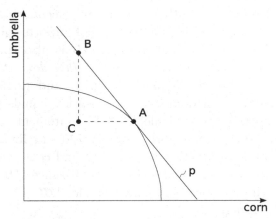

Figure 3.1. Production point A maximizes the value of production given relative price p (the absolute value of the slope of the tangent line).

---

[1]In general, the absence of a subscript on a price denotes a relative price — except when I use a partial equilibrium model in which there is only one price. With $p = \frac{p_1}{p_2}$, p is the "relative price of commodity 1". Where I associate "corn" with commodity 1 and "umbrellas" with commodity 2, I also call p the relative price of corn.

conditions, at a competitive equilibrium level of production, the tangent of the PPF equals the negative of the relative commodity price faced by producers. Section 3.4 provides details about this assertion.

A line in the "corn–umbrella" plane, e.g. the line with slope $-p$ through A in Figure 3.1, is the set of umbrella and corn combinations whose value equals the value of point A under relative price p. For example, the value of the bundles at A and B are equal, evaluated at the relative price p. Firms produce at point A, obtaining revenue that they distribute to factors of production. Some of those factors may be fixed, so part of the revenue may be distributed as pure rent; this possibility is immaterial to our purposes. Because all revenue is distributed, total income to society is sufficient to purchase any bundle on the line through AB. This line is the graph of the national income accounting identity, which states that the value of consumption equals income.

Chapter 2 emphasized that the income accounting identity is equivalent to the constraint that the value of imports equal the value of exports. Therefore, the line through AB is also the balance of payments constraint *under the assumption that domestic and world prices are equal.* We saw (equations (2.14) and (2.15)) that the statement "the value of domestic consumption equals the value of domestic production" is equivalent to the statement "the value of imports equal the value of exports" when world and domestic relative prices are equal. If production occurs at A and consumption occurs at point B, imports of umbrellas equal the distance CB and exports of corn equal the distance AC. The triangle ABC is often referred to as a "trade triangle".

Now we determine the level of consumption. Under the assumptions listed above, a competitive equilibrium and the solution to problem of a social planner who maximizes the weighted sum of individuals' utility produce the same levels of production and consumption. Using this result, we represent equilibrium consumption as the level that maximizes a social welfare function. Indifference curves are the level sets of this social welfare function.

The "income expansion path" (IEP) is the set of points that satisfy the optimality condition that the marginal rate of substitution equals the relative price:

$$\frac{U_1\left(x_1, x_2\right)}{U_2\left(x_1, x_2\right)} = \frac{p_1}{p_2} = p, \tag{3.1}$$

where $U\left(x_1, x_2\right)$ is the social welfare of consumption at $\left(x_1, x_2\right)$ and the subscript U_i denotes a partial derivative. Figure 3.2 graphs level sets for this utility function and shows budget constraints for fixed p and three different levels of income. The tangency between each indifference curve and the budget constraint with the slope $-p$ is a point on the IEP. When it is important to emphasize that the IEP depends on the relative price that consumers face, we write the function as IEP(p). The IEP is the locus of tangencies of the indifference curves and the budget constraints. For the special case of homothetic preferences, the IEP is a ray from the origin.

A change in p causes the IEP to shifts toward the axis of the commodity that becomes relatively cheaper. To illustrate this claim, the student should identify the tangencies between the three

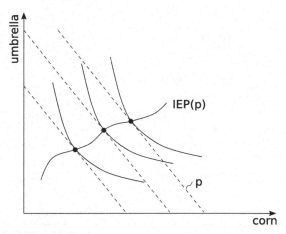

Figure 3.2. The IEP(p) is the locus of tangencies between different indifference curves an lines with slope $-p$. The IEP has positive slope when neither good is inferior.

indifference curves in Figure 3.2 associated with a higher relative price of corn (a larger value of p). Convexity of the indifference curves implies that these tangencies occur on the respective indifference curves above the IEP shown in the figure. These three new points lie on the IEP associated with the higher p, and each point lies above the IEP associated with the initial p. The increase in p means that umbrellas have become relative cheaper; the steps above show that this change causes the IEP to shift toward the umbrella axis. This relation requires only that the indifference curves are convex.

Figure 3.3 combines the information in Figures 3.1 and 3.2, showing the production and consumption points and the trade triangle, given the exogenous price p. The assumptions about technology and market behavior mean that the price determines the production point, A. This production point and the price then determine the BOP constraint. The price and preferences determine the IEP. Equilibrium requires that the consumption occurs on both the BOP and the IEP. The equilibrium consumption point is therefore B.

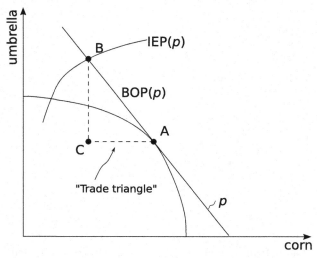

Figure 3.3. At price p equilibrium production occurs at A, consumption at B, and the trade triangle is $\triangle ABC$.

Point C completes the trade triangle, making it easy to identify the levels of imports and exports.

This construction makes it simple to identify the autarchic (relative) price, p^a and to understand why a country gains from being able to trade at a relative price that is either higher or lower than the autarchic price. To find the autarchic price, find the indifference curve that is tangent to the PPF. The absolute value of the slope of the point of tangency is the autarchic relative price. The statement that welfare increases if the country is able to trade at any price other than its autarchic price, means that under trade this country is on a higher indifference curve compared to the autarchic indifference curve.

To illustrate this claim, pick any price that differs from the autarchic price and see how the production and consumption points change, relative to the production and consumption points at the autarchic price. For example, at a price p greater than the autarchic price, production moves southeast along the PPF, as factors move into the corn sector. At this higher price, umbrellas are relatively cheaper, so the IEP moves toward the umbrella axis. The BOP constraint is a line tangent to the production point with slope equal to the world price. The consumption point under trade is given by the intersection of this BOP constraint and the new IEP.

A sketch helps to confirm that the consumption point with trade lies above the autarchic indifference curve. Creating this sketch gives students a bit of practice working with these figures. Using the PPF and an indifference curve, identify the autarchic production and consumption point. Pick a world price different from the autarchic price, and identify the corresponding production and consumption points. Show that if the with-trade consumption point were to lie below the autarchic indifference curve, then the indifference curves under autarchy and under trade must cross. Because the indifference curves cannot cross, the with-trade consumption point must lie above the autarchic indifference curve. Thus, trade increases utility relative to autarchy.

3.3 The Effects of Taxes and Tariffs

We can use the construction in Section 3.2 to identify the levels of production, consumption and trade under various taxes.[2] Before proceeding, it is worth noting the difference between a *unit* and an *ad valorem* tax/subsidy/tariff. The former is a tax paid on each unit of a commodity, and the latter is a tax expressed as a fraction of the price of the product. If the pre-tax price of a good is P and consumers pay a unit tax of u, consumers face the price $P + u$. If these consumers face an *ad valorem* tax of t, then they face the price $(1 + t)P$. These two taxes lead to the same price if $P + u = (1 + t)P$, i.e. if $u = tP$. Thus, an *ad valorem* tax of t, together with a price P, corresponds to a unit tax of tP.

Section 3.2 stressed the assumption that there are no commodity or trade taxes (and no other distortions); here we introduce taxes. There are three relative prices in this model: (i) the ratio of prices that producers *receive*, i.e. "the relative producer price" (denoted p^{pr}), (ii) the ratio of prices that consumers *pay*, i.e. "the relative consumer price" (denoted p^c), and (iii) the ratio of prices on the world market, or the "world relative price" (denoted p^w). Absent trade or commodity taxes, these relative prices are equal. (In our example, p is the ratio of the price of corn over the price of umbrellas.) Taxes on trade, production, or consumption break the equalities.

For example, if world prices are fixed at $p^w = \frac{p_c^w}{p_u^w}$ and there are no trade or production taxes, producers face the relative price $\frac{p_c^w}{p_u^w}$. If, instead, corn producers receive a unit production subsidy s, then they receive the price $p_c^w + s$, so relative producer prices are $p^{pr} = \frac{p_c^w + s}{p_u^w}$. If, however, umbrella producers must pay a unit tax t, then they face the price $p_u^w - t$, and relative producer prices are $p^{pr} = \frac{p_c^w}{p_u^w - t}$. The two policies lead to the same relative producer price if $\frac{p_c^w + s}{p_u^w} = \frac{p_c^w}{p_u^w - t}$, i.e. if $s = p_c^w \frac{t}{p_u^w - t}$. This example shows that a producer

---

[2]Before reading this discussion of taxes in a general equilibrium setting, some students may benefit from reading Section 3.7. This section contains simpler material on taxes in a partial equilibrium setting in a closed economy. It is included in order to make these lecture notes reasonably self-contained.

tax in one sector has the same effect on relative producer prices as a (particular) producer subsidy in the other sector. Because of the equivalence of the two policies, we sometimes speak of a tax/subsidy policy. The production point (in this model) depends only on the relative producer price, so the tax and the subsidy are equivalent. Either policy implies

$$p^{pr} > p^c = p^w.$$

A production tax drives a wedge between producer and consumer (relative) prices, but maintains equality between consumer and world prices.

A trade policy, in contrast, drives a wedge between domestic and world prices, but (absent consumer or producer taxes) maintains equality between consumer and producer (relative) prices. For example, suppose that the country imports corn and imposes a tariff on corn; once again, because only relative prices matter, this policy is equivalent to taxing exports of umbrellas. This policy implies

$$p^{pr} = p^c > p^w. \tag{3.2}$$

The equality between domestic consumer and producer prices, in the presence of trade restriction, is worth emphasizing. If the country is incompletely specialized (as we assume in this chapter) and imports corn, then domestic production of corn satisfies some of the domestic demand for corn, and corn imports satisfy the remaining demand. Here, consumers purchase corn from both domestic and world markets, so the (tariff inclusive) price that they pay must be the same in both markets: $p_c^c = (1 + \tau) p_c^w = p_c^{pr}$, where $\tau > 0$ is the tariff on corn imports. Similarly, umbrella producers sell umbrellas in both domestic and foreign markets, so the price that they receive must be the same in the two markets: $p_u^c = p_u^w = p_u^{pr}$. For $\tau > 0$, these equalities imply equation (3.2).

Finally, a consumption tax on corn (or a consumption subsidy on umbrellas) implies

$$p^c > p^w = p^{pr}.$$

This policy does not affect the equality between producer and world prices, but it increases the relative consumer price of corn. Different policies drive wedges between different pairs of relative prices.

The fact that only relative prices matter means that a tax on imports and a tax on exports have the same qualitative effect; similarly, a subsidy on exports and a subsidy on imports have qualitatively the same effect. This equivalence is known as the Lerner Symmetry Theorem ("taxes on imports are equivalent to taxes on exports").

To confirm this theorem, let $p^w = \frac{p_c^w}{p_u^w}$ be the world relative price of corn. If the country imports umbrellas and imposes an *ad valorem* tariff τ on imports, or an *ad valorem* tax t on exports, the domestic relative prices in the two cases are

$$\text{(tariff)} \ p^{d,\text{tariff}} = \frac{p_c^w}{(1+\tau)\,p_u^w}; \quad \text{(export tax)} \ p^{d,\text{tax}} = \frac{(1-t)\,p_c^w}{p_u^w}.$$

(The superscript d denotes "domestic".) If $(1+\tau)^{-1} = 1 - t$, i.e. if $t = \frac{\tau}{1+\tau}$, then the two policies have the same effect on domestic relative prices, and thus the same effect on the equilibrium.

3.3.1 *Comparative static questions*

Armed with the information above, consider the following comparative static questions. In each case assume that the country is "small", i.e. it's policies do not affect the world relative price; a large country is able to affect the world relative price. For this experiment, we hold fixed p^w, the world relative price. A "lump sum transfer" is a direct transfer of income that does not create a distortion. In contrast, indirect transfers of income arising from policies that change relative prices create a distortionary cost. These types of transfers are sometimes referred to as "leaky buckets": they move income from one person to another, but in the process some of the income is lost — much as a leaky bucket moves water from one location to another, but in the process loses some of the water.

The answers to the three questions posed below describe how curves and equilibrium points change in the different policy scenarios. For each question, students should construct a figure that matches the written description. This exercise promotes careful reading, provides practice in constructing these figures, and contributes much more to understanding and intuition compared to merely looking at figures that have already been created. In each case, students can begin with Figure 3.3.

3.3.1.1 *A consumption tax*

Suppose that the small country initially exports corn. What is the effect on production, consumption, trade and welfare of a small consumption tax/subsidy that increases consumers' relative price of corn. Assume that the tax revenues (or subsidy payments) are distributed (financed) in a lump sum.

Answer: This policy might be a tax on corn consumption or a subsidy on umbrella consumption. In either case, it increases the relative price of corn, causing the IEP to move toward the umbrella axis, the commodity that has become relatively cheaper. The policy does not alter the production point or the BOP constraint, because producer and world relative prices are unchanged. Umbrella consumption increases, corn consumption falls, and both imports and exports increase. The new consumption point, given by the intersection of the new IEP path and the (unchanged) BOP constraint, lies below the indifference curve in the pre-tax scenario. The policy reduces welfare.

3.3.1.2 *A trade tax*

What is the effect on production, consumption, trade and welfare if the country imports umbrellas and imposes a small tariff, and distributes tariff revenues in a lump sum?

Answer: Under this policy, the relative price of corn is the same for consumers and for producers, but this relative price is lower than the world relative price of corn; the tariff increases the relative price of umbrellas, the imported good. The tariff moves the IEP toward the corn axis (because consumers' relative price of corn has decreased) and the production point moves up the PPF toward the umbrella axis (because producers' relative price of corn has decreased.) The BOP shifts in, in a parallel fashion (because the small country has no effect on world price), to intersect the new production point. The new consumption point is given by the intersection of the new IEP and the new BOP constraint.

Umbrella production increases and corn production falls. The new consumption point lies below the indifference curve corresponding to the original consumption point, so welfare (real income) falls. Both the substitution effect (a higher relative price of umbrellas) and the income effect (a lower real income) reduce umbrella consumption. The policy's effect on corn consumption is ambiguous: the substitution effect promotes increased corn production (due to the lower relative price of corn) but the income effect tends to decrease corn consumption. Either of those two effects might dominate.

3.3.1.3 *A trade tax with a very leaky bucket*

What is the effect on production, consumption, trade and welfare if the country imports umbrellas and imposes a small tariff, but instead of distributing the tariff revenue the country throws it into the sea (or saves it for the future)?

Answer: The relative price faced by producers determines the production point. This relative price depends on the tariff, but not on what is done with the tariff revenue. Therefore, the production point and the BOP constraint are the same as in question (ii). The IEP depends on the consumers' relative price but not on income, and therefore does not depend on what is done with the tariff revenue; the IEP is the same as in question (ii). However, by throwing the tariff revenue into the sea instead of returning it to consumers in a lump sum, income is lower relative to the scenario in question (ii). Therefore, the consumption point and welfare are different than in question (ii).

Because the country throws away (or saves) part of its income (the tariff revenue), it must run a BOP *surplus*. To identify the equilibrium consumption point, begin with the recognition that income consists of two components: (a) the income from sale of factors of production, and (b) the tariff revenue. For this problem, (b) is thrown away, so the only source of consumers' income comes from the sale of their factors of production. Amount (a) equals the value of production.

To identify the equilibrium consumption point, begin by identifying the production point under the tariff: the point on the PPF whose tangency equals producers' relative price. (Students should add this tangency line to their version of Figure 3.3.) The value of every consumption pair on this tangency line equals the value at the production point, which equals payments to factors of production. This line is the consumers' budget constraint when they do not receive any tariff revenue. The intersection of this budget constraint and the IEP gives the equilibrium consumption point. This point lies below the BOP constraint, so the country is running a BOP surplus, as claimed above. Welfare is obviously lower when the tariff revenue is thrown away, rather than returned to the consumers in a lump sum. The country produces at the same point and is on the same IEP in the two scenarios, but because consumers' income is lower when the tariff revenue is thrown away, consumption of both goods is also lower in that scenario.

3.3.1.4 *Comparing Scenarios (ii) and (iii)*

Scenarios (ii) and (iii) involve opposite extreme assumptions. Scenario (ii) assumes that the "bucket" that transfers tariff revenue to consumers has no leaks, and Scenario (iii) assumes that the bucket is so full of leaks that none of the transfer reaches consumers. In both cases, the tariff reduces welfare, but (not surprisingly) the welfare loss is greater when the government transfers tariff revenue to consumers inefficiently, or not at all.

Question (ii) is relatively straightforward to answer, because when the tariff revenue is returned to consumers in a lump sum we can find the equilibrium consumption point (and therefore welfare) without having to calculate the tariff revenue; we simply find the intersection of the BOP line and the IEP. This procedure works because when the tariff revenue is returned to consumers, the country is in balance of payments equilibrium: the value of its imports equals the value of its exports. In contrast, when the tariff revenue is not returned to consumers (Question (iii), the country runs a positive) balance of payments: the value of its imports is less than the value of its exports. In this case, we need additional information to find the consumption point, as the answer to Question (iii) shows.

3.3.1.5 *An algebraic perspective*

Now we show algebraically that when the country returns the tariff revenue to consumers, it is in balance of payments equilibrium; when the country throws away the tariff revenue, it runs a balance of payments surplus. Consider the case of the tariff on umbrella imports. Suppose that the world prices of the two commodities are p_c^w and p_u^w and the country imposes an *ad valorem* tariff on umbrellas of τ, so the domestic prices are p_c^w and $(1 + \tau) p_u^w$.

First consider the case where the country returns all tariff revenue to consumers. Denote the equilibrium levels of domestic production (supply) and consumption (demand) of the two commodities as S_c, S_u, D_c, D_u. The revenue from the sale of domestic production (evaluated at domestic prices) equals the returns to factors of production, $p_c^w S_c + (1 + \tau) p_u^w S_u$. The tariff revenue equals $\tau p_u^w (D_u - S_u)$. Total revenue (national income) equals the sum of these two, which equals

$$p_c^w S_c + (1 + \tau) p_u^w S_u + \tau p_u^w (D_u - S_u) = p_c^w S_c + p_u^w S_u + \tau p_u^w D_u.$$

The left-hand and the right-hand sides of this equation express national income in two ways. The left side equals the value of domestic production evaluated at *domestic* prices, plus the tariff revenue. The right side equals the value of domestic production evaluated at *world* prices, plus the tax revenue that would be obtained by charging a unit tax, τp_u^w, on each unit of umbrellas *consumed* (not the level imported).

The value of consumption, at domestic prices,

$$p_c^w D_c + (1 + \tau) p_u^w D_u,$$

equals total revenue because by assumption consumers spend all of their income. Expenditures equal revenue means

$$p_c^w S_c + p_u^w S_u + \tau p_u^w D_u = p_c^w D_c + (1 + \tau) p_u^w D_u \Longleftrightarrow$$

$$p_c^w S_c + p_u^w S_u = p_c^w D_c + p_u^w D_u \Longleftrightarrow$$

$$p_c^w (S_c - D_c) = p_u^w (D_u - S_u).$$

The last equality states that the value of exports equals the value of imports *at world prices.* Therefore, if tariff revenues are returned to consumers, and if consumers spend all of their income, *then the country must be in balance of payments equilibrium.* Here, to identify the equilibrium level of consumption, we can use the BOP constraint (together with the IEP). We do not need to identify the level of tariff revenues.

If the tariff revenue is thrown into the sea, the equality of income $(p_c^w S_c + (1 + \tau) p_u^w S_u)$ and expenditures $(p_c^w D_c + (1 + \tau) p_u^w D_u)$ implies

$$p_c^w S_c + (1 + \tau) p_u^w S_u = p_c^w D_c + (1 + \tau) p_u^w D_u \Longleftrightarrow$$

$$p_c^w S_c + p_u^w S_u = p_c^w D_c + p_u^w D_u + \tau p_u^w (D_u - S_u) \Longleftrightarrow$$

$$p_c^w (S_c - D_c) - p_u^w (D_u - S_u) = \tau p_u^w (D_u - S_u) > 0.$$

This inequality states that the value of exports minus the value of imports is positive, i.e. the country is running a balance of payments surplus.

3.4 Technical Details

The technical information summarized in this section reminds students of the relation between a competitive equilibrium and the solution to a social planner's problem. The material also emphasizes that in a competitive equilibrium without distortions, factor prices equal the shadow value of the factor: the marginal increase in the value of output due to an increase in the supply of a factor. Subsequent chapters use this equality. Here we assume that there are no taxes or other distortions. We establish a number of facts that we used in constructing the previous figures in this chapter, and that we will refer to in subsequent chapters:

  (i) In a competitive equilibrium the slope of the PPF is equal to the negative of the ratio of marginal products.

  (ii) In the social optimum, the slope of the PPF equals the negative of the relative commodity prices.

(iii) A competitive equilibrium reproduces the social optimum if firms in both sectors face the same factor prices; moreover, the factor prices in the competitive equilibrium equal the *shadow prices* (defined below) for the social planner's optimization problem.

(iv) When competitive firms in the two sectors face different factor prices, production occurs at a point inside the PPF.

    Item (i) is useful for demonstrating items (ii) and (iii). Items (ii) and (iii) are important because they imply that the point at which production occurs (under the assumption of perfect competition and convex technology) is given by the point where the tangent to the PPF equals the relative price faced by producers. (That ratio is the price of the commodity on the horizontal axis over the price of the commodity on the vertical axis.) We used this relation above; here we demonstrate that it holds in a competitive equilibrium. Item (iv) is important because it emphasizes the assumption that firms in different sectors face the same factor prices. When this assumption does not hold, production occurs inside the PPF.

3.4.1 *The slope of the PPF equals the negative of the ratio of marginal products*

Suppose that there are two factors of production, L and K; production functions in the corn and umbrella sectors are $C(K_c, L_c)$ and $U(K_u, L_u)$. The full employment conditions are $K_c + K_u = K$ (the aggregate stock of capital) and $L_c + L_u = L$ (the aggregate stock of labor). Consider the problem

$$\max C(K_c, L_c)$$

$$\text{subject to } U(K_u L_u) \geq U, \quad L_c + L_u \leq L, \quad K_c + K_u \leq K,$$

where U is a feasible level of umbrella production. The Lagrangian is

$$\mathcal{L} = C(U) = C(K_c, L_c) + \lambda \left(U(K_u L_u) - U \right)$$
$$+ \mu \left(K - K_c - K_u \right) + \nu \left(L - L_c - L_u \right).$$

The first-order conditions to this problem imply[3]

$$\lambda = \frac{C_L}{U_L} = \frac{C_K}{U_K}. \tag{3.3}$$

The envelope theorem implies

$$\frac{dC}{dU} = -\lambda.$$

These results imply that

$$\frac{dC}{dU} = -\frac{C_L}{U_L} = -\frac{C_K}{U_K}, \tag{3.4}$$

which says that the slope of the PPF equals the negative of the ratios of the marginal products of the factors.

---

[3]In order to avoid using subscripts in subscripts, the notation C_L (for example) means

$$\frac{\partial C(K_c, L_c)}{\partial L_c}.$$

3.4.2   *At the social optimum, the slope of the PPF equals the negative of the relative commodity prices*

Now consider the social planner's problem of maximizing the value of production, given the relative price of corn p:

$$\max pC(K_c, L_c) + U(K_u L_u)$$
$$\text{subject to } L_c + L_u \leq L, K_c + K_u \leq K. \tag{3.5}$$

The Lagrangian is

$$\mathcal{L}(p, K, L) = \max[pC(K_c, L_c) + U(K_u L_u)$$
$$+ \rho(K - K_c - K_u) + \omega(L - L_c - L_u)]. \tag{3.6}$$

The variables ρ and ω are the Lagrange multipliers corresponding to the capital and labor constraints. The Lagrangian $\mathcal{L}(p, K, L)$ equals the *maximized* value of national income, given the relative commodity price and the supply of factors. The first-order conditions to the maximization problem (3.6)

$$U_K = \rho = pC_K \quad \text{and} \quad U_L = \omega = pC_L, \tag{3.7}$$

imply

$$\frac{1}{p} = \frac{C_L}{U_L} = \frac{C_K}{U_K}. \tag{3.8}$$

Because p is the relative price of corn, $\frac{1}{p}$ is the relative price of umbrellas. The fact that the planner maximizes the value of production means that the production point is on the PPF: it is not feasible to produce at points above the PPF and it is not efficient to produce at points below the PPF. Equations (3.4) and (3.8) imply that at the optimal production point, the slope of the PPF equals the negative of the relative price of umbrellas, i.e. the relative commodity price. (With umbrellas on the vertical axis, the slope of the PPF is $\frac{dU}{dC}$, which equals $-\frac{U_L}{C_L} = -\frac{U_K}{C_K}$, which equals p, by equations (3.4) and (3.8).) The optimal production point changes in response to a change in p.

3.4.3 *The competitive equilibrium and the social optimum*

We want to show that the outcome of the social planner's *optimization problem* is identical to the outcome in the *equilibrium problem*.[4] To find the competitive equilibrium, use the profit maximizing conditions in each sector. Let umbrellas be the numeraire good (with price 1) and the price of corn be p (as above) and let w and r be the prices of labor and capital, respectively in a competitive equilibrium. Both sectors face the same factor prices, by assumption. The profit maximizing conditions (value of marginal product equals factor price) in the two sectors are

$$U_L = w = pC_L \Rightarrow \frac{1}{p} = \frac{C_L}{U_L},$$
$$U_K = r = pC_K \Rightarrow \frac{1}{p} = \frac{C_K}{U_K}. \tag{3.9}$$

These profit maximizing conditions reproduce the optimality conditions for the social planner, equation (3.8). The necessary conditions for the social planner's problem, and the equilibrium conditions in the competitive equilibrium both require

$$\frac{1}{p} = \frac{C_L}{U_L}, \qquad \frac{1}{p} = \frac{C_K}{U_K},$$
$$L_c + L_u = L, \quad K_c + K_u = K.$$

The last two equations (the full employment conditions) are optimality conditions in the social planner's problem, and they are equilibrium conditions in the equilibrium problem. The four unknowns

---

[4]An equilibrium problem (often) requires finding an outcome that solves the optimality condition of *more than a single agent*. In our setting, the solution to the equilibrium problem has to satisfy the necessary condition to the optimization problems of consumers and of (perhaps many) producers in more than one sector. The problem also has to satisfy equilibrium conditions such as the requirement that aggregate demand for a factor equals aggregate supply. Not all equilibrium problems, e.g. those associated with certain games, can be solved as a single optimization problem.

(labor and capital in the two sectors) satisfy the same equations at a social optimum and at a competitive equilibrium.

For the social planner's problem, the envelope theorem implies

$$\frac{\partial \mathcal{L}(p, K, L)}{\partial K} = \rho \quad \text{and} \quad \frac{\partial \mathcal{L}(p, K, L)}{\partial L} = \omega. \tag{3.10}$$

The constraint multipliers for capital and labor, ρ and ω, equal the marginal increase in the maximal value of output, due to a marginal change in the supply of capital and labor, respectively. These multipliers are often referred to as the "shadow values" or "shadow prices" of capital and labor, respectively. The concept of a shadow value will be important later in this course.

Because the arguments of the functions C_L, C_K, U_L, U_K are the same in the solution to the social planner's problem and in the competitive equilibrium, equations (3.7) and (3.9) imply

$$\omega = w \quad \text{and} \quad \rho = r.$$

The factor prices in the competitive equilibrium are equal to the Lagrange multipliers ρ and ω from the social planner's problem. As noted above, these Lagrange multipliers equal the shadow value of the constraint (the amount by which national income would increase, due to an increase in the supply of the factor). We conclude that in a competitive economy without distortions, e.g. taxes and subsidies or market failures such as externalities, the factor price equals the shadow value of the factor.

3.4.4 *If firms face different factor prices, production is below the PPF*

Firms in the corn and umbrella sectors might face different factor prices for a variety of reasons; perhaps the use of a particular factor is subsidized in *one* sector. For example, let w_c and w_u be the (different) subsidy-inclusive prices of labor, faced by firms in the two sectors, and let r be the common price of capital. Nothing in this setting suggests that workers earn different amounts in the two sectors. Instead, the subsidy-inclusive price that firms pay is different. For example, workers earn \$20/h in both sectors, but due to a subsidy, firms in one sector pay only \$19/h. The profit maximizing conditions (value of marginal product equal to factor price) in the two sectors imply

$$\frac{C_L}{C_K} = \frac{w_c}{r} \neq \frac{w_u}{r} = \frac{U_L}{U_K}. \tag{3.11}$$

The second equality in equation (3.4) is a necessary condition for the production point to lie on the PPF. Equation (3.11) shows that this necessary condition is not satisfied at a competitive equilibrium when firms in different sectors face different prices. There, the equilibrium production point lies below the PPF.

3.5 Import Demand/Export Supply Functions

This section revisits the material discussed in Section 2.11 of Chapter 2, except that here we use a strictly concave production possibility frontier rather than the linear frontier in the Ricardian model. This change eliminates the flat portion of the import demand and export supply function in Figure 2.11, and it means that we have to consider the effect of a price change on equilibrium production when the country is not specialized. In the Ricardian model, a country is specialized for all relative prices not equal to the country's autarchic relative price. If a country is specialized, a small change in the price does not change the country's production point.

As in Section 2.11 of Chapter 2, once we have the import demand and export supply functions, we can determine the equilibrium in a two-country model. Here we consider the possibility of multiple equilibria, introducing the meaning of *stability* of an equilibrium. For this discussion we assume that there are no taxes or trade restrictions. Once we know how to determine the curves in the absence of those policies, it is easy to determine them with the policies.

If we fix the world price at any level p, and if we know that at that level the country wants to import M units of corn, then the balance of payments constraint means that the country exports $X = pM$ units of umbrella. This equality is an example of Walras' Law: the value of total excess demand must be 0. If there is excess domestic demand for one commodity (corn in this example), there must be excess domestic supply of some other commodity. This relation holds for any number of commodities. It is an identity, not an equilibrium condition; that is, it holds for any p, not merely for the equilibrium p.[5]

Figure 3.4 illustrates the excess demand and supply of corn. The vertical axis shows the relative price of corn, p. The positive half of the figure shows the import demand for corn, and the negative half shows the export supply. "Negative imports" are the same as exports. The statement that at a particular price a country wants to import -2 units of corn, means that the country wants to export 2 units of corn. A country's import demand function (the level of imports as a function of the relative price of imports) — is an *excess demand* function: the difference between domestic demand and domestic supply. If excess domestic demand for a commodity is -2, then excess domestic supply of that commodity is $+2$. This fact enables us to draw the import demand and export supply functions in the same figure.

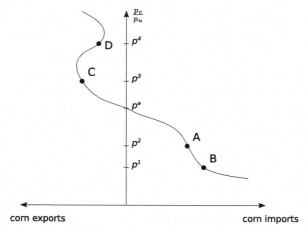

Figure 3.4.   The export demand function (the right panel) has a negative slope. The export supply function may be (but is not necessarily) backward bending.

---

[5]If I own corn and take relative prices as given, then my demand for a certain number of umbrellas implies a willingness to sell a certain amount of corn — regardless of whether anyone wants to buy it.

We used Figure 3.3 to explain how to find the autarchic price, shown in Figure 3.4 as p^a. At this price, excess domestic demand for corn is 0, i.e. import demand and export supply are 0. Recall the three equilibrium conditions used to find the relation between trade and prices: (i) Production occurs at the tangency of the PPF and the line whose slope equals the negative of the domestic producer price; (ii) The country is on its BOP constraint; (iii) Consumers are on the IEP. Using these equilibrium conditions and Figure 3.3, we can see how equilibrium demand and supply, and thus excess demand, depends on the price at which a country trades. Figure 3.4 shows that if the country faces a world price lower than its autarchic price, $p = p^2 < p^a$, the country imports corn. The magnitude of its imports equals the distance between the vertical axis and point A. This distance equals one of the sides of the country's trade triangle in Figure 3.3.

Three things happen if the world price falls to $p^1 < p^2$. First, production shifts into umbrellas, because the producer relative price of corn has fallen: the domestic supply of corn falls. Second, the terms of trade improve, causing the BOP constraint to slide around the BOP, enabling the country to consume more of each good; thus, income rises. The income effect encourages increased consumption of both commodities. Third, the fact that corn has become relatively cheaper means that there is a substitution effect, which also encourages the consumption of corn. Thus, the production effect, the income effect, and the substitution effect all increase the excess demand for corn. Therefore, demand for corn imports rises as the price of imports falls (e.g. to point B in Figure 3.4).

The import demand function has a negative slope. In this respect, the import demand function looks like a typical partial equilibrium (Marshallian) demand curve. However, there are important differences. The partial equilibrium demand curve treats other prices and income as constant. In contrast, the import demand function graphs a general equilibrium relation. A change in the price of imports changes both production and real income. The import demand (and the export supply) functions incorporate this production and income effect.

The export supply function is a bit more interesting, because it is not necessarily monotonic. Consider a world price $p^3 > p^a$. Using the now-familiar equilibrium conditions, you can show that the country exports corn at this price; exports are positive, e.g. at the point C in Figure 3.4. Now consider a higher price, $p^4 > p^3 > p^a$. As we increase the price from p^3 to p^4 we again have a production effect, an income effect, and a substitution effect. However, the income effect works in the opposite direction to the other two effects, making the net change ambiguous. The higher relative price of corn attracts resources into the corn sector, increasing domestic corn supply; this is the production effect. The higher price of corn creates a substitution effect, leading to lower demand for corn. Both of these effects promote higher excess supply of corn. However, the country is a corn exporter for prices above p^a, so a higher price means an improvement in its terms of trade, i.e. higher income. The higher income encourages increased demand for corn. If this income effect is strong enough it can overcome the production and substitution effects. In that case, a higher price of corn reduces the export supply, as shown at point D. There can be more than a single turning point in the export supply function, as Figure 3.4 illustrates.

3.6   The Equilibrium World Price and Stability

We begin by using the tools developed above to determine the set of equilibrium world prices. We then introduce the concept of stability, and explain why it is useful. The next subsection formalizes the concept of stability. We then remind students of how the second order condition in an *optimization* problem is used to answer comparative static questions. This digression makes it easy to understand, in Section 4.3 of Chapter 4, how the stability condition in an *equilibrium* problem is used to answer comparative static questions. We conclude this section by showing that stability implies that elasticities of import demand and export supply satisfy a particular relation known as the Marshall–Lerner condition.

3.6.1 *Finding the set of equilibrium prices*

The previous section showed how to construct the import demand/export supply function for a particular country. We find the set of equilibrium world prices by finding prices at which the import demand for one country equals the export supply of the other country (for a given commodity).

Figure 3.5 graphs M, the import demand function for Home and X^* the export supply function for Foreign. The figure does not show the export supply for Home or the import demand for Foreign, as these are irrelevant because of Walras' Law. An equilibrium world price equates Home import demand for corn and Foreign export supply for corn. Walras' Law insures that the equality of world supply and demand for corn guarantees the equality of supply and demand for umbrellas. Each country is on their balance of payments constraint, so the world excess demand for umbrellas is 0 if and only if the world excess demand for corn is 0. Figure 3.5 shows a situation where there are three equilibrium prices, p_1, p_2

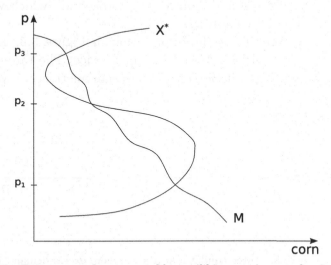

Figure 3.5. Prices p_1 and p_3 are stable equilibirum prices, and price p_2 is an unstable equilibrium price.

and p_3. Each of these three equilibrium prices equate supply and demand.

3.6.2 *Introducing the concept of stability*

The equilibrium conditions in the static model determine the set of equilibrium prices. But the static model says nothing about what happens at non-equilibrium prices, and it cannot assess whether one equilibrium price is "more plausible" than another equilibrium price. Consequently, when there are multiple equilibria, the static model, by itself, is no help in answering comparative static question such as "How does a change in technology or policy alter the equilibrium price?" To overcome this limitation, we need more structure: an additional assumption. Economists create this structure by imbedding the static model in a dynamic framework, known as a tatonnement process. This process describes how price changes over time if the current price happens to be out of equilibrium. This description makes it possible to answer comparative static questions because it eliminates certain equilibrium prices from consideration. We now provide the foundation for this procedure, which we later use in Section 4.3 of Chapter 4.

Figure 3.6 reproduces the information in Figure 3.5, graphing the world excess demand, $M - X^*$ against price. The tatonnement process is based on the fiction of a "Walrasian auctioneer" who calls

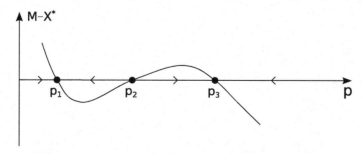

Figure 3.6.   There are three equilibrium prices, where excess demand is 0. The prices p_1 and p_3 are stable and the price p_2 is unstable. The arrows in the different intervals on the price axis show the direction of change in price if the Walrasian Auctioneer calls out a price in a particular interval.

out a price; agents then announce how much they want to buy or sell at that price. If supply exceeds demand $(M - X < 0)$, the auctioneer lowers the previous price. The arrow pointing to the left in Figure 3.6 indicates this change. The auctioneer raises the previous price, as indicated by an arrow pointing to the right, if demand exceeds supply at that price $(M - X > 0)$.

With this process, beginning with any non-equilibrium price, the economy moves toward either p_1 or p_3; these two prices are therefore "stable". However, the economy would move away from p_2, which is "unstable". Another way to say this is that if the auctioneer begins at a price close to a stable equilibrium price, the process causes the price to converge to that stable equilibrium. In contrast, the process moves the price away from an unstable equilibrium.[6]

Note that at a stable equilibrium, world excess demand has a negative slope. At an unstable equilibrium the slope is positive.

In asking comparative static questions we assume that prior to the change (e.g. in technology or policy) the economy is at or close to a stable equilibrium, e.g. at price p_1 or p_3, but not p_2. The basis for this assumption is that even if the economy somehow arrived at the unstable price p_2, any nudge would cause it to move away from that price, toward either p_1 or p_3. Therefore, we would not expect the economy to remain long at p_2, even if it somehow reached that point. In contrast, if the economy begins at any non-equilibrium price, it always moves toward either p_1 or p_3. Once it reaches one of these stable prices, even if it somehow gets nudged away from it, it would return to that price. This reasoning suggests that the economy would be at or close to a stable equilibrium "most of the time".

3.6.3 *Formalizing the concept of stability*

We can formalize the story of the Walrasian auctioneer by adding explicit dynamics. Suppose that we assume that price adjusts

---

[6]In Figure 3.5, Foreign's export supply function has a positive slope at both stable equilibria. Students should use an example to verify that there can be a stable equilibrium at which that export supply function has a negative slope, provided that the import demand function intersects the demand function "from below".

according to the following differential equation[7]

$$\dot{p} \equiv \frac{dp}{dt} = F\left(M(p) - X^*\left(\frac{1}{p}\right)\right) \equiv f(p). \tag{3.12}$$

The argument of the function F is excess demand; the argument of the function f is the (relative) price. We assume that $F\left(\cdot\right)$ is continuously differentiable, $F\left(0\right) = 0$ if and only if $M - X^* = 0$, and $F\left(\cdot\right) > 0$ if and only if $M - X^* > 0$. The price does not change if excess demand is zero, and price increases if excess demand is positive. Therefore, the derivative of F with respect to excess demand, evaluated where excess demand equals 0, is positive. The assumption that F has the same sign as excess demand means that there is no loss of generality in replacing the function F by the identity function:

$$F\left(M(p) - X^*\left(\frac{1}{p}\right)\right) \equiv M(p) - X^*\left(\frac{1}{p}\right).$$

(Only the sign of the time derivative in equation (3.12) matters, not its magnitude.) With this simplification, equation (3.12) becomes

$$\dot{p} = \frac{dp}{dt} = M(p) - X^*\left(\frac{1}{p}\right) \equiv f(p). \tag{3.13}$$

Hereafter we assume that equation (3.13) describes the time derivative of price.

An equilibrium price is a solution to $f(p) = 0$. We have seen that there may be multiple equilibria. An equilibrium is stable if and only if, beginning in the neighborhood of that equilibrium, the price moves toward the equilibrium. Therefore, if the current price is below the equilibrium price, it must be the case that $\dot{p} = f(p) > 0$, and if the current price is above the equilibrium price, it must be the case

---

[7]We write $X^*\left(\frac{1}{p}\right)$ instead of $X^*\left(p\right)$ in equation (3.12) in order to remind students that if p is Home's relative price of imports then $\frac{1}{p}$ is Foreign's relative price of imports. It helps to get in the habit of thinking of a country's import demand and export supply as depending on the relative price of their imports.

that $\dot{p} = f(p) < 0$. *At a stable equilibrium* p^*, $f'(p^*) < 0$: the slope of the excess demand function is negative, as shown in Figure 3.6.[8]

This dynamic model means that we can re-interpret Figure 3.6 as showing the direction of change of p (rather than excess demand); this interpretation justifies the arrows on the price axis in that figure. For example if the price is $p < p_1$ then price is increasing, i.e. $\dot{p} > 0$. The arrows on the p axis show the direction of change (over time) of p. An arrow pointing to the right means that price is increasing. In Figure 3.6, there are two stable equilibria, p_1 and p_3. The price p_2 is also an equilibrium price, but it is an *unstable* equilibrium.

3.6.4 *An analogy: stability and second order conditions*

Optimization problems and equilibrium problems are different, but have important features in common. In an optimization problem we find a maximum (or a minimum). In an equilibrium problem we find the value of a variable or vector (e.g. a price) that satisfies an equilibrium condition (e.g. excess demand equals 0). Sometimes (but not always) it is possible to recast an equilibrium problem as an optimization problem; for example in some cases we can find a competitive equilibrium by solving the maximization problem of a fictitious social planner.

Economists frequently want to know how the solution to an optimization problem or an equilibrium problem changes when a parameter changes. In an optimization problem we use the second order condition, and in an equilibrium problem we use the stability condition to answer the question. This subsection emphasizes the similarity of these two approaches. An asterisk on a variable indicates either the optimal or the equilibrium value of that variable, depending on the context.

For example, suppose that we have the optimization problem

$$\max_{x} \pi(x, \alpha),$$

---

[8]We exclude the knife-edge (non-generic) cases where the excess demand function is tangent to the price axis.

where α is a parameter. We want to know how the optimal x, call it $x^* = x(\alpha)$ depends on α. The first-order condition is

$$\pi_x(x, \alpha) = 0. \tag{3.14}$$

To find $\frac{dx^*}{d\alpha}$ we differentiate the first-order condition, equation (3.14) and rearrange to obtain

$$\frac{dx^*}{d\alpha} = -\frac{\pi_{x\alpha}(x, \alpha)}{\pi_{xx}(x, \alpha)}. \tag{3.15}$$

By the second-order condition $(\pi_{xx}(x, \alpha) < 0)$ we obtain

$$\text{sign}\left(\frac{dx^*}{d\alpha}\right) = \text{sign}\left(\pi_{x\alpha}(x, \alpha)\right). \tag{3.16}$$

Figure 3.7 shows the graph of $\pi_x(x, \alpha)$ as a function of x. Because of the second-order condition, we know that this function has a negative slope in the neighborhood of the optimum. If, as shown in this example, $\pi_{x\alpha}(x, \alpha) > 0$, then an increase in α causes the graph of $\pi_x(x, \alpha)$ to shift up (as shown by the dotted curve in Figure 3.7). In this case, the optimal level of x increases, as shown. This graphical demonstration is an alternative to the mathematics that leads to equation (3.16).

In summary, the optimum is given by the root of a function, $\pi_x(x, \alpha)$. By the second-order condition, we know that in the neighborhood of the optimum the graph of the function (over x)

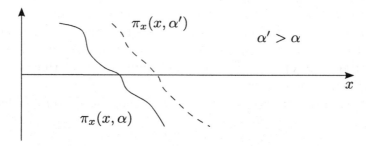

Figure 3.7.   By concavity of π in the neighborhood of a local maximum, the graph of π_x has a negative slope in that neighborhood. A change in α increases or decreases the maximizing x, depending on whether an increase in α shifts π_x up or down.

has a negative slope. Therefore, to determine the effect of α on the optimal x we need only determine how a change in α affects the graph of $\pi_x(x, \alpha)$.

We follow an analogous procedure to determine the comparative statics in an equilibrium problem. However, with an equilibrium problem we use an equilibrium condition instead of a first-order condition, and we use a stability condition instead of a second-order condition. For example, suppose that the economy depends on a parameter α; this parameter may represent technology, a policy, or something else. At the equilibrium price, excess demand, is zero: $f(p, \alpha) = 0$. Equation (3.13) describes the price adjustment: $\dot{p} = f(p, \alpha)$, implying the stability condition $f_p(p, \alpha) < 0$. To determine the effect of α on the equilibrium price we totally differentiate the equilibrium condition and then rearrange, using the stability condition, to obtain

$$\frac{dp^*}{d\alpha} = -\frac{f_\alpha(p^*, \alpha)}{f_p(p^*, \alpha)} \Rightarrow \text{sign}\left(\frac{dp^*}{d\alpha}\right) = \text{sign}\left(f_\alpha(p^*, \alpha)\right). \qquad (3.17)$$

Compare the two parts of equation (3.17) with equations (3.15) and (3.16). The equilibrium condition $f(p, \alpha) = 0$ is analogous to the first-order condition $\pi_x(x, \alpha) = 0$, and the stability condition $f_p(p, \alpha) < 0$. is analogous to the second-order condition $\pi_{xx}(x, \alpha) < 0$. Without the stability condition, information about $\text{sign}(f_\alpha(p^*, \alpha))$ would not help in answering the comparative static condition.

3.6.5 *The Marshall–Lerner condition*

No trade course would be complete without mention of the Marshall–Lerner condition, so here it is. We saw above that stability of an equilibrium world relative price requires that the excess demand function $M - X^*$ has a negative slope in the neighborhood of the equilibrium. This requirement of a negative slope can be rewritten as a condition on elasticities, known as the Marshall–Lerner condition.

The elasticity of demand for imports is the percentage increase in import demand resulting from a percentage fall in the (relative) price of imports. In the two-commodity model, there is a simple relationship between a country's import demand elasticity and its export supply elasticity. Define M as imports, p as relative price of imports (i.e. the number of units of the export good a county must export in order to import one more unit of the import good), and X as exports. The elasticity of demand for imports is

$$\eta = -\frac{dM}{dp}\frac{p}{M} = -\frac{dM}{M}\frac{p}{dp} = -\frac{\hat{M}}{\hat{p}}. \tag{3.18}$$

The hat notation means "proportional change"; e.g. $\hat{M} \equiv \frac{dM}{M}$. The use a negative sign in the definition of demand elasticity is just a convention. The elasticity of supply of exports is

$$\nu = -\frac{dX}{dp}\frac{p}{X} = -\frac{dX}{X}\frac{p}{dp} = -\frac{\hat{X}}{\hat{p}}. \tag{3.19}$$

The reason for the negative sign in this definition is that an increase in the price of imports implies a decrease in the price of exports. Recall that all of these prices are relative prices.

The relation between the elasticities is given by

$$\eta - \nu = 1. \tag{3.20}$$

The intuition behind this equation is based on the fact that the value of imports has to equal the value of exports; a 1% increase in the relative price of imports increases the value of imports by $1 - \eta$ percent, so the value of exports must change by $-\nu$ percent.

To derive equation (3.20), begin with the condition for balance of payments equilibrium

$$pM = X.$$

Take logs of this equation and differentiate the result to obtain

$$\hat{p} + \hat{M} = \hat{X}.$$

Divide by $\hat{p}$ to obtain

$$1 + \frac{\hat{M}}{\hat{p}} = \frac{\hat{X}}{\hat{p}}. \tag{3.21}$$

Substituting the definitions in equations (3.18) and (3.19) into equation (3.21) reproduces the relation shown in equation (3.20).

Equation (3.20) implies that if $\eta < 1$ (i.e. import demand is inelastic) then $\nu < 0$ (i.e. the export supply function bends backward. The export supply function "turns around" at the price where the elasticity of import demand equals 1. If a country's demand for imports is inelastic, then a fall in the price of the country's imports causes the country to spend less on the good (because the rise in demand is less than proportional to the fall in price). If the country spends less on imports then it needs to sell less to pay for those imports. Thus, a fall in the price of imports (equivalently, a rise in the price of exports) causes the level of exports to fall if and only if the demand for imports is inelastic.

Our derivation of the import demand/export supply function discussed the features that determine the slope of the export supply function. The export supply function is "more likely" to bend back if domestic supply of the export good is less elastic, and if the income effect is large relative to the substitution effect.

The Marshall–Lerner condition is

$$\eta + \eta^* > 1. \tag{3.22}$$

Here, a starred variable indicates the value of that variable for Foreign. An equilibrium is stable if and only if inequality (3.22) holds at the equilibrium. This condition states that stability requires that the sum of the countries' elasticities of demand is greater than 1. To derive this condition, recall that we already established graphically that an equilibrium is stable if and only if the slope of the world excess demand is negative at the equilibrium price. That is, we showed that stability is equivalent to the condition

$$\frac{d\left(M - X^*\right)}{dp} < 0. \tag{3.23}$$

Thus, we need to show that equations (3.22) and (3.23) are equivalent. Take the derivative in equation (3.23) and use the fact that 0 excess demand requires $M = X^*$ at an equilibrium:

$$\frac{d\left(M - X^*\right)}{dp} = \frac{M}{p}\left(\frac{p}{dp}\frac{dM}{M} - \frac{p}{X^*}\frac{dX^*}{dp}\right)$$

$$= \frac{M}{p}\left(-\eta - \frac{p}{X^*}\frac{dX^*}{dp}\right). \quad (3.24)$$

Now remember that Home's relative price of imports is p, so Foreign's relative price of imports is $\frac{1}{p}$. To help keep track of things, write $\rho = \frac{1}{p}$, Foreign's relative price of imports. Foreign's export supply is $X^*(\rho)$. Use the chain rule to write

$$\frac{dX^*}{dp} = \frac{dX^*}{d\rho}\frac{d\rho}{dp} = -\frac{dX^*}{d\rho}\frac{1}{p^2}.$$

Using this fact, write

$$\frac{p}{X^*}\frac{dX^*}{dp} = -\frac{p}{X^*}\frac{dX^*}{d\rho}\frac{1}{p^2} = -\frac{1}{X^*}\frac{dX^*}{d\rho}\frac{1}{p} = -\frac{\rho}{X^*}\frac{dX^*}{d\rho} = \nu^*. \quad (3.25)$$

The last equality follows from the definition of the export supply elasticity, equation (3.19). Using equation (3.25) we can rewrite equation (3.24) as

$$\frac{d\left(M - X^*\right)}{dp} = -\frac{M}{p}\left(\eta + \nu^*\right). \quad (3.26)$$

Finally, using the relation (3.20) to replace ν^* by $\eta^* - 1$ we obtain

$$\frac{d\left(M - X^*\right)}{dp} = -\frac{M}{p}\left(\eta + \eta^* - 1\right).$$

From this relation we conclude that the slope of the excess demand function is negative if and only if the Marshall–Lerner condition is satisfied.

3.7   A Review of Taxes in the Simplest Setting

Section 3.3 of Chapter 3 introduces taxes in an open economy general equilibrium setting. Students who have either not seen or have forgotten basic facts about taxes in the (much simpler) partial equilibrium closed economy setting will benefit from the material below. This material discusses tax incidence, tax equivalence, and the approximation of the welfare cost of revenue-raising taxes.[9] Section 5.4 of Chapter 5 notes that the tax equivalence discussed here has a direct general equilibrium analog.

In a *closed* economy, the competitive equilibrium outcome is the same regardless of whether consumers or producers are directly responsible for paying a tax. The equilibrium price and quantity and thus the consumer and producer surplus and the tax revenue do not depend on which agent has the statutory obligation to pay the tax. Both producers and consumers "effectively" end up paying part of the tax.

For example, suppose that in the absence of a tax the equilibrium price is $12 and the supply and demand is 100 units. If a tax of $2 per unit is imposed on consumers, will the price consumers pay rise to $12 + $2 = $14? In general, the answer is "no". The tax does increase the price that consumers pay, but (in general) this higher price decreases the amount that they demand. In order for producers to want to decrease the amount that they supply, the price that producers receive (in general) falls. The percent (or fraction) of the tax that consumers pay is called the consumer incidence of the tax, and the percent (or fraction) that producers pay is the producer incidence.

If, for example, the $2 tax causes the tax-inclusive price that consumers face to rise from $12 to $13.50, then demand falls as consumers move up the demand curve. In order for supply to fall by enough to maintain supply equal to demand, the price that producers receive must have fallen. In this example, the producer price must have fallen to $11.50, because the tax drives a $2 wedge between the consumer (tax-inclusive) price and the producer price. The difference in the tax-inclusive price paid by consumers and the price received by producers is $13.50 − $11.50 = $2, the amount of the unit tax.

---

[9]Some of this material is included in Chapter 10 of my textbook Natural Resources as Capital, Karp 2017. There I use it as a prelude for discussing taxes applied to natural resources in a partial equilibrium dynamic setting.

Consumers "effectively" pay the share $\frac{13.5-12}{\text{tax}} = \frac{1.5}{2} = 0.75$, or 75% of the tax, and producers "effectively" pay the remaining 25% of the tax. The tax causes the consumer price to raise by 75% of the tax, and it causes the producer price to fall by 25% of the tax. In this example, the tax incidence on consumers is 75% and the tax incidence on producers is 25%. In general, the tax incidence depends on the elasticities of supply and demand, a relation we derive below. However, the tax incidence and the equilibrium quantity and price *do not* depend on whether the tax is directly levied on consumers or producers. This equivalence between the producer and consumer taxes arises simply because, in a closed economy (no trade) supply equals demand.

3.7.1   *Tax equivalence*

This section uses a partial equilibrium model to show that consumer and producer taxes are equivalent for non-traded goods. Figure 3.8 shows a supply and demand curve (the heavy line) in the absence of taxes. Consumers and producers face the same equilibrium price p^*.

Under a tax, the consumer and producer prices are different, so we can no longer use the same axis to measure both prices. We have

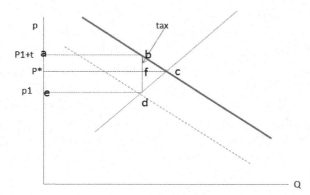

Figure 3.8.   Upward sloping line: supply function. Heavy downward sloping line: demand function with no tax. Light downward sloping line: demand function with tax. The tax equals the distance $\parallel bd \parallel$.

to be clear about what the vertical axis now measures. Suppose that we introduce a consumer unit tax of ν. We continue to let the vertical axis be the price that producers receive and we continue to denote the producer price by p. Therefore, the tax does not alter the location of the supply curve.

With the producer price p, the tax causes the consumer price to be $p + \nu$. The original demand function, the heavy downward sloping line, shows the relation between quantity demanded and the *price that consumers pay*. However, under the tax, we decided to use the vertical axis to represent the price that producers receive. Because the price that consumers pay and the price that producers receive are not the same under a tax, we cannot use the original demand function to read off the quantity demanded. Supply is a function of p and demand is a function of $p + \nu$, and one axis cannot represent both of these.

We want to have the supply and demand curves on the same graph, in order to determine the equilibrium by finding the intersection between these two curves. If we hold the tax ν fixed and consider the quantity demanded to be a function of the *producer* price, p, the original demand curve shifts down by ν, resulting in the light dashed demand function shown in Figure 3.8. This "new" demand function contains exactly the same information as the original demand function; it merely shows demand as a function of the producer price rather than the consumer price, recognizing that the consumer price is $p + \nu$. The vertical distance between the original demand function and the demand function under the tax is ν, as the figure shows. This figure shows linear supply and demand functions, merely for easy viewing. Regardless of the shape of the demand function, the unit tax ν shifts the demand function down by ν units.

The intersection of the original supply function and the new demand function occurs at the price p_1, the equilibrium producer price in the presence of the tax. We obtain the equilibrium quantity by reading off the quantity associated with this price, q_1. The equilibrium consumer price is $p_1 + \nu$. Note that

$$p_1 < p^* < p_1 + \nu.$$

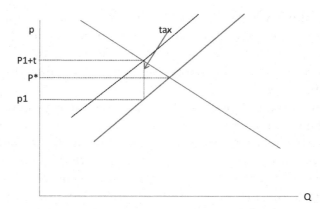

Figure 3.9.   Heavy upward sloping line: supply function. Light upward sloping line: supply function under tax. Downward sloping line: demand function.

The tax incidence for producers in this example is $\frac{p^* - p_1}{\nu}100$ and the tax incidence for consumers is $\frac{p_1 + \nu - p^*}{\nu}100$. Both tax incidences lie between 0% and 100%, and they sum to 100%:

$$\frac{p^* - p_1}{\nu}100 + \frac{p_1 + \nu - p^*}{\nu}100 = 100.$$

Figure 3.9 shows the effect of a unit tax ν when producers pay the tax. In this graph we let the vertical axis represent the price that consumers pay. The price that producers receive is the consumer price minus the tax. Using the same reasoning as in Figure 3.8, we see that the producer tax shifts the supply curve (as a function of the consumer rather than the producer price) up by the amount ν.

As an exercise, students should reconstruct Figures 3.8 and 3.9 and then construct a third figure by superimposing Figure 3.9 over 3.8, in that way convincing themselves that the equilibrium prices and quantities are the same, regardless of which agent has the statutory obligation to pay the tax.

3.7.1.1 *Algebraic confirmation*

To confirm this result algebraically, denote the producer price as p^s (for supply) and the consumer price as p^c (for consumption) and write the "market price" as p. If consumers have the statutory obligation to pay the tax, the prices are $p^s = p$ and $p^c = p^s + \nu$ (producers receive the market price and consumers pay this price plus the tax). If producers pay the tax, $p^s = p - \nu$ and $p^c = p$ (consumers pay the market price and producers receive this price minus the tax). We want to confirm that prices are the same regardless of which agent has the statutory obligation to pay the tax.

If consumers pay the tax, supply equals demand implies

$$S(p) = D(p + \nu). \tag{3.27}$$

Let $p^*(\nu)$ be the (unique) price that solves this equation: the equilibrium producer price when consumers have the statutory obligation to pay the tax. This price is a function of ν. Thus, $p^*(0)$ is the equilibrium price when $\nu = 0$. When consumers (directly) pay the tax, the price producers receive (the "supply price") equals $p^*(\nu)$ and the price consumers pay equals $p^*(\nu) + \nu$.

If, instead, producers pay the tax, the equilibrium condition is

$$S(p - \nu) = D(p). \tag{3.28}$$

Substitute $p = p^* + \nu$ into this equation to write equation (3.28) as

$$S(p^*) = D(p^* + \nu).$$

The last equation reproduces equation (3.27) evaluated at $p = p^*$, the unique solution to that equation. Thus, the two equations (3.27) and (3.28) lead to the same producer and consumer prices — the fact that we set out to confirm.

3.7.2 *Approximating tax incidence*

Calculating the exact tax incidence requires that we find the equilibrium price in the absence of the tax, and the equilibrium price(s) under the tax, and compare the two. We can use supply and demand elasticities, evaluated at the zero-tax equilibrium, to approximate the tax incidence for small taxes:

$$\text{elasticity of supply } \theta = \frac{dS(p)}{dp}\frac{p}{S},$$
$$\text{elasticity of demand } \eta = -\frac{dD(p)}{dp^c}\frac{p}{D}, \tag{3.29}$$

where it is understood that the elasticities are evaluated at the *equilibrium price in the absence of a tax*. Using these definitions, we can totally differentiate the condition that supply equals demand, equation (3.27), and then convert to elasticities and solve the resulting equation for $\frac{dp}{d\nu}$ to obtain an expression for the change in equilibrium price due to a change in the tax, starting from a zero tax:

$$\frac{dp}{d\nu} = -\frac{\eta}{\theta + \eta}. \tag{3.30}$$

This intermediate result and the elasticity definitions produce the approximations for tax incidence:

$$\text{producers' approx. tax incidence: } \frac{\eta}{\theta + \eta}100,$$
$$\text{consumers' approx. tax incidence: } \frac{\theta}{\theta + \eta}100. \tag{3.31}$$

These expressions imply, for example, that (all else equal) a lower demand elasticity increases the consumer tax incidence and lowers the producer tax incidence. Students can visualize this result using a figure with supply and demand functions where producers have the statutory obligation to pay the tax as in Figure 3.9. Hold the supply function and the tax fixed and rotate the demand function clockwise around the with-tax equilibrium. This rotation makes the demand function steeper, i.e. it reduces the demand elasticity. From this figure it will be apparent that the reduction in demand elasticity increases the consumer tax incidence.

3.7.3 *Deadweight cost of taxes*

As long as the elasticities of supply and demand are both positive, both consumers and producers bear some of the incidence of the tax. The tax causes consumers' after-tax price to rise, and producers' after-tax price to fall. Thus, the tax reduces both consumer and producer surplus. In Figure 3.8, the area of the trapezoid $abcp^*$ measures the loss in consumer surplus due to the tax, and the area of the trapezoid p^*cde is the loss in producer surplus. Tax revenue equals the area of rectangle $abde$. Social welfare is the sum of producer and consumer surplus and tax revenues. A higher tax lowers consumer and producer surplus and increases the tax revenue. In Figure 3.8, the loss in consumer plus producer surplus, minus the gain in tax revenue, equals the area of the triangle bce. This triangle is society's deadweight cost of the tax.

For linear supply and demand functions, the deadweight loss is literally a triangle, making its area easy to measure. For general supply and demand functions, we can use the elasticities to obtain an approximation of the deadweight cost. This approximation uses the formula for a triangle, $\frac{1}{2} \times base \times height$. The height of the triangle is simply the tax, ν (see Figure 3.8). Denote the base of this triangle as $-\Delta q$; the Δ is read "the change in", so $-\Delta q$ is the change in quantity demanded, expressed as a positive quantity. (We want the base to be a positive number. The tax decreases quantity, so $\Delta q < 0$, and $-\Delta q > 0$.) Therefore, the approximation for deadweight loss, DWL, is

$$DWL = \frac{1}{2} \left(-\Delta q\right) \nu. \tag{3.32}$$

We can use elasticities, and some algebra, to approximate the change in quantity as

$$-\Delta q \approx \theta \frac{q}{p} \frac{\eta}{\theta + \eta} \qquad \Delta \nu = \theta \frac{q}{p} \frac{\eta}{\theta + \eta} \nu. \tag{3.33}$$

The last equality uses the fact that $\Delta \nu = \nu - 0 = \nu$, because the we are taking the approximation at the zero-tax equilibrium. With this result, and using equation (3.32), we have the approximation expressed using elasticities

$$DWL = \frac{1}{2} \frac{\theta \eta}{\theta + \eta} \frac{q}{p} \nu^2. \tag{3.34}$$

The approximation of deadweight loss requires only estimates of the supply and demand elasticities, observation of quantity and

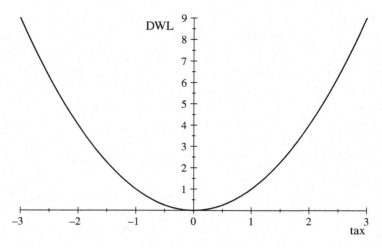

Figure 3.10.   The graph of the approximation of deadweight loss.

price, and knowledge of the magnitude of the tax. Equation (3.34) illustrates an important and general result in economics. The deadweight loss is approximately proportional to the *square* of the tax. The deadweight loss increases with the magnitude of the tax, but it increases faster than the tax. Figure 3.10 illustrates this relation, setting $\frac{\theta\eta}{\theta+\eta}\frac{q}{p}$ equal to 1.

This relation is important because it means that extremely small taxes cause essentially no deadweight loss. However, as the tax increases, the deadweight loss increases rapidly. For example, doubling a tax increases the approximate deadweight loss by a factor of $2^2 = 4$. Tripling tax increases the approximate deadweight loss by a factor of $3^2 = 9$. Therefore, eliminating an extremely small tax leads to a negligible increase in social welfare. But eliminating a tax that is not small may lead to a substantial increase in social welfare. Notice also that the deadweight loss is symmetric around 0: a small subsidy creates the same deadweight loss as does a small tax.

3.7.4   *The open economy*

The discussion above applies to a closed economy, where domestic supply equals domestic demand. With trade, of course, domestic supply and demand are not equal. Consumer and producer taxes are not equivalent in an open economy; tax incidence is entirely different in open and closed economies. For a small open economy, world prices are fixed. Consumers bear 100% of the incidence of a consumer tax, and producers bear 100% of the incidence of a producer tax.

Chapter 4

Applications: Empirics, Transfers, and Leakage

4.1 Introduction

This chapter discusses three applications of the methods introduced in Chapter 3. The first application concerns econometric estimates of the effect of trade liberalization on economic growth. The use of a proxy as a substitute for missing data on liberalization can lead to a mispecified regression equation. This possibility is easily seen using the theoretical constructs above, but was not always recognized in the empirical literature.

The second application concerns the "Transfer Problem". A Home country might make a transfer to Foreign, e.g. in the form of war reparations or aid. (If we had a dynamic model, we could also consider a loan.) We use the concept of stability, introduced in Section 3.6 of Chapter 3, to show how the price-effect of this transfer depends on economic fundamentals. We then consider the effect of the transfer on Home's welfare.

The third application concerns an environmental problem known as "leakage". Stricter environmental regulations, e.g. a carbon tax or a ceiling on carbon emissions, likely increase the costs of producing "dirty" (e.g. carbon-intensive) goods. Stricter environmental regulation imposed by one country, or a group of countries, might shift production of this dirty good to trading partners that did not change their environmental policies, raising pollution there. In this case, some of the pollution reduction achieved by the stricter environmental regulation "leaks" in the form of increased pollution in non-regulating countries. We use both partial and general equilibrium models to describe leakage. The partial equilibrium model ignores income effects, and the general equilibrium model includes them. The two types of models might lead to qualitatively different conclusions about leakage.

4.2 Import Substitution vs. Export Promotion

Different development strategies, import substitution (prominent in Latin America) and export promotion (prominent in Southeast Asia) were followed in the 1960s–1980s. The former protects the import-competing sector, discouraging imports, and the latter promotes exports. From the Lerner Symmetry Theorem (Section 3.3 of Chapter 3), we know that a tax on imports is equivalent to a tax on exports. Therefore, the import substitution policy is implicitly a tax on exports — exactly the opposite of an export promotion policy. A diagram shows some important similarities and differences between the two policies, making it easy to see why a particular estimation strategy used to determine the effect of trade liberalization on economic growth can produce misleading conclusions.

Figure 4.1 shows the PPF for a small country that faces world prices p^w, equal to the absolute value of the slope of the two parallel lines. With free trade, production is at point A and consumption is at point A'. The figure also shows production and consumption under the import substitution policy (B and B', respectively) and under the export promotion policy (C and C', respectively). The import substitution policy increases the relative price of umbrellas, causing the production of umbrellas to rise, and the consumption share of umbrellas to fall. The export promotion policy has the opposite effect.

The figure is constructed to represent a circumstance where both national income, measured at world prices, and also the level of utility (indicated by the indifference curve through points B' and C'), are the same under the two policies. In general, there is no reason to

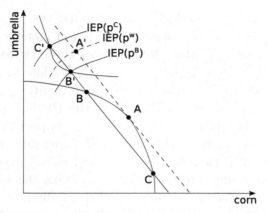

Figure 4.1. Welfare is the same under the import tax and the export tax. Eliminating the trade policy has the same effect on welfare, but different effects on the volume of trade.

suppose that two policies would lead to the same level of national income. Even if they did, there is no reason to suppose that the resulting welfare levels would be the same under the two policies. The figure has these special characteristics (same income and utility under the two policies) in order to keep it simple.[1]

The level of national income at world prices is the value of production (= the value of consumption, by virtue of the BOP constraint) at world prices. Choosing umbrellas as the numeraire, the level of national income at world prices equals the vertical intercept of the BOP constraint.

The figure is constructed as follows. Under free trade the country imports umbrellas. I choose an import substitution policy (here, a tariff) that promotes increased production of umbrellas, moving the production point to B. The solid line through B shows the BOP constraint under this policy. The domestic price that supports

---

[1]I do not want to leave students with the impression that two policies that lead to the same value of national output (evaluated at world prices) also lead to the same level of utility. In general, they do not, because the consumer prices are different under the two policies. I have constructed this example so that the two policies do lead to the same level of welfare — a very unlikely outcome — just to make a point simply.

production at B is denoted $p^B < p^w$. Because the policy lowers the domestic relative consumer price of corn (i.e. it increases the relative price of umbrellas) the IEP shifts toward the corn axis, as shown by $IEP(p^B)$. Consumption occurs at point B'. The figure shows the indifference curve through this consumption point.

The BOP constraint also intersects the PPF at point C. The price equal to the tangent at C, $p^C > p^w$, supports production at C. Because B and C lie on the same BOP constraint, they result in the same value of national income at world prices, even though the two production points are quite different. With the higher relative price of corn, the $IEP(p^C)$ shifts toward the umbrella axis, as shown. I assume that $IEP(p^C)$ intersects the BOP constraint exactly where that constraint intersects the indifference curve, at point C'. This assumption is very special, but the purpose of this diagram is to make a simple point. The assumptions mean that both national income and welfare are the same under the two policies, even though one policy encourages import substitution and the other promotes exports.

The levels of the policies (as distinct from the level of national income) need not be the same at the two points. For example, if point B is supported using an *ad valorem* tariff on umbrellas of τ, the domestic relative price of corn is

$$p^B = \frac{p_c^w}{(1 + \tau)p_u^w} = \frac{p^w}{1 + \tau}.$$

Similarly, if the point C is supported using an export subsidy on corn of s, then the domestic relative price of corn is

$$p^C = (1 + s)p^w.$$

The levels of the policies are the same, i.e. $s = \tau$, if and only if

$$\frac{p^w}{p^B} = \frac{p^C}{p^w}. \tag{4.1}$$

There is no reason to suppose that this equality holds. The assumption that the value of national income at world prices is equal at points B and C and equality (4.1) are unrelated; for any pair of tax and subsidy, either one, neither one, or both, might hold.

It might seem as though an export promotion policy would lead to higher welfare, because it appears to play to the country's strength; it promotes its comparative advantage rather than discouraging it. The figure shows that there is no intrinsic reason why an export promotion policy should be better or worse than an import substitution policy. Both types of policies involve a production and a consumption distortion. The removal of each policy (in this example) creates the same increase in national income and in the level of utility.

An empirical literature asks whether a more liberal trade regime promotes economic growth. All of the models that we discuss are static, and all of the policy experiments involve comparative statics: we examine the effect of a change in a policy on the *level*, not the rate of change, of some endogenous variable, e.g. income or welfare. In order to discuss growth formally, we would need a dynamic model. The relation between a change in a level and a change in growth depend on the specific dynamic model. For example, a change in policy regime might lead to a higher level of income in the short run, but slower growth.

Many empirical specifications rely on intuition from static models, rather than on an explicit dynamic model. The static model suggests that a more liberal trade regime is associated with higher real income (a level). The static model implies that *a change* in trade policy leads to a change in income; in particular, more liberalization leads to higher income, i.e. greater growth. This implication suggests that the change in income (a measure of growth) should be regressed against the *change* in the trade policy (if the underlying model is static). There are empirical models that regress growth on policy levels (or their proxies) and others that regress growth on changes in policy levels (or their proxies).

There are a variety of problems with this type of regression. I want to make a point only about the problem that arises from the lack of reliable data on policy levels. Due to this data problem, many empirical applications use "openness", defined as the ratio of the value of imports plus exports to GNP, as a measure of how liberal the policy is. This measure is endogenous (as, presumably, is the level of the policy), so an instrumental variable technique is needed in order to obtain unbiased parameter estimates. If all countries use import restrictions, the relation between the trade policy and openness is monotonic: a higher tariff leads to a smaller measure of openness. In that case, openness is a reasonable proxy for the level of trade intervention.

However, if some countries use import substitution and other countries use export promotion policies, the relation between the level of the policy and the measure of openness is non-monotonic. In this case, openness is not a good proxy for the level of the trade restriction. For example, in Figure 4.1, if one country liberalizes by removing its tariff (moves from B to A) the measure of openness rises; if the other country liberalizes by removing its export subsidy (moves from C to A), the measure of openness falls. Both countries have become more liberal, i.e. have moved from a regime of trade intervention to one of free trade. In the first case, the measure of openness accurately reflects this change, and in the second case it does not.

The relative success of the Southeast Asian economies compared to those of Latin America might be taken as evidence in favor of export promotion policies relative to import substitution policies. It is clear from the above discussion that the theoretical justification for preferring one policy to the other cannot rest on the type of static model that we have considered. Some kind of market failure, or technological non-convexity (e.g. increasing returns to scale in a sector) is needed to justify intervention. The infant industry argument (or some version of it) has been used to support both kinds of policies. The infant industry argument does not provide (an obvious) reason to support one kind of policy over another: it depends on which sector has the infants that would benefit most from temporary protection.

The limited size and growth potential of the domestic market, relative to the world market, is a more plausible reason for favoring export promotion. If an industry needs to reach a minimum size in order to achieve economies of scale, and if domestic demand for the commodity that this industry produces is small, it might not be possible to achieve the efficient scale under an import substitution policy.

4.3 The Transfer Problem

This section introduces a well-studied topic in international trade. It also shows the role played by the stability assumption (AKA the Marshall–Lerner condition in this context) in addressing comparative statics general equilibrium questions. We ask the following two questions: (1) What are the short run effects, on equilibrium terms of trade, of a financial transfer from one country to another? (2) Is it possible that a country would actually be made better off as a consequence of making a transfer, because of improved terms of trade generated by increased demand for its exports?

4.3.1 *Price-effects of the transfer*

To address the first question, suppose that Home makes a transfer of T dollars to Foreign. How does this transfer affect the terms of trade in the short run? (The long run effects will depend on whether the transfer has to be repaid, as with a loan, or never repaid, as with war reparations.)

The post-WWI peace treaty between Germany and the Allies, which required Germany to make substantial war reparations, was the historical context that motivated this question. Keynes argued that Germany would suffer a "secondary burden" as a result of these reparations, meaning that the transfer would lead to a deterioration in Germany's terms of trade (i.e. a fall in the price of its exports). This argument was based on the belief that in order to generate a surplus that would allow it to make the payments, Germany would have to increase its exports. These increased exports (a shift out in its export supply function) would cause its terms of trade to deteriorate. (See Figure 3.5 and notice that shifting out the export supply function causes the price of exports to fall, provided that the initial equilibrium is stable.)

This argument is not compelling, because in order to generate a trade surplus Germany could either increase exports or decrease imports — or do some combination of both. If it generates the trade surplus by decreasing its imports — that is, if it enacts a policy that causes its import demand function to shift in — its terms of trade improve (again, see Figure 3.5). This improvement in the terms of trade, arising from the transfer, is known as a "secondary blessing".

Thus, casual reasoning cannot tell us whether the balance of payments surplus that Germany must run in order to finance the transfer leads to an improvement or a deterioration in its terms of trade (a secondary blessing and a secondary burden, respectively). Casual reasoning suggests that the answer is likely to be ambiguous. However, a little analysis helps to explain the ambiguity in an economically meaningful way.

Choose Home's export good as the numeraire, and set the relative price of its imports equal to p Denote $D(y, p)$ and $S(p)$ as Home's demand and supply of its import good, where y is Home's income. Demand depends on both the relative price and income, but supply depends only on the relative price. Define m as Home's marginal propensity to consume its import good. If Home has one more dollar of income, it spends the fraction of that dollar on the import good:

$$m = p\frac{\partial D(y,p)}{\partial y} = p\left[\frac{\partial(D(y,p) - S(p))}{\partial y}\right].$$

The first equality is the definition of m. The second equality follows because $\frac{\partial S(p)}{\partial y} = 0$, due to the fact that supply depends on price but not on income. This equality means that we can interpret m either as Home's marginal propensity to consume its import good, or as Home's marginal propensity to import.

If Home gets one extra dollar, it will spend the fraction m on imports. The units of $\frac{\partial D(y,p)}{\partial y}$ are $\frac{\text{units of import good}}{\text{dollars}}$ and the units of p are $\frac{\text{dollars}}{\text{units of import good}}$. The parameter m is unit free (a "pure number") because the units of the product $\frac{\text{units of import good}}{\text{dollars}} \times \frac{\text{dollars}}{\text{units of import good}}$ cancel.

We define m^* analogously, as Foreign's marginal propensity to consume its import good. Foreign's import good is the numeraire good, so its relative price equals 1. It is worth emphasizing that m is a partial derivative; it holds prices constant.

If Home transfers T to Foreign, then at constant prices, Home's income falls by T and Foreign's income increases by T. At constant prices, the change in Home's expenditure on imports is $-mT$.

At constant prices, the change in Foreign's expenditure on its own import good is m^*T, so the change in Foreign's expenditure on Home's import good is $(1 - m^*)T$.

The transfer does alter prices; otherwise there would be no secondary burden or blessing. We want to determine the sign of the price change. For this purpose, it is sufficient to determine whether the transfer would create excess demand or excess supply for the good imported by the donor *at the initial equilibrium price, p.* This simplicity arises from two assumptions. First, we assume that the initial price is a stable equilibrium, and we rely on the tatonnement process corresponding to the Walrasian Auctioneer: price remains constant if and only if excess demand is zero, and price rises if and only if excess demand is positive at a given price. Second, we assume that the transfer is small enough that the sign of its effect can be learned from a derivative.[2]

To determine how the transfer affects the world price, we ask "What would happen if we made the transfer and *did not allow the price to change*? Would there be excess demand or excess supply for home imports?" The answer to this question, together with the above assumptions, tells us how the price must change in order to clear markets.

Figure 4.2 illustrates the argument. The initial equilibrium price occurs at the intersection of the price axis and the graph of excess demand, the solid curve, $M - X^*$. The stability assumption implies that this curve has a negative slope in the neighborhood of the equilibrium p. The transfer will cause this curve to change in some way — we have not yet shown how. If the transfer causes the excess demand curve to shift up (to the dotted curve), then the new equilibrium price must be higher than the initial price. If the transfer causes the excess demand curve to shift down (to the dashed curve), then the new equilibrium price must be lower than the initial price.

---

[2]If instead the transfer was extremely large, it might cause the equilibrium to jump from the neighborhood of one stable equilibrium to the neighborhood of a different stable equilibrium. Our assumption that the transfer is small means that the post-transfer equilibrium price is in the neighborhood of the original equilibrium price.

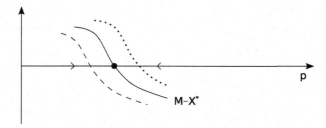

Figure 4.2. The direction of change in a stable equilibrium depends on whether the exogenous change (here, the transfer) shifts the excess demand function up or down.

We need only know whether the curve shifts up or down. Because these curves are continuous, it is sufficient to know whether the post-transfer curve is higher or lower than the original curve *at the initial equilibrium price*. This question is much easier than determining whether the new curve is higher or lower than the original curve at an *arbitrary* price.

The algebraic treatment in Section 4.3.1 shows the role of the Marshall–Lerner condition. The graphical argument below shows the role of the assumption that world excess demand has a negative slope at the initial equilibrium. Section 3.6.5 of Chapter 3 shows that the Marshall–Lerner condition is equivalent to a downward sloping world excess demand. Thus, we use the stability assumption for comparative statics regardless of whether we use a graphical or an algebraic approach.

4.3.1.1 *The graphical approach*

Here, we will see the importance of being able to evaluate the post-transfer world excess demand curve at the initial price. Denoting (as above) domestic supply and demand as S and D and income as y (with stars to indicate variables for Foreign), we can write the world excess demand as

$$M - X^* = D(p, y) + D^*(p, y^*) - S(p) - S^*(p) \equiv f(p, T). \quad (4.2)$$

Home and Foreign income, y and y^*, depend on both price and the transfer, so the function f also includes both arguments.

Holding price fixed at the original $(T = 0)$ equilibrium, the transfer has no effect on supply; but the transfer changes demand due to the income effect. At the initial price, the transfer reduces Home's expenditure on its import good by mT and the transfer increases Foreign's expenditure on Home's import good by $(1-m^*)T$. Aggregate expenditure on Home's import good (at the original price) changes by $(1 - m^* - m)T$, so aggregate demand for Home's import good changes by the quantity $\frac{(1-m^*-m)T}{p}$. (Dividing by price converts expenditures into quantity.) At the initial price, this expression is positive if and only if $(1 - m^* - m) > 0$, i.e. $1 > m^* + m$. If this inequality holds, then the excess demand function has shifted up in the neighborhood of the initial price, as shown by the dotted curve in Figure 4.2. In this case, the equilibrium price of Home's import good has increased, and Home suffers a Secondary Burden from the transfer. (Its imports become more expensive.) In contrast, if $1 < m^* + m$, then the transfer shifts down the excess demand for Home's import good, as shown by the dashed curve. The transfer creates a fall in the relative price of Home's import good: Home obtains a Secondary Blessing.

4.3.1.2 *The mathematical derivation*

To give students practice working with formal rather than graphical methods, this section derives the conclusion above using mathematics. Equation (4.2) shows $f(p,T)$ as the excess demand function. An equilibrium price p^* must satisfy $f(p^*,T) = 0$. We want to determine the price-effect of a small transfer, a change from $T = 0$ to $T > 0$. The initial equilibrium price (before the transfer, i.e. for $T = 0$) satisfies

$$f(p^*, T)_{|T=0} = f(p^*, 0) = 0.$$

Totally differentiate this equation and evaluate at $T = 0$ to obtain

$$f_p(p^*, T)_{|T=0}dp^* + f_T(p^*, T)_{|T=0}dT = 0$$

$$\implies \frac{dp^*}{dT} = -\frac{f_T(p^*, 0)}{f_p(p^*, 0)}. \tag{4.3}$$

Compare equations (3.15) and the second line of (4.3). The stability condition implies that $f_p(p^*, 0) < 0$, so we conclude

$$\text{sign}\left(\frac{dp^*}{dT}\right) = \text{sign}(f_T(p^*, 0)). \qquad (4.4)$$

Section 3.6.4 of Chapter 3 illustrated this procedure. Notice the similarity between equations (4.4) and (3.16). The former signs the comparative statics expression for an equilibrium problem and the latter is a comparative statics expression for an optimization problem.

I repeat the relation between the marginal propensity to consume Home's imports and the demand for Home's imports:

$$p\frac{\partial D}{\partial y} = m, \quad p\frac{\partial D^*}{\partial y^*} = 1 - m^*. \qquad (4.5)$$

Multiplying equation (4.2) by p (to convert from units of quantity to units of money), and using equation (4.5) we can write the derivative $pf_T(p^*, 0)$ as

$$pf_T(p^*, 0) = p\left(D_y(p, y)\frac{dy}{dT} + D^*_{y^*}(p, y^*)\frac{dy^*}{dT}\right)$$

$$= (-m + 1 - m^*).$$

The sign of $f_T(p^*, 0)$ is the same as the sign of $(1 - m - m^*)$. We conclude that $\frac{dp^*}{dT} > 0$ if and only if $1 - m - m^* > 0$. We reached the same conclusion using graphical analysis.

4.3.2 *Welfare effects of the transfer*

Home gives Foreign T units of income, equivalent to T units of the numeraire good. If this gift results in a deterioration of Home's terms of trade (a secondary burden) then Home faces the secondary burden of higher import prices, as well as the primary burden of lower nominal income. In this case, it is obvious that Home's welfare falls and Foreign's welfare increases as a result of the transfer. The interesting question is whether, in the event that Home enjoys a secondary blessing (an improvement in its terms of trade) that blessing can be so large that Home is actually better off as a consequence of the transfer.

In this two-country model, the answer is "no": the transfer strictly lowers Home's welfare. (With three or more countries, there are special cases where the transfer does improve Home's welfare.) I will prove a slightly weaker result: Home's welfare could not be at the same level before and after the transfer.[3] For this claim there is a simple proof by contradiction. I assert the contrary of what I want to prove (the "hypothesis") and derive a contradiction, thus showing that the hypothesis must be false, i.e. the statement that I want to prove must be true.

Consider the case where Home imports food. Figure 4.3 shows the total world demand for the commodity, $D + D^*$ and the total world supply, $S + S^*$. The initial equilibrium price is at the intersection of those curves.

Here are the steps of the argument.

(i) Hypothesis: After the transfer, Home is just as well off as before the transfer.

(ii) Therefore, the price of Home imports (food) must have fallen. (Home needs to be compensated for the transfer. If it makes the transfer and it's term's of trade deteriorated, Home would necessarily be worse off.)

(iii) Because the supply function has not shifted (supply depends on price, not income), the demand function must have shifted in (so that the equilibrium price of food is lower).

---

[3]Why is this result only "slightly" weaker than showing that the transfer lowers Home's' welfare? Consider a model that depends continuously on some parameter α (which might affect tastes or technology or something else). We know that there are circumstances where the transfer lowers Home's welfare, e.g. where Home suffers a secondary burden. Let Γ be the set of α such that the transfer lowers Home's welfare; Γ is nonempty. If there is a non-empty set, denoted Δ, for which the transfer raises Home's welfare, then continuity implies the existence of a boundary between the two sets where the transfer does not alter Home's welfare. The argument in the text shows that this boundary does not exist. Therefore, Δ is empty: the transfer cannot increase Home's welfare.

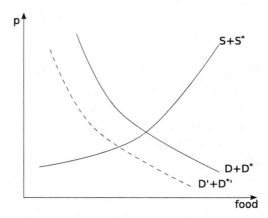

Figure 4.3. If the equilibrium price falls as a result of exogenous change, this change must shift down the aggregate demand function, as shown.

(iv) Therefore the equilibrium level of (world) aggregate consumption of Home's import good (food) must have decreased (see Figure 4.3).

(v) Because free trade is efficient (the transfer is just that — a transfer, not a distortion), the recipient must also be just as well off as before the transfer (efficiency argument): each country is on the same indifference curve as before the transfer.

(vi) Because each country is on the same indifference curve (real income is unchanged in both countries — there is a substitution but not an income effect) and the price of Home imports has decreased, each country's consumption of Home imports (food) has increased. Therefore aggregate consumption of food has increased.

(vii) Statements (iv) and (vi) are contradictory, so the hypothesis (i) must be false.

4.4 Leakage

Two common ways of modeling pollution both begin with the observation that polluting firms produce joint products: the good that they actually intend to produce, and pollution, a bad. Define the Business As Usual (BAU) level of pollution as the level that the firm would choose, absent regulation.

The simplest approach inverts the firm's joint production function to write the good as a function of usual inputs and of pollution. Denote $(S, E) = F(K, L)$ as the joint production function of good S and pollution E, given inputs K, L. For given levels of inputs, this production function defines a curve showing the maximum level of S for any E, $S = G(E; K, L)$. The function G is a standard production function, treating pollution, E, as an input, along with the standard inputs K, L. The BAU pollution level is $E^*(K, L) = \max_E G(E; K, L)$; if pollution is unregulated (e.g. the price of pollution is zero), the firm emits $E^*(K, L)$, the level that minimizes the cost of production. Using the production function, define the minimal cost of producing S units, given the emissions level E, as $C(S, E)$; this "restricted cost function" suppresses the prices of factors K, L.

A different approach introduces a separate activity, abatement. The firm produces the joint outputs and then, if regulated, undertakes the abatement activity to reduce pollution, e.g. through an end-of-pipeline apparatus. In most cases, the two models are equivalent. I use the first approach.

I first consider a partial equilibrium setting. This material shows how to use comparative statics to approximate leakage. I then use a general equilibrium setting to show how to use the machinery developed in Chapter 3 to study leakage. Leakage is positive in the partial equilibrium model, but the general equilibrium model shows that leakage might be negative. With *negative* leakage, stricter environmental policy in a group of countries lowers pollution in the countries that do not change their policy. The comparison of the partial and general equilibrium analysis illustrates the possibility that including income effects can overturn conclusions developed in a partial equilibrium setting. In both settings we assume that there are no trade restrictions and that transport costs are zero.

4.4.1 *Partial equilibrium*

This section illustrates use of a standard partial equilibrium model to show how the magnitude of leakage depends on economic parameters. It also provides another example of the use of comparative statics.

There are n countries; m insiders adopt a carbon policy (e.g. a carbon tax or a ceiling) that increases their cost of producing the carbon-intensive commodity, and $n - m$ outsiders face no carbon constraint. All countries have the same demand function, and there is free trade. Leakage is defined as the number of units of increased outsider emissions per unit of insiders' decreased emissions. If each insider reduces emissions by de and each outsider increases emissions by dE, leakage equals

$$L = \frac{(n - m)dE}{mde}.$$

Evaluating this derivative at the BAU level of emissions gives an approximation of leakage for small policy levels, i.e. for those that lead to small reductions in the insiders' pollution level.

In country $j \in \{i, o\}$ (for insiders and outsiders) the industry cost function is $C^j(S, E)$, where S equals j's output (supply) of the carbon-intensive commodity and E equals its emissions: $C_S^j > 0$, $C_{SS}^j > 0$, and $C_{EE}^j > 0$. For E less than the BAU level, $C_E^j < 0$: increased emissions lower costs. We do not need to consider emissions above the BAU level, because firms would never choose such levels. The j index allows insiders and outsiders to have different cost functions, and thus different supply functions and carbon intensity, even before the insiders reduce emissions. Outsiders choose E to minimize costs, so their level of emissions satisfies

$$C_E^o(S^o, E^o) = 0, \tag{4.6}$$

where S^o equals the outsider's supply and E^o their emissions; insiders emit at the constrained level, $E^i = e$. Country j's inverse supply function equals

$$p = C_S^j(S^j, E^j),$$

where p is the common price. Insiders and outside have different levels of E, so they have different supply functions even if they have the same cost function. Each country has the demand function $D(p)$,

Table 4.1. Notation for the partial equilibrium model of leakage.

Parameter name	Meaning
θ	Elasticity of BAU emissions wrt output
η	Absolute value of elasticity of demand
ϕ^j, $j = i, o$	Elasticity of supply wrt price in country $j = i, o$
ρ	Elasticity of output wrt constrained emissions (at constant price)
s^j, $j = i, o$	Output in country j relative to average output per country
S^j, $j = i, o$ and $\bar{S}$	Output in country j and average output per country
$\lambda = \frac{m}{n}$	Fraction of countries that constrain emissions
δ	$\frac{\text{outsider's emission intensity}}{\text{insider's emission intensity}} = \left(\frac{E}{S^o}\right) / \left(\frac{e}{S^i}\right)$

implying the market clearing condition

$$nD(p) = mS^i + (n - m)S^o. \qquad (4.7)$$

Differentiating the market clearing condition (4.7) with respect to e (the insiders' emissions level), yields $\frac{dp}{de}\frac{e}{p}$. I then differentiate outsiders' equilibrium condition (4.6) to find $\frac{dE}{dS^o}$. These expressions, the definition of elasticity of supply with respect to price, $\phi^o = \frac{dS^o}{dp}\frac{p}{S^o}$, the elasticity of BAU emissions with respect to output, $\theta = \frac{dE}{dS^o}\frac{S^o}{E}$, and notation in Table 4.1, yield the approximation of leakage[4]:

$$L = (1 - \lambda) \frac{\theta \rho s^i}{\lambda \frac{\phi^i}{\phi^o} s^i + (1 - \lambda)s^o + \frac{\eta}{\phi^o}} \frac{E}{e}$$

$$= \frac{\theta \rho \delta (1 - \lambda s^i)}{\frac{\eta + \phi^i}{\phi^o} + (1 - \lambda s^i)\left(1 - \frac{\phi^i}{\phi^o}\right)}. \qquad (4.8)$$

---

[4]Both ρ and θ depend on the cost function, but one is not the inverse of the other. For example, it might be the case that under BAU one unit of output creates one unit of emissions, in which case $\theta = 1$. Unless production happens to be Leontieff, a one unit reduction in the emissions ceiling reduces output by less than one unit.

The first equality shows that leakage is positive (because the denominator is positive). If demand is more elastic than supply, then $\frac{\eta}{\phi^o} > 1$. The second line of equation (4.8) provides a number of intuitive results. For example, leakage increases with outsiders' relative carbon intensity, δ. Leakage depends on the fraction of insiders, λ, multiplied by the average production share of an insider, s^i, not on the two share parameters independently. We do not expect counterintuitive results from a partial equilibrium setting, so the main value of a formula like equation (4.8) is to estimate leakage based on estimates of fundamental parameters, without the need to construct a full model. The model makes it easy to determine the sensitivity of leakage estimates to changes in parameters.

The elasticity of the estimate of leakage, with respect to δ, equals 1. If outsiders are more carbon intensive than insiders, $\delta > 1$. The symmetric example below sets $\delta = 1 = s^o$, i.e. I evaluate the estimate of leakage at a point where the insiders and outsiders are identical before the former reduce their emissions. If, for example, the outsiders are 30%, more carbon intensive then the insiders, then the estimates below increases by 30%. The elasticity of the estimate of leakage with respect to s^o equals

$$\frac{dL}{ds^o}\frac{s^o}{L} = \frac{1}{1 + \left(\frac{((\phi^o - \phi^i)(1-\lambda))s^o}{\eta + \phi^i}\right)},$$

which is less than 1 if $\phi^o - \phi^i > 0$. Thus, if the typical outsider produces a smaller fraction of the carbon intensive good than the typical insider ($s^o < 1$), then the estimate of leakage below (L^{SYM}) exaggerates leakage.

By evaluating the approximation in equation (4.8) at a symmetric equilibrium, where $\delta = s^o = 1$, the expression for leakage simplifies to

$$L^{\text{SYM}} = \theta\rho\left(\frac{1 - \lambda}{\lambda\frac{\phi^i}{\phi^o} + (1 - \lambda) + \frac{\eta}{\phi^o}}\right). \tag{4.9}$$

Not surprisingly, leakage decreases in the membership ratio, λ. A higher ratio the insiders' price elasticity of supply, relative to outsiders' price elasticity of supply ($\frac{\phi^i}{\phi^o}$) also reduces leakage. The upper bound on the estimate of leakage is $\theta\rho$. Given a range of parameter values, we can calculate the range of leakage for this approximation.

4.4.2 *General equilibrium*

The partial equilibrium model takes as given income and all prices other than the price of the dirty commodity. The model described below emphasizes income effects arising from a policy change. The policy change likely creates other general equilibrium effects, e.g. changes in factor prices, that lead to the change in income. However, we do not need to consider those other changes explicitly to evaluate the consequence of the policy change.

A country has a clean sector, y, and a dirty sector, x. Both sectors use inputs such as capital and labor. The relative price of the dirty good is p. The dirty sector produces joint outputs: the dirty good, x, and emissions, z. As described above, we can think of pollution, z, as an "input" in the dirty sector (by inverting the joint production function).

Home imposes an emissions tax, t, exogenous to the model, making emissions endogenous. A larger tax corresponds to a stricter environmental policy. The Rest of World (ROW) trading partner has fixed (possibly non-existent) policies. I describe ROW using an excess supply or demand function for the dirty good. From the standpoint of a firm in Home, t is the price of a unit of pollution. The prices of other factors of production, e.g. capital and labor, respond to the level of regulation, but as noted above we do not have to explicitly consider those changes.

Positive leakage means that stricter domestic environmental policy increases pollution abroad. Leakage requires that the higher pollution tax shifts out a country's excess demand for the dirty good in the neighborhood of the equilibrium commodity price. This shift leads to increased dirty-good production, and therefore increased pollution, abroad. Thus, a necessary and sufficient condition for positive leakage, arising from a small increase in the pollution tax, is that the higher tax shift out the country's excess demand for the dirty good *at the initial equilibrium price.*

We saw above that in a partial equilibrium setting, a stricter environmental policy raises production costs, shifting in (and up) the domestic supply curve, without altering the demand curve. The higher tax therefore shifts up the partial equilibrium excess demand curve (domestic demand minus domestic supply), causing positive leakage. Positive leakage is inherent to partial equilibrium models, where the question is its magnitude, not its sign. The similar appearance of partial and general equilibrium excess demand curves may lead to the mistaken impression that leakage is always positive in a general equilibrium setting.

I assume that agents in Home have identical homothetic preferences. Therefore, the IEP is a ray from the origin: at a fixed commodity price, expenditure shares are constant. Agents consume both goods. I also assume that pollution has no effect on the ratio of marginal utility of the two goods. Therefore, pollution affects commodity demand only via its effect on income and/or price.

Merely to simplify the exposition, suppose that Home is small, so it faces a fixed world relative price.[5] If the higher tax shifts out Home's import demand function for the dirty good, then production of this good increases in ROW, increasing ROW pollution, leading to positive leakage. If the higher tax shifts in Home's import demand function for the dirty good, then production of this good decreases in ROW, decreasing ROW pollution, leading to negative leakage.

The tax-induced reduction in pollution in Home decreases the supply of a factor of production (pollution), causing the PPF to shift in. The original production point is no longer feasible, given the

---

[5]If home is large, the world price is endogenous. If, for example, Home imports the dirty good, and if its pollution policy leads to a reduction in its import demand for the dirty good (because demand for the good falls by more than supply falls, at the initial price), then at a stable equilibrium the world relative price of the dirty good falls. This reduction worsens Foreign's terms of trade, lowering Foreign's income, lowering its demand for the dirty good at the initial price. In this case, the income effect in Foreign reinforces the income effect at Home, and also tends to reduce pollution, thereby lowering leakage.

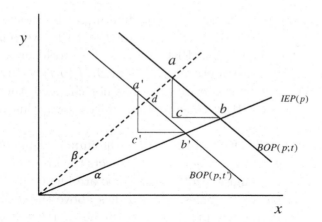

Figure 4.4. The balance of payments constraint before, $BOP(p;t)$, and after, $BOP(p;t')$, the increase in emissions tax, $t' > t$. Corresponding consumption points are b and b'. The initial production point is a and the post-tax increase production point lies somewhere on $BOP(p;t')$.

reduction in pollution. Therefore, the higher pollution tax, $t' > t$, changes the country's equilibrium production point and also reduces its real income, changing domestic demand for the two goods. The tax-induced change in imports therefore involves a production effect and an income effect. These two effects jointly determine the sign of leakage. Because of the small country assumption and free trade, there is no price effect.

Figure 4.4 shows why leakage might be either positive or negative. Home, facing relative price p and an emissions tax t, produces at a. Point a lies on the country's production possibility frontier (not shown, to reduce clutter) at the initial tax. The dashed line, with slope β, shows the set of points where relative production of the dirty and clean good equals the ratio at point a. At the initial equilibrium the consumption point is b and the trade triangle, Δabc, shows imports, the length $\| cb \|$. The point $(\| cb \|, p)$ lies on the country's import demand function, at the initial tax.

The tax-induced decrease in the level of emissions causes the PPF to shift in: with lower emissions, a given level of dirty good production requires more of the other inputs (e.g. capital and labor), lowering the amount of those inputs available to produce the clean good.

At this level of generality, we cannot determine the exact effect of the higher tax (and lower emissions) on the PPF: we only know that it lies below the original PPF. Because the world price has not changed, the BOP constraint shifts in, from $BOP(p; t)$ to $BOP(p; t')$, as shown. Because the domestic price has not changed, the country remains on the same IEP; consumption moves down this IEP to a point such as b'.

To determine the effect of the tax on the import demand for the dirty good, we need to know how the tax affects the production point. By construction, triangles $\Delta a'b'c'$ and Δabc are identical. From the property of congruent triangles, point a' lies above the dashed line, northwest of d. If the new production point lies northwest of a' (on $BOP(p, t')$) then the dirty sector has contracted more than the clean sector; moreover, this difference in contraction rates is sufficient to offset the reduction in demand for the dirty good caused by the tax-induced fall in income. The net effect is to increase imports of the dirty good at the original price p: imports exceed $\| cb \|$. In this case, the higher pollution tax shifts out the import demand curve for the dirty good, just as in a partial equilibrium model, resulting in positive leakage.

However, if the new production point lies southeast of a' (on $BOP(p, t')$) then the higher tax shifts in the import demand function for the dirty good, leading to negative leakage. For production points southeast of a' (i.e. if the clean sector contracts more than the dirty sector) the income effect dominates the production effect. Point d on the dashed curve corresponds to a situation where the tax causes an equal proportional contraction in both sectors. A sufficient condition for negative leakage is therefore that the production point lie at or southeast of d, and that the country is initially importing the dirty good.

4.4.3 *The math behind the result*

Denote $\varepsilon^{x,t}(t; p)$ and $\varepsilon^{y,t}(t; p)$ as, respectively, the (total) tax elasticity of dirty and clean good domestic production. The modifier "total" means that the elasticities take into account any change in factor prices due to the higher tax; the commodity price is constant because this is a small country. A higher tax reduces equilibrium emissions, causing the production possibility frontier to move towards the origin. Therefore, a higher tax must reduce the supply of at least one of the two goods: at least one elasticity is negative. Denote $\psi(t; p) = \frac{x}{y}(t; p)$ as the equilibrium relative domestic production of the dirty good, for a given emissions tax and price, so

$$\frac{d\psi}{dt} \frac{t}{\psi} = \varepsilon^{x,t}(t; p) - \varepsilon^{y,t}(t; p). \tag{4.10}$$

If $\varepsilon^{y,t} = \varepsilon^{x,t}$, then a higher tax causes the production point to move southwest down the dashed line in Figure 4.4. If $\varepsilon^{y,t} > \varepsilon^{x,t}$ then the higher tax causes a smaller percent reduction in the clean sector than in the dirty sector, and the new production point lies above the dashed line. If $\varepsilon^{y,t} < \varepsilon^{x,t}$, the new production point lies below the dashed line.

The line $BOP(p; t)$ in Figure 4.4 shows the country's BOP constraint at the initial production point, a, corresponding to the initial tax, t. The line $IEP(p)$ shows the country's Income Expansion Path, a straight line due to homothetic preferences; the slope of this line is α, a constant because the commodity price is constant for this experiment. The ratio $\frac{\alpha(p)}{\alpha(p)+p}$ is the share of the clean good in expenditures. The figure shows the case $\beta > \alpha$, where the country imports the dirty good. At a fixed commodity price, a higher tax changes the production point, lowering the value of national income, causing the balance of payments constraint to shift in, and changing the consumption point and the level of dirty-good imports.

Appendix A establishes that an increase in the tax shifts out the import demand function, causing positive leakage, if and only if

$$\frac{\beta}{\alpha} \varepsilon^{y,t} > \varepsilon^{x,t}. \tag{4.11}$$

If a higher tax reduces production of the dirty good ($\varepsilon^{x,t} < 0$) and increases domestic production of the clean good ($\varepsilon^{y,t} > 0$), then inequality (4.11) is satisfied for all $\frac{\beta}{\alpha}$, so the higher tax causes positive leakage. In the implausible case where a higher tax increases production of the dirty good ($\varepsilon^{x,t} > 0$) and decreases domestic production of the clean good ($\varepsilon^{y,t} < 0$), then inequality (4.11) is never satisfied, so the higher tax causes negative leakage.

In the plausible case where the higher tax reduces supply of both goods, there is no presumption that leakage is positive. The parameter β and the elasticities $\varepsilon^{x,t}$ and $\varepsilon^{y,t}$ depend on the tax, the production side of the economy (factor supplies, production functions), and the world price. The parameter α depends only on preferences and the world price; a smaller α increases the share of the dirty good in consumption.

In order to understand the role of α, take the case where both $\varepsilon^{x,t}$ and $\varepsilon^{y,t}$ are negative. In this case, a change in preferences that reduces α makes it "more likely" that leakage is negative. The explanation for this result relies on the relation between α and the income elasticity of demand for the two commodities. Denoting national income as I, and D^x and D^y as consumption of goods x and y, the income accounting identity requires $pD^X + D^y = I$. Differentiating with respect to I and using $D^y = \alpha D^x$ gives a relation between the elasticities of demand with respect to income, for the clean and for the dirty goods:

$$p\frac{\partial D^x}{\partial I}\frac{I}{D^x} + \alpha\frac{\partial D^y}{\partial I}\frac{I}{D^y} = \frac{I}{D^x} = \alpha\frac{I}{D^y}.$$

As $\alpha \to 0$, the economy spends all income on the dirty good, and the income elasticity of demand of the dirty good equals 1. In this case, a reduction in income due to the higher tax causes a proportional reduction in demand for the dirty good, and (using the assumption $\varepsilon^{x,t}$ and $\varepsilon^{y,t}$ are negative) necessarily leads to negative leakage. At the other extreme, as $\alpha \to \infty$, the income reduction resulting from the higher tax has no effect on domestic consumption of the dirty good (equal to zero), but (by assumption $\varepsilon^{x,t} < 0$) reduces domestic production of the dirty good. ROW production of the dirty good therefore increases, leading to positive leakage.

The important feature of this model is that the stricter environmental policy lowers income, lowering demand for both the clean and the dirty good. In plausible circumstances, production of both goods also falls with the higher tax. Therefore, the effect of the tax on the import demand for the dirty good depends on the relative magnitude of the tax-induced change in the demand for the dirty good and the domestic supply of that good. If the percent decrease in the demand for this good exceeds the percent decrease in its domestic supply, the import demand for the dirty good falls, leading to reduced pollution in the trading country: leakage is negative.

Chapter 5

The Theory of the Second Best

5.1 Introduction

The "theorem" or "theory" (it goes by both names) of the second best (TOSB) is important in many fields of economics. The theory states that if there are two or more distortions (market imperfections), decreasing one of the distortions does not necessarily improve welfare. Many "counter-intuitive" results in economics are simply special cases of this general result.

After providing an abstract description of the TOSB, this chapter works through a several examples chosen for their intrinsic interest and their ability to illustrate the TOSB. A partial equilibrium example shows that a policy that is optimal in the presence of a single distortion might lower welfare when there is a second, additional distortion. The second example shows that if an economy begins with a trade restriction and a distortionary domestic tax, reducing the trade restriction (a distortion) has ambiguous welfare effects. I then consider the consequences of missing insurance markets and the resulting inability to insure against revenue volatility arising from, for example, weather-induced supply shocks. An economy begins with two missing markets, the absence of an insurance market and the inability to trade. Opening the international market without insurance markets can lower welfare. Section 5.3 of this chapter provides several examples where growth can lead to lower welfare. This material uses a rather unintuitive or unnatural definition of

113

"distortion". However, it helps in showing the unifying power of the TOSB. The final section shows that the failure to achieve an exogenous constraint optimally comprises a distortion, thereby creating another setting for the TOSB to be relevant.

To promote a general interpretation of the term "distortion", I prefer to leave it somewhat vague. A precise but abstract definition begins with an optimization problem, possibly that of a social planner or a firm. If the agent has n decision variables ($\mathbf{x} \in R^n$), there are n first-order conditions of the form $f_i(\mathbf{x}) = 0$, $i = 1, 2, \ldots, n$. Assuming that agent's maximization problem is concave, these first-order conditions are sufficient for an optimum. If the i'th first-order condition is not satisfied, then $f_i(\mathbf{x}) = d_i$, with $d_i \neq 0$. In this context, d_i is the distortion. It can be positive or negative. This interpretation shows that distortions are in the eye of the beholder. Something that seems like a distortion to one agent seems like a good thing to another agent — it depends on whose optimization problem we have in mind. This feature is especially important to keep in mind when we discuss immizerizing growth.

5.2   The TOSB in an Abstract Setting

Figure 5.1 illustrates the theory in an abstract setting, showing its generality. The two panels in the figure illustrate two possibilities. In each panel, the axes d_1 and d_2 represent two distortions. A larger (absolute) value of d_i is a larger distortion. For example, consider a small country with $n \geq 3$ sectors (so there are at least two relative prices) that imposes trade restrictions but no other distortionary taxes; for this country, free trade is efficient. The trade restrictions might be positive or negative, e.g. some importing sectors might be taxed and other subsidized. These policies arise from political lobbying. If d_1 and d_2 are the tariffs in two sectors, both of these count as distortions from the standpoint of social welfare, although not, of course, from the standpoint of the industries that lobby for them. If $d_i < 0$, sector i imports are subsidized.

The curves in Figure 5.1 are iso-welfare curves, with higher welfare on curves closer to the origin. The maximum welfare is

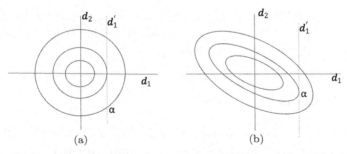

Figure 5.1.　In panel (a) the decrease in the second distortion (resulting in a move from point α toward point β) increases welfare. In panel (b) this change lowers welfare.

achieved when both distortions are completely removed: $d_1 = d_2 = 0$. In Figures 5.1(a) and 5.1(b), welfare increases as we move along either axis toward the origin: we pass through higher iso-welfare curves on this trajectory. If we are on the d_1 axis, for example, the other distortion (d_2) is constant at 0. In that case, we are in a world with only one distortion, and decreasing that distortion raises welfare. In addition, the level sets are convex, reflecting the assumption that the underlying maximization problem is concave.

We represent a world with two distortions by a point off the axes, such as point α. Once again, removing both distortions, i.e. moving to the origin, increases welfare. Suppose, however that we hold d_1 and consider the piecemeal reform of removing only the second distortion. The geometric representation is that we move North along the dotted vertical line beginning at α until $d_2 = 0$. In Figure 5.1(a), this piecemeal reform improves welfare, because as we move along the dotted line away from α, toward the horizontal axis, we pass through higher iso-welfare curves. In panel b, the corresponding trajectory takes us through lower iso-welfare curves. Lowering $|d_2|$ lowers welfare: Removing the "distortion" d_2 decreases efficiency. In panel b, the original point α gives the optimal level of d_2, given that d_1 is fixed at d_1'. Any movement along the vertical dotted line away from α decreases welfare.

The critical difference between the two panels is that in panel a the optimal level of d_2 is always 0, i.e. the optimal level of d_2 is independent of the level of d_1. In panel b, the optimal level of d_2 depends on the level of d_1. In general, there is no reason to think that panel a is more plausible than panel b.

5.3   A Famous Example

We begin with the canonical example of the TOSB. Although this example is unrelated to trade, its simplicity is a great virtue. Figure 5.2 shows the inverse demand function $p = 20 - 3q$, the solid line, and the corresponding marginal revenue curve, $MR = 20 - 6q$, the dashed line. Average and marginal costs are constant at $c = 2$. Each unit of production (or consumption) creates 6 dollars of environmental damages. In this example, pollution is proportional to output, and social environmental costs are proportional to pollution. The only way to reduce pollution costs is to reduce output. The private cost of production is therefore 2 and the social cost of production, which includes environmental damages, is $2 + 6 = 8$.

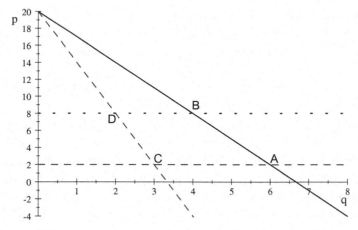

Figure 5.2.   A: the competitive equilibrium with no pollution tax. B: the competitive equilibrium with the optimal (Pigouvian) tax $t = 6$. C: the monopoly equilibrium with no pollution tax. D: the monopoly equilibrium with the *non-optimal tax $t = 6$*.

An untaxed competitive industry sets price equal to marginal cost and produces at point A. The monopoly sets marginal revenue equal to marginal cost, and produces at point C. In a competitive industry, the optimal tax, also known as the Pigouvian tax, is $t = 6$. This tax causes firms to face the social cost of production. The socially optimal level of production and the price occur at point B.

If the monopoly where charged the same tax, $t = 6$, it's tax-inclusive cost of production also equals the social cost. The monopoly facing $t = 6$ produces at point D. Absent the tax, the monopoly produces too little, relative to the socially optimal level: point C lies to the left of point B. The tax causes the monopoly to reduce output even more, lowering social welfare: the tax that is optimal in a competitive setting ($t = 6$) lowers social welfare if imposed on the monopoly.

This example illustrates the basic point of the theory of the second best: a policy that improves matters in one circumstance might make things worse in another circumstance. This general statement is useful as a caution, but it is not surprising, and it does not directly help to determine the optimal policy. The optimal policy depends on the specifics of the problem.

5.4 Trade Liberalization with a Commodity Tax

The material in this section provides practice using several tools developed in Chapter 3, it illustrates the theory of the second best, and it also serves as background to material in Section 6.5 of Chapter 6. The example shows that trade liberalization in the presence of fixed domestic taxes might either increase or decrease a county's welfare. This conclusion is useful when thinking about trade policy, because almost always there are distortions, e.g. taxes, beyond the control of the officials setting trade policy. Those officials must treat the commodity taxes as fixed.

Intuition about the circumstances under which trade liberalization increases or lowers welfare, in the presence of other fixed distortions, is much more valuable than simply recognizing that the reform might have either effect. The starting point is to ask whether the reduction of one distortion (arising from the trade restriction) ameliorates or exacerbates the fixed distortions (arising from the fixed domestic taxes). If reducing one distortion ameliorates the loss due to other distortions, the policy change necessarily improves welfare. However, if reducing one distortion exacerbates the other distortions, we have to assess the relative magnitudes of these two changes to determine whether the policy reform increases welfare.

In our example, a small country can produce food, the numeraire good, and cloth. Figure 5.3 identifies point A as the untaxed autarchic production and consumption point. The equilibrium (consumer = producer) price that supports this equilibrium is the tangent at A, shown as p^a.

Suppose that this *closed* country imposes an *ad valorem* tax of $t > 0$ on cloth consumption, and returns all revenue to consumers in a lump sum.[1] Denote the autarchic relative price that producers face under the tax as p^{at}. Consumers face the relative price $(1 + t)\, p^{at}$.

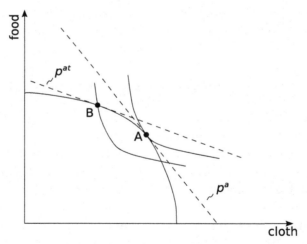

Figure 5.3. In a closed economy, the tax on cloth consumption shifts the production (= consumption) point from A to B.

---

[1]This example resembles the tax model discussed in Section 3.7 of Chapter 3 because it begins with the closed economy; it resembles the tax model discussed in Chapter 3.3 of Chapter 3 because it uses a general equilibrium setting.

The tax makes cloth more expensive for consumers, so they consume less cloth. Consumption moves to a point like B. Because supply = demand for both commodities in autarchy, production must also shift to point B. In order for producers to want to produce at this point (involving less cloth), the producer relative price of cloth must have fallen:

$$p^{at} < p^a < (1+t)\, p^{at}.$$

The first equality follows from comparing the slopes of the tangents to the PDF at points A and B. The second equality follows from comparing the slopes of the indifference curves through points A and B. For a fixed commodity tax, the ratio between consumer and producer (relative) price is fixed at $1+t$ – regardless of whether the economy is closed or open. The change in relative prices induced by the tax increases equilibrium consumption and production of food, even though the tax lowers real income.

Figure 5.3 provides a general equilibrium illustration of tax incidence, discussed in a partial equilibrium setting in Section 3.7 of Chapter 3. The tax on cloth raises the relative price of cloth that consumers face and lowers the relative price of cloth that producers face. Both consumers and producers bear some of the incidence of the tax, just as in the partial equilibrium setting.

In the partial equilibrium setting, we saw that consumer and producer taxes are equivalent for a closed economy. This equivalence also holds in a general equilibrium setting: there is an *ad valorem* production tax on cloth (denote it as T) that would leads to the equilibrium at point B. Denote p^{at} as the equilibrium autarchic relative producer price under the consumption tax t and $(1+t)\, p^{at}$ as the consumer relative price. Pick a producer tax T that satisfies $(1-T)\,(1+t) = 1$, so $T = \frac{t}{1+t}$. With this tax, when consumers face the relative price $p^{aT} = (1+t)\, p^{at}$ and producers face the relative price $(1-T)\, p^{aT} = (1-T)\,(1+t)\, p^{at} = p^{at}$, both agents face the same prices as they did under the consumption tax. Production and consumption occur at the same point. Revenue from sales of commodities plus tax revenue and utility are the same under the two taxes. The consumer *ad valorem* tax t and the producer *ad valorem* tax $T = \frac{t}{1+t}$ are equivalent.

Now consider the "second best" question under the fixed consumption tax: What happens to welfare if the economy opens up to trade? The theory of the second best alerts us to the possibility that relaxing one distortion (the trade restriction) in the presence of a second fixed distortion (the consumption tax) may have ambiguous effects on welfare.

By assumption, the country imposing the trade restriction and the consumption tax is small, so a change in its policies has no effect on the world relative price of cloth, p^w (the price of cloth over the price of food). We begin with an *ad valorem* consumption tax, t, and an *ad valorem* trade tax, τ. This combination of policies eliminates trade because we assume that the trade policy is prohibitive. A change in anything that affects domestic demand and supply, such as a change in the consumption tax, would change the magnitude of the prohibitive tariff.

It is important to be clear about what it means to liberalize trade. Let τ be the *ad valorem* trade policy, p^w the world relative price of cloth, and p^{pr} the domestic relative price of cloth. With a trade policy τ, $p^{pr} = (1 + \tau) p^w$. If $\tau > 0$, then the domestic producer price of cloth exceeds the world price. In this case, the policy corresponds to a tax on cloth imports or a subsidy on cloth exports; trade liberalization corresponds to a decrease in the trade policy, or $d\tau < 0$. That decrease would result in a fall in the domestic producer and consumer price of cloth, causing the country to begin to import cloth. If $\tau < 0$ then the domestic producer price of cloth is below the world price. In this case, the policy corresponds to a tax on cloth exports; trade liberalization corresponds to a higher (closer to zero) value of τ, or $d\tau > 0$.[2] Trade liberalization leads the country to

---

[2]Do not confuse the situation discussed here with the Lerner Symmetry Theorem, introduced in Section 3.3 of Chapter 3. That theorem states that a tax on imports is equivalent to a tax on exports. Here we are picking a particular good, cloth, and considering the two possibilities where, absent the trade restriction, the country would import cloth or it would export cloth. If, for example, the country would import cloth absent the trade restriction, then the Lerner Symmetry Theorem states that the trade policy could be either a tariff on cloth imports or a tax on food exports.

begin to export cloth. In both of these two cases, trade liberalization requires a smaller *absolute value* of τ.

In summary, we hold fixed a positive consumption tax, $t > 0$, and we assume that initially the trade tax is prohibitive. The trade tax might involve either $\tau > 0$ or $\tau < 0$. We consider the effect of reducing the absolute value of τ.

An example may help. With food as the numeraire, suppose that the domestic consumer price of cloth is 45 and the producer price is 30. This price difference is supported by a unit consumer cloth tax of 15, or an *ad valorem* tax t that solves $(1 + t)\,30 = 45$, or $t = 0.5$. Suppose that the world price of cloth is 32, so absent the prohibitive trade policy, the country would export cloth. In this case, the prohibitive *ad valorem* tariff solves $(1 + \tau)\,32 = 30$, or $\tau = -0.062\,5$; the unit trade policy solves $32 + u = 30$, or $u = -2$.

We first use graphical methods to show that in one scenario (soon to be identified) a small trade liberalization unambiguously increases the country's welfare. In another scenario, this small trade liberalization has an ambiguous welfare effect. The graphs enable us to identify these two possibilities, and to match them with the answer to the question: "Does liberalization cause the country to become a cloth exporter or a cloth importer?" We then use calculus to obtain a more detailed description of the welfare change from trade liberalization, and better intuition.

5.4.1 *The Graphical Analysis*

Figure 5.4 simplifies Figure 5.3 by eliminating the zero-tax autarchic equilibrium, but still showing the autarchic production = consumption point a under the consumption tax t, along with the associated indifference curve U. Under this tax, absent trade, the producer relative price of cloth is p^{at}, the slope of the tangent of the PPF at the production point a; the consumer relative price is $(1 + t)\,p^{at}$, the slope of the indifference curve through a. A small trade liberalization changes domestic relative price, but given the fixed consumption tax, the ratio of consumer to producer price remains constant at $1 + t$; therefore, the domestic producer and consumer relative prices of cloth

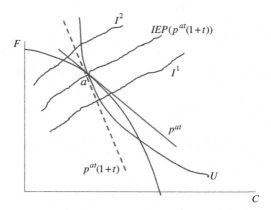

Figure 5.4. In the presence of the fixed consumption tax and the prohibitive trade policy, the consumption and production point is at a. If the small trade liberalization leads to cloth imports, the liberalization unambiguously increases welfare. The welfare effect is ambiguous if liberalization leads to cloth exports.

move in the same direction following a trade reform. We consider two cases: case (i) where the trade reform lowers the domestic producer and consumer prices of cloth, and case (ii) where the reform raises those prices.

Case (i): When the trade reform lowers the consumer relative price of cloth, the reform increases welfare. The lower consumer price causes the Income Expansion Path to shift down, toward the curve labeled I^1. The production point moves north west along the PPF, away from point a. In this configuration, trade liberalization causes the country to import cloth.

The following argument shows that the trade reform increases welfare. Consumption occurs where the new IEP (e.g. I^1) intersects the BOP constraint (not shown to reduce clutter). The BOP intersects the PPF north west of point a. What do we know about the slope of the BOP constraint? The domestic relative producer price of cloth is $p^{pr} = (1 + \tau)\,p^w$. Because the reform lowers this domestic price, the prohibitive trade policy is $\tau > 0$: reform implies a reduction in τ. Provided that the post-reform level of τ is nonnegative (which we know to be the case, because the reform is small), the post-reform domestic producer price of cloth remains above the world price. Therefore, the absolute value of the tangent to the post-reform production point is greater than the world price. That is, the BOP is flatter than the tangent at the new production point. Adding the BOP constraint described here to Figure 5.4, it is apparent that the BOP intersects the IEP above the pre-reform indifference curve. The reform raises welfare.

Case (ii): If the trade reform increases consumers' relative price of cloth, then the IEP shifts up, toward the curve labelled I^2. With a higher (post-reform) relative price of cloth, production moves south east, away from point a on the PPF. Because $p^{pr} = (1 + \tau) p^w$, in order for the reform to increase the domestic price of cloth, it must be the case that $\tau < 0$, so $p^{pr} < p^w$. Therefore, the BOP at the new production point is steeper than the tangent to the PPF at that point. (The slope of this tangent is the domestic relative producer price.) However, we cannot guarantee that the intersection of this BOP constraint and the new IEP lies above the original indifference curve. Therefore, we cannot guarantee that the trade liberalization increases welfare.

Discussion: The primary distortion created by the fixed commodity tax is the reduction in cloth consumption, relative to the no-tax autarchic equilibrium. (The autarchic consumption point under the tax is to the north-west of the zero-tax autarchic consumption point, on the PPF; see Figure 5.3.) If the trade liberalization increases cloth consumption, as in Case (i), it necessarily increases welfare. However, if the trade liberalization lowers cloth consumption, the welfare effect is ambiguous.

5.4.2 *The mathematics*

Denote the trade tax revenue as $R = \tau p^w \left(C^{\text{con}} - C^{\text{prod}} \right)$, where superscripts "prod" and "con" denote production and consumption of cloth, C. I refer to R as "trade tax revenue" instead of "tariff revenue" because I want to include the possibility that the country is using either a tariff or an export tax. By the Lerner Symmetry Theorem, an export tax and an import tariff are equivalent. In order to avoid using different notation or terminology depending on whether the country is a cloth importer or an exporter under free trade, I consider the case where the trade policy τ applies to cloth, which might be either imported or exported after the trade liberalization. Under the prohibitive trade policy, $\left(C^{\text{con}} - C^{\text{prod}}\right) = 0$ so $R = 0$.[3]

Trade liberalization increases trade tax revenue:

$$dR = p^w \tau d \left(C^{\text{con}} - C^{\text{prod}}\right) + p^w \left(C^{\text{con}} - C^{\text{prod}}\right) d\tau$$

$$= p^w \tau d \left(C^{\text{con}} - C^{\text{prod}}\right) > 0. \tag{5.1}$$

The first equality follows from the definition of the differential of R and the second equality follows from the fact that at a prohibitive trade policy, $\left(C^{\text{con}} - C^{\text{prod}}\right) = 0$. To confirm the inequality in (5.1), consider the two possibilities. If the prohibitive trade policy involves a tariff on cloth ($\tau > 0$) then liberalization results in imports of cloth. Because initially cloth imports are 0, it must be the case that $d\left(C^{\text{con}} - C^{\text{prod}}\right) > 0$. If the prohibitive trade policy involves an export tax on cloth ($\tau < 0$) then liberalization results in exports of cloth. Because initially cloth exports are 0, it must be the case that $d\left(C^{\text{con}} - C^{\text{prod}}\right) < 0$. In both cases, the product of τ and $d\left(C^{\text{con}} - C^{\text{prod}}\right)$ is positive.

---

[3]The prohibitive trade tax drives imports and exports to zero, without the need for additional trade restrictions. For example, suppose that the country would export cloth under free trade. In this case, $\tau < 0$. A higher export tax corresponds to $d\tau < 0$, i.e. a higher $|\tau|$, or, equivalently, a larger import tariff. (Remember the Lerner Symmetry theorem). As we increase the export tax, (equivalently, increase the import tariff) cloth exports fall. The prohibitive tariff/tax drives exports exactly to zero. If we were to further increase the export tax, then agents would want to begin importing cloth (and exporting food). Thus, an export tax (equivalently, an import tariff) above the "prohibitive" level has the same effect as an export subsidy to food. If the government refuses to pay an export subsidy, then increases in the export tax (larger $|\tau|$) maintains trade at zero. In that case, a small change in the export tax has no effect on anything. Thus, the comparative static question is non-trivial only if we begin at a trade tax less than or equal to the prohibitive tax. The analysis below relies on the assumption that we begin with zero trade. Thus, we have to begin at exactly the prohibitive tax.

A road map may be helpful at this point. For the purpose of finding the welfare effect of trade liberalization, we begin with the recognition that welfare depends on consumption, which depends on prices and income. Liberalization changes both of these variables. We first determine the effect of liberalization on income, taking into account the fact that income depends on prices, which change with the trade policy. To simplify the differential of income, we use the fact that at a competitive equilibrium, the marginal rate of transformation, $\frac{dF^{\text{prod}}}{dC^{\text{prod}}}$, equals the negative of the producer relative price. Next, we totally differentiate the indirect utility function, and rearrange the resulting differential to obtain an expression for the change in utility measured in monetary units (rather than in utils). At this step we use Roy's equation and the previous expression for the differential of income. We then simplify the measure of the change in utility. This step uses the fact that initially the trade policy is prohibitive, implying that initially consumption equals production for each commodity. After obtaining the mathematical results, we use economic logic to interpret them.

To save notation, denote the producer relative price of cloth by p (rather than p^{at} above) and the consumer relative price of cloth by $p^{\text{con}} = (1 + t)p$. The consumption tax and the trade policy create wedges between consumer and producer relative price and between both domestic prices and the world price. The domestic producer price is $p = (1 + \tau)p^w > 0$, so $\tau > -1$. Let $V(y, p^{\text{con}}) = V(y, p(1 + t))$ be the indirect utility function, where y is income. Our goal is to find how welfare changes when there is a *small* liberalization in trade policy, leading to a change in domestic prices. The economy has three sources of income: the sale of goods, and tax revenue from the consumption tax and the trade tax. Income equals

$$y = pC^{\text{prod}} + F^{\text{prod}} + tpC^{\text{con}} + R.$$

We hold the consumption tax t fixed and differentiate this expression to find the change in income when the trade tax, τ, changes. The differential is

$$dy = pdC^{\text{prod}} + dF^{\text{prod}} + C^{\text{prod}}dp + tC^{\text{con}}dp + tpdC^{\text{con}} + dR.$$

The first two terms on the right side can be written as

$$pdC^{\text{prod}} + dF^{\text{prod}} = \left(p + \frac{dF^{\text{prod}}}{dC^{\text{prod}}}\right)dC^{\text{prod}} = 0.$$

The second equality here uses the fact that at a competitive equilibrium, the tangent of the production possibility frontier, $\frac{dF^{\text{prod}}}{dC^{\text{prod}}}$, equals the negative of the producer (relative) price. Using this result and $dp = p^w d\tau$ (because for the small country the world price is fixed), we write the differential of income as

$$dy = C^{\text{prod}}p^w d\tau + tC^{\text{con}}p^w d\tau + tpdC^{\text{con}} + dR. \qquad (5.2)$$

Recall that the consumer relative price is $p^{\text{con}} = (1+t)(1+\tau)p^w$ and that t and p^w are fixed while τ changes: its absolute value is being reduced. Therefore, $dp^{\text{con}} = (1+t)p^w d\tau$. The differential of the indirect utility function, $V(y, p^{\text{con}})$, equals

$$dV = V_y dy + V_p dp^{\text{con}} = V_y dy + V_p(1+t)p^w d\tau$$

$$\Longrightarrow \frac{dV}{V_y} = dy + \frac{V_p}{V_y}(1+t)p^w d\tau \qquad (5.3)$$

$$\Longrightarrow \frac{dV}{V_y} = dy - C^{\text{con}}(1+t)p^w d\tau.$$

The second equality in the first line uses the differential for dp^{con}; the second line follows from dividing both sides of the previous equality by the marginal utility of income, V_y; the third line uses Roy's equation. The ratio $\frac{dV}{V_y}$ is a measure of the change in utility expressed in units of income. The numerator is in units of utils and the denominator is a ratio of units of utils over units of money.

Substituting equation (5.2) into the expression for the change in utility gives

$$\frac{dV}{V_y} = C^{\mathrm{prod}}p^w d\tau + tC^{\mathrm{con}}p^w d\tau + tpdC^{\mathrm{con}} + dR - C^{\mathrm{con}}(1+t)p^w d\tau$$

$$= \left(C^{\mathrm{prod}} - C^{\mathrm{con}}\right) p^w d\tau + (tC^{\mathrm{con}}p^w d\tau$$

$$- C^{\mathrm{con}}tp^w d\tau) + tpdC^{\mathrm{con}} + dR$$

$$= tpdC^{\mathrm{con}} + dR. \tag{5.4}$$

The change in welfare equals the sum of two terms. From equation (5.1), $dR > 0$: a reduction of the trade restriction, beginning with a prohibitive trade restriction, increases revenue from the trade tax. The consumption tax, t, is positive, so the first term, $tpdC^{\mathrm{con}}$, is positive if $dC^{\mathrm{con}} > 0$ and negative if $dC^{\mathrm{con}} < 0$.

If the trade policy is a tariff on cloth imports ($\tau > 0$), then a small degree of liberalization ($d\tau < 0$) reduces the domestic relative price of cloth and also increases national income, increasing consumption of cloth, so $dC^{\mathrm{con}} > 0$. In this case, both terms in the last line of equation (5.4) are positive, so trade liberalization unambiguously improves welfare. Thus, a necessary condition for liberalization to lower welfare is that the trade policy is an export tax ($\tau < 0$); in this case, liberalization increases the domestic price of cloth.

If $\tau < 0$, then the welfare effect of liberalization is uncertain. To help sign the aggregate welfare effect when $\tau < 0$, we use $p = (1+\tau)p^w$ and the second line of equation (5.1) to write

$$\frac{dV}{V_y} = tpdC^{\mathrm{con}} + dR = t(1+\tau)p^w dC^{\mathrm{con}} + p^w \tau d\left(C^{\mathrm{con}} - C^{\mathrm{prod}}\right)$$

$$= p^w \left[(t + \tau + t\tau)dC^{\mathrm{con}} - \tau dC^{\mathrm{prod}}\right]. \tag{5.5}$$

Recall that in this scenario, $\tau < 0$. Reduction of the export tax increases the domestic relative producer price of cloth, increasing cloth production: $dC^{\mathrm{prod}} > 0$. Using this fact, a necessary and sufficient for the second line of equation (5.5) to be negative is

$$(t + \tau + t\tau)\frac{dC^{\text{con}}}{dC^{\text{prod}}} < \tau. \qquad (5.6)$$

There are two possibilities: (i) $t + \tau + t\tau < 0$ and (ii) $t + \tau + t\tau > 0$.

We now establish that if the welfare effect is negative, then (i) cannot hold. Assume to the contrary that the welfare effect is negative and (i) holds. Inequality (i) implies

$$\frac{\tau}{(t + \tau + t\tau)} > 1 \Leftrightarrow \tau < t + \tau + t\tau \Leftrightarrow 0 < t(1 + \tau).$$

The last inequality always holds, because $p = (1 + \tau)p^w > 0$, so $\tau > -1$. If the welfare effect is negative and $\tau < 0$ and $t + \tau + t\tau < 0$, then equation (5.6) implies

$$\frac{dC^{\text{con}}}{dC^{\text{prod}}} > \frac{\tau}{(t + \tau + t\tau)} > 1. \qquad (5.7)$$

Inequality (5.7) (and $dC^{\text{prod}} > 0$) implies $dC^{\text{con}} - dC^{\text{prod}} > 0$, or $dR = \tau \left(dC^{\text{con}} - dC^{\text{prod}}\right) < 0$, which we know to be false. Therefore, if trade reform lowers welfare (inequality (5.9) holds), we conclude that $t + \tau + t\tau < 0$.

Thus far, we have shown that *necessary* conditions for liberalization to lower welfare include

$$\tau < 0 \quad \text{and} \quad t + \tau + t\tau > 0. \qquad (5.8)$$

Combining these necessary conditions with inequality (5.6), we have the *necessary and sufficient* condition for trade liberalization to lower welfare:

$$\frac{dC^{\text{con}}}{dC^{\text{prod}}} < \frac{\tau}{t + \tau + t\tau} < 0. \qquad (5.9)$$

The necessary conditions involve only the levels of the tax and trade policy. The necessary and sufficient condition states that the fall in cloth consumption, relative to the increase in cloth production, must be sufficiently large relative to a function of the policies.

5.4.3 *The economic interpretation*

Now, we provide the economic interpretation of the mathematical results. The economy begins with two distortions, a consumption tax and a prohibitive trade restriction, and slightly liberalizes trade. This liberalization increases revenue (initially zero) from the trade tax, leading to a first order increase of dR in welfare, measured in units of money. The consumption tax causes equilibrium cloth consumption to be too low, relative to the zero-tax autarchic scenario. If trade liberalization ameliorates that consumption distortion, i.e. if trade liberalization leads to an increase in cloth consumption, then liberalization unambiguously improves welfare.

Trade liberalization does reduce the consumption distortion if liberalization leads to a lower consumer price of cloth; that in turn requires that the world relative price of cloth is lower than the producer autarchic relative price of cloth, i.e. it requires that the trade policy is a tariff on cloth imports ($\tau > 0$).

The situation where trade liberalization has an ambiguous welfare effect is more interesting.[4] That situation requires trade liberalization to reduce cloth consumption, which in turn requires that liberalization leads to a higher relative price of cloth. In this case liberalization leads to cloth exports; here the trade policy is a cloth export tax ($\tau < 0$).

However, $\tau < 0$ is only a necessary condition for trade liberalization to lower welfare. A second necessary condition is $t + \tau + t\tau > 0$, which can be written as $\frac{t}{1+t} > -\tau$. The left side of this inequality increases from 0 to 1 as the consumption tax increases, and we have noted that $-\tau < 1$. Thus, the second necessary condition puts a

---

[4]There is an important difference between being unable to sign a comparative statics expression (here, the change in welfare) and being able to state that the sign is ambiguous. For example, if you are told that X and Y are two positively valued functions, then without more information you cannot sign the difference, $X - Y$. If, however, you can additionally show that in some cases $X > Y$ and in some cases the inequality is reversed, then you can make the stronger statement that the sign of the difference is ambiguous. Here, "ambiguous" is *not* a synonym for "I don't know the sign of $X - Y$"; instead it means "I *do* know that in some cases $X - Y > 0$ and in some cases $X - Y < 0$".

ceiling on the prohibitive trade tax relative to the consumption tax: the prohibitive trade tax cannot be "too large".

As the introduction to this chapter notes, a "distortion" can be viewed as a wedge that prevents a necessary condition for efficiency to hold. The first best price is simply the world price. The wedge associated with the consumption distortion is $t(1+\tau)p^w$, the amount by which the consumer price differs from the first best price; the wedge associated with the trade distortion is $p^w\tau$.

We noted (e.g. in Section 3.7.3 of Chapter 3) that the welfare cost of a distortion is convex in the magnitude of the distortion. If the trade distortion is small, the welfare gain from its reduction is also small. Thus, if the second necessary condition holds ($\frac{t}{1+t} > -\tau$), the gain from liberalizing trade is "more likely" to be small relative to the loss from exacerbating the consumption distortion. In this case, trade liberalization might reduce welfare.

These comments relate to the necessary conditions for trade liberalization to reduce welfare. The necessary and sufficient condition for liberalization to reduce welfare (equation (5.9)) requires a substantial reduction in cloth consumption relative to the increase in cloth production, where the meaning of "substantial" depends on the policy levels (via the right-hand side of equation (5.9)). In this case, the worsened consumption distortion dominates the improved trade distortion, and trade liberalization lowers welfare.

5.5 Trade, Price Volatility, and Missing Markets

Trade in the absence of insurance markets provides another illustration of the theory of the second best. Revenue volatility is an important feature of many commodity markets. Markets partially insure suppliers against revenue risk arising from supply shocks (e.g. due to weather or pests), and trade reallocates price variability across countries.

5.5.1 *Revenue variability*

Even if the Marshall Lerner condition is satisfied (Section 3.6.5 of Chapter 3), so that an equilibrium is stable in the technical sense, a small shift in domestic supply or demand might lead to a large change in the equilibrium price. Where there are frequent changes in underlying supply or demand and one or both of these curves are inelastic, there may be a high degree of price variability. A shift in one of the domestic supply and demand curves in Figure 4.3 causes the equilibrium price to change.

Primary (i.e. agricultural and natural resource) commodities form a large component of the exports of a few Developing Countries (DC's). Demand for these exports tends to be inelastic, as is short run supply. The prices of these DC exports are sensitive to small changes in supply or demand, leading to revenue instability.

In the 1960s and 1970s attempts were made to stabilize the price of many primary commodities using International Commodity Agreements (ICAs) that relied on buffer stocks and supply controls. The ICAs had a number of drawbacks. Price ceilings defended by buffer stocks are vulnerable to speculative attack; as the stock is drawn down to defend the price ceiling, the market may believe that an imminent stock-out will cause the ceiling to be breached. The belief that the price will soon be much higher increases speculative demand, putting added pressure on the buffer stock. In this case, self-fulfilling beliefs may lead to a price spike that would not have occurred absent the buffer stock mechanism. In addition, buffer stocks tend to crowd out private storage, reducing a market-based source of stabilization.

Buffer stocks are also used to defend price floors. These can be very expensive, often requiring an agency to purchase and store large volumes to prevent the price from falling below the floor. A credible price floor, by reducing risk to producers, puts further downward pressure on prices by encouraging additional production. Supply controls attempt to limit supply to prevent this downward pressure. However, supply controls encourage cheating amongst signatories, for the usual reasons in cartels. Producers outside the agreement, facing less competition from the signatories, have added incentive to increase production.

Although both sides of the market may agree in principle on the value of stable prices, consumers benefit from low prices and producers benefit from high prices, so the political will to defend the floor or ceiling may vanish. In the early 2000s calls to reintroduce ICAs (e.g. in a well-publicized Oxfam report) received little support.

Other remedies to the risk from price volatility include the creation of futures markets and the use "commodity bonds", which denominate debt in, for example, barrels of oil or pounds of coffee rather than dollars. Both of these are means of transferring risk. A. Dixit wrote a series of papers in the late 80s and early 1990s (in REStud, JIE, QJE) which show that trade policies may be ineffective in improving a competitive equilibrium in the absence of insurance markets, largely because the government does not have better information than markets.

Markets provide partial insurance against the variability in price that arises from supply fluctuations. Denote industry supply as Q and industry revenue as $R(Q) = P(Q)Q$, where $P(Q)$ is the inverse demand function. The change in revenue caused by a change in supply is

$$\frac{dR}{dQ} = P(Q)\left(1 - \frac{1}{\eta}\right), \tag{5.10}$$

where η is the elasticity of demand (expressed as a positive number). If η is large (i.e. the inverse demand function is quite flat), a change in Q leads to negligible change in price; in this case, the change in revenue is proportional to the change in quantity sold. If η is small (the inverse demand function is steep) then an increase in quantity leads to a large fall in price; in this case the change in revenue might be small or even negative. For $\eta = 1$ revenue does not change as the quantity changes. In the special case of unitary elasticity of demand, the market provides perfect income insurance for producers. More generally, the market provides some revenue insurance for producers. To the extent that an individual producer's quantity is positively correlated with aggregate quantity, the market therefore provides partial revenue insurance for an individual producer.

Trade "reallocates" many things (e.g. production, pollution, unemployment). It also reallocates risk. Figure 5.5 provides a partial equilibrium example of two countries that produce and consume

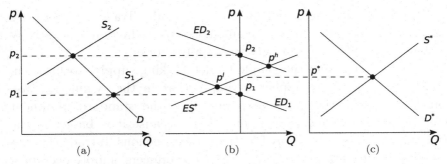

Figure 5.5. Panel (a) shows Home (random) supply and demand, and panel (c) shows Foreign supply and demand. Panel (b) shows home (random) excess demand and foreign excess supply.

the same good; supply in one country is random. Under trade, the variance of world price is between the variance of each autarchic price.

Figure 5.5(a) illustrates the supply and demand of Home, where supply is random: it is given by S_1 half the time, and S_2 half the time. In autarchy, Home price fluctuates between p_1 and p_2. Figure 5.5(c) shows the supply and demand of Foreign, where supply is non-stochastic. The autarchy price in Foreign is p^*. Figure 5.5(b) shows the nonstochastic excess supply of Foreign, S^*, and the excess demand of Home, ED_1 and ED_2. With trade, the world price fluctuates between p^l and p^h. Home has less price variability with trade, and Foreign has more. Trade reallocates price instability. Because price variability creates risk for agents, trade reallocates risk.

This example with asymmetric countries suggests that when trade leads to the import of price volatility, trade may reduce welfare for the country that imports the volatility. However, one country may import price instability for some commodities, and export price instability for other commodities. The increased price instability for some commodities may then be worth the decreased instability for others. In order to use a single commodity model to illustrate this situation it is more appropriate to treat Home and Foreign symmetrically, so that each has random supply. In such a (symmetric) model, each country's average (expected) exports (and imports) are zero, but in most states of nature they trade. Trade reduces price instability in each country; the amount of the reduction is negatively related to the correlation between supply shocks.

This extension of the simple model, making supply stochastic in both countries, may appear to imply that in the symmetric case at least, price variability does not alter the standard argument for trade. That conclusion is incorrect, because it is based on the assumption that the supply functions are exogenous. If trade changes the distribution of prices, it can change producers' supply decisions, and thus change the supply function in every state of nature (e.g. in every weather condition).

5.5.2 *Pareto inferior trade*

Newbery and Stiglitz[5] illustrate a situation in which all agents in both (symmetric) countries might be worse off under free trade than under autarchy. Their result can be interpreted as an illustration of the theory of the second best.

Their model contains a representative producer and a representative consumer in each of two countries. The risk averse producer allocates land (the only input) between a "safe crop" and a "risky crop". After the farmer makes this land allocation decision, the random weather shock occurs, determining the output of the risky crop. The output of the safe crop is deterministic, and depends only on the amount of land devoted to its cultivation. The consumer is risk neutral, with preferences that imply an elasticity of demand for the risky crop equal to 1.

First, consider the equilibrium under autarchy. The assumption of unitary elasticity of demand for the risky crop means that a 10% decrease in supply causes a 10% increase in equilibrium price. Consequently, the farmer's revenue from the risky crop is non-stochastic under autarchy. Any decrease in supply is exactly compensated by an increase in price, leaving revenue unchanged.

---

[5]Newberry and Stiglity, *Review of Economic Studies*, 1984, pp. 1–12, Pareto Inferior Trade.

With unitary elasticity of demand, the implicit insurance provided by the market is "complete", in the sense that the farmer's revenue is certain. The farmer facing no revenue uncertainty from producing the risky crop behaves as if she has full insurance, allocating the socially optimal amount of land to the risky crop. Consumers are risk neutral by assumption.

Now consider the free trade equilibrium. Suppose that two countries are exactly the same, except that the random shock to supply is perfectly negatively correlated: when there is good weather in one country, there is bad weather in the other. Because the two countries are identical in each period prior to the realization of their respective random variables, the farmers in each country make the same land allocation decision (before the weather shock is realized). However, given the negative correlation in the supply shock, when output is high in one country, it is low in the other country. Thus, under trade, aggregate output of the risky crop is non-stochastic; under free trade the price of the risky crop is also non-stochastic.

Under autarchy the farmer faces price uncertainty but no income uncertainty. With trade, the farmer faces no price uncertainty, but substantial income uncertainty. Of course, the farmer cares about income, not the price *per se*. The risk averse farmer allocates less land to the risky crop when there is trade (and the accompanying revenue risk) compared to in autarchy (where there is no revenue risk). The land allocation is socially optimal in the riskless autarchic scenario, but not in the risky trade scenario. Therefore, the introduction of trade causes the land allocation to depart from the optimum.

In expectation the consumer is worse off with trade, because although trade provides price stability (which is unimportant to the risky neutral consumer) it reduces the supply of the risky crop (which under autarchy was at the first best level). The farmer is worse off because she faces income risk with trade. Both of the agents in both of the countries have lower expected welfare with trade than under autarchy.

This model incorporates many unrealistic assumptions, but these serve only to make the result (relatively) transparent. The Pareto Inferior result is not knife-edge, so it survives a small weakening of any of the assumptions. The intuition for the result is that there is no insurance market: markets are incomplete. This missing market is unimportant under autarchy, because the spot market provides a perfect substitute for the missing insurance market. With trade, and non-stochastic aggregate supply, the spot market no longer serves this function. Trade opens up one market (international sales) but effectively closes down the (implicit) insurance market.

This possibility is an example of the theory of the second best. We can view one distortion as the missing insurance market and the other distortion as a prohibitive tariff. Reducing the tariff to 0 can make all agents worse off, and thus decreases social welfare in both countries. Absence of complete (e.g. insurance) markets means that there is an *a priori* case for government intervention; competition, together with free trade, is not necessarily constrained efficient.

This example of Pareto-inferior trade is primarily useful as a means of sharpening our intuition about second-best settings. However, in order to determine whether missing insurance markets provide a plausible argument for trade policy, it is important to ask why the markets are incomplete. If the reasons have to do with informational problems such as adverse selection or moral hazard, and if the government does not have better information than private agents, trade policy may be powerless to improve upon a competitive equilibrium. The theory of the second best tells us that insurance arguments *might* provide a justification for trade policy. However, the fact that these markets are incomplete certainly does not provide a presumption that trade restrictions are welfare improving.

5.6 Immizerizing growth

Immizerizing growth describes a situation where growth makes a country poorer. I consider two examples. In the first example, growth shifts out a country's export supply function, leading to a fall in its terms of trade large enough to offset the benefits from growth. The second example assumes that growth occurs in an environment where the government achieves an exogenous constraint in a suboptimal manner. I also use this example to discuss the Principle of Targeting. Clarete and Whalley[6] present an empirical model of the two possibilities discussed below.

The possibility that growth is immizerizing is another example of the theory of the second best — but the connection may not be obvious. There are two sources of possible confusion. First, growth might be immizerizing for the country that experiences the growth, *not for the world at large.* It is important to keep in mind whose welfare change we are examining. Second, representing growth as arising from a reduction in a distortion is not essential, but it helps to emphasize that the theory of the second best is applicable more generally than might be obvious. With a bit of practice, many or even most "surprising" results in economics can be seen as applications of the theory of the second best. Most problems can be understood without applying the lens of the theory of the second best, but that lens provides a unifying device for apparently unrelated problems.

Imagine that an economy has some factor of production, or some technology locked away, e.g. the country has a prohibitive tax on this factor or technology, so that producers do not use it. We can think of this tax or prohibition as being a distortion. Getting rid of this distortion makes producers want to use the factor or technology. Thus, getting rid of the distortion is "like" growth. Of course, the two are not literally the same, but they are formally the same: getting rid of the distortion makes the factor or the technology available, as does growth, causing the PPF to shift out.

5.6.1 *A growth-induced decline in the terms of trade*

A growth-induced decline in the terms of trade can lower a country's welfare. Note that here we are speaking of a reduction in welfare for the agent (the firm or industry or country) that experiences the growth. *Aggregate welfare* (i.e. for consumers or producers in

---

[6]Clarete and Whalley, "Immizerizing Growth and Endogenous Protection", *Journal of Development Economics*, 45 (1994), pp. 121–133.

the partial equilibrium setting, or for all countries in the general equilibrium setting) increase as a consequence of growth.

5.6.1.1 *Partial equilibrium setting*

Consider first a partial equilibrium model with a downward sloping demand and an upward sloping industry marginal cost = supply curve. Here, we can think of growth as a reduction in industry marginal costs. Because this marginal cost curve gives industry supply, growth is equivalent here to an outward shift in the supply function. At the competitive equilibrium, the demand and supply curves intersect; producer welfare is measured by producer surplus. The reader should draw a demand curve and a supply (= marginal cost) curve and observe the change in producer surplus due to an outward shift in the supply function (= growth). Growth might either increase or decrease producer surplus, depending on the exact manner in which the supply function shifts, and on the demand function. Growth is more likely to reduce producer surplus if demand is very inelastic, where the outward shift in the supply function leads to a large fall in price.

If growth occurs to a monopoly instead of to competitive firms, then growth never reduces industry profits. The monopoly can continue to produce at the pre-growth level, and obtain higher profits due to the reduction in marginal costs. In general, it is optimal for the monopoly to change the production level.

In order to interpret this situation as an example of the theory of the second best we need to identify a second distortion, in addition to the "distortion" that keeps the technology locked away. Although the competitive equilibrium maximizes social surplus, it does not maximize industry profits, except in the special case where demand is perfectly elastic. From the standpoint of the industry, the competitive equilibrium is not optimal; it is a second best outcome. The distortion, i.e. the feature that reflects the fact that the industry is not at its first best level of output is that in the competitive equilibrium price equals marginal cost, whereas in the first best (*from the standpoint of producers*) outcome, marginal revenue equals marginal cost. From the standpoint of producers collectively, optimality requires $MR = P(1 - \frac{1}{\eta}) =$ marginal cost, whereas in the competitive equilibrium $P =$ marginal cost. The difference between the monopoly first order condition and condition for the competitive equilibrium is the "distortion" $d = P/\eta$. The competitive equilibrium is a departure from the first best (from the producers' standpoint) outcome, and this departure can be viewed as a "distortion". Agriculture in many countries, including in the US, has been subject to this kind of immizerizing growth.

5.6.1.2 *General equilibrium setting*

In a general equilibrium setting, the exporting country plays the role taken by the industry in the partial equilibrium example. The assumption that the exporting country is "large" corresponds to the assumption (in the partial equilibrium setting) that the industry faces a downward sloping demand function. In the general equilibrium trade setting, the assumption that the exporter is large means that it's trading partner has an imperfectly elastic excess demand for imports. Therefore, anything that changes the location of the exporter's excess supply function also changes the world equilibrium price.

Figure 5.6 illustrates immizerizing growth in a general equilibrium context. Suppose that p is the original world equilibrium relative price (before growth). Figure 5.6 shows growth as being primarily in the export sector (corn). The PPF frontier shifts out, but it shifts out mostly for corn, the export commodity of the country that grows.

Recall the steps used to derive a country's export supply curve using its PPF, IEP, and BOP constraint (and the resulting trade triangle). Using graphical examples, students should convince themselves that export-biased growth can "easily" shift out a country's export supply curve, causing its export price to fall from p to a level like p' in Figure 5.6. The fall in price is greater, the less elastic is the import demand function that the country faces.

The fact that the equilibrium price falls means that the IEP shifts toward the axis of the export good, as shown in Figure 5.6.

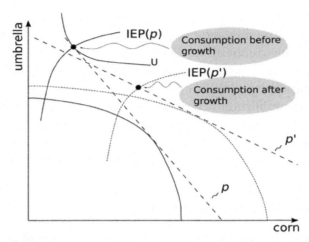

Figure 5.6. Immizerizing growth due to deterioration of terms of trade: price of exports falls from p to p'.

Production also shifts. Possibly more of the import commodity is produced (relative to the initial equilibrium) but much more of the export commodity is produced. In the example in this figure, the consumption point at the after-growth equilibrium is below the indifference curve at the pre-growth equilibrium; growth leads to a decline in welfare. This example depends on the assumptions that growth is predominately in the export sector (corn), and that the Rest-of-World import demand for corn is very inelastic.

As in the partial equilibrium model above, we can think of the second distortion as arising from the country behaving as a price taker, when in fact it has market power. Of course, this behavior is not a distortion from the perspective of world welfare; it is a distortion only from the perspective of the country whose welfare we are evaluating.

5.7 Exogenous Constraints and the Principle of Targeting

Immizerizing growth can also occur where an exogenous constraint, such as target level of domestic production of a particular commodity, is achieved in a suboptimal manner. These exogenous targets are

sometimes referred to as noneconomic constraints, to indicate that
the source of the constraint is outside the model. However, "exogenous" seems like a better descriptor.

In the example here, a country imports food and faces fixed world
prices. Nothing that happens in this small country changes the world
price. Therefore the source of immizerizing growth must be different
here than in the previous example.

Denote as F^s the domestic production of food; suppose that the
country has an exogenous target of F^* units of food production,
i.e. it requires that $F^s \geq F^*$. Perhaps the country chooses this
target to ensure food security, but such considerations are extra-
neous to the model. This target (the constraint) is binding, in the
sense that under free trade, the level of food production is less
than F^*.

In the current context, the constraint should *not* be regarded as
a distortion; it is a fact of life (exogenous). This constraint lowers
national income, but we make no judgement as to whether the
constraint is a good or a bad thing. The added food security might
be worth the welfare cost. A distortion arises if the constraint is
achieved suboptimally, causing an *additional* loss in national income,
above the loss necessary to achieve the target. This additional loss is
the manifestation of the distortion.

The "Principle of Targeting" says that the policy intervention
should be as direct as possible. Here, because the policy objective
involves food production, policy should alter *producer* prices by
means of a tax/subsidy. Recall that a subsidy on food production
and a tax on cloth production are equivalent, because only relative
prices matter. Consumer prices should not be affected by an optimal
policy. A tariff is therefore a non-optimal policy.

Suppose that the country ignores the Principle of Targeting and
achieves the target using a particular second-best instrument, a tariff.
Figure 5.7 shows IEP associated with the tariff-inclusive relative price
of cloth as p. The PPFs through A and B correspond to the pre- and
the post-growth technologies. The price p is less than the world price
of cloth (given by the slope of the BOP constraint through points A
and B) so production in the food sector is subsidized, or equivalently,

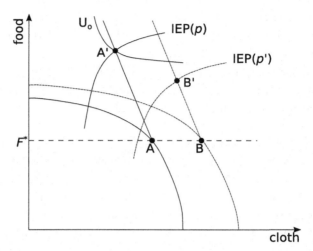

Figure 5.7. Growth can lower welfare when an exogenous target is achieved using a second best policy instrument.

production in the cloth sector is taxed. The tariff achieves the target level of F^*, and utility is U_0.[7]

Now suppose that there is unbalanced growth, concentrated in the cloth sector. Figure 5.7 shows the PPF flatter at B than at A. Therefore, to maintain production of food at F^* using a trade policy, the tariff must increase. (It is important to understand why the last sentence is true: What has to happen to the domestic relative price, i.e. the tariff inclusive price, in order to maintain production at F^* after growth?) The larger tariff means that the distortion that consumers face (the wedge between domestic and world prices) increases. Because world prices are fixed, the domestic relative price of food increases. Consequently, the IEP shifts down from IEP(p) to IEP(p') as shown. In Figure 5.7, the income expansion path shifts down so much, that utility after growth (with the larger tariff) is lower than utility before growth.

---

[7]As an exercise, students should find the level of utility that would have been achieved had the exogenous constraint been satisfied using a first-best production tax/subsidy instead of the trade policy. The comparison of welfare under the first-best and the second-best policies illustrates the Principle of Targeting.

The fact that growth requires a larger tariff on food imports shows up in Figure 5.7 as a slightly flatter tangent at point B than at A. Because the production point depends on relative prices, this flattening means that the economy requires a lower relative price of cloth (a higher relative price of food) to maintain food production at F^*. This construction does not explain the source of the change, and therefore does not suggest whether the change is plausible. It might be tempting to argue that given the entire production possibility frontier has shifted out, it would not be necessary to increase the relative price of food to maintain the same (or greater) level of food production. Section 7.4 of Chapter 7 explains this feature. Here we merely foreshadow that explanation. The type of growth illustrated by Figure 5.7 is consistent with increased production of both goods. However, at the original price p (that supports production at A') the growth makes increased production of cloth much more profitable than production of food. This increased incentive to produce cloth draws factors of production away from the food sector, decreasing food production at the original price. To maintain food production at the constrained level, society must increase the relative price of food, thereby dampening the tendency for higher cloth production to draw factors away from the food sector.

In this example, the distortion is policy-induced: an exogenous target is achieved in a suboptimal manner. This fact means that the country starts out in a "second best" (read: "suboptimal") setting. Whenever a change occurs in a second-best setting, be alert to the possibility that the change causes a "counter-intuitive" (but not any more!) result.

Chapter 6

The Ricardo–Viner Model

6.1 Introduction

The two-sector Ricardo–Viner or "Sector-Specific Factors" model assumes that both commodities require a sector-specific input (e.g. land for corn and machines for umbrellas) as well as a mobile factor. In contrast, the Ricardo model assumes that there is a single factor of production, which is mobile across sectors. The Heckscher–Ohlin–Samuelson (HOS), studied in the next chapter, assumes that there are two or more factors of production, all of which are mobile across sectors. We can interpret HOS as a long run model and the Ricardo–Viner model as a medium run model.

I first outline the model and discuss its comparative statics properties. Then I use the model for two second-best applications: (i) trade in the presence of imperfect property rights and (ii) trade in the presence of a minimum wage. I close this chapter by studying an "intermediate" model in which the sector-specific factors can adjust slowly across sectors. This extension serves as a bridge between the Ricardo–Viner and the HOS models.

6.2 Equilibrium in the Basic Model

The building block in this model is the optimality condition that the value of the marginal product of labor (the mobile factor) is equal to the wage. Because labor can move freely from one sector to the

145

other, the wage in the two sectors must be equal (as in the Ricardo model). Producers maximize profits by hiring labor up to the point where labor's value of marginal product equals the wage; therefore, the values of marginal product of labor are equal in the two sectors.

Let K_c and K_u be the amount of sector-specific capital in the corn and umbrella sector; L_c and L_u are the stocks of labor in the two sectors. Let $C(K_c, L_c)$ and $U(K_u, L_u)$ be the sectoral production functions, and denote partial derivatives using subscripts, so C_L and U_L are the marginal products of labor in corn and umbrellas. (To conserve notation, I do not use subscripts on the subscripts, but the meaning should be clear from the context.) These marginal products are functions of the labor and the amount of capital in the sector. I assume that the production function in each sector is concave in labor and that the inputs are technical substitutes, i.e. an increase in either factor in a sector increases the marginal product of the other factor in that sector. In the corn sector, for example, these assumptions mean:

$$C_{LL} < 0 \quad \text{and} \quad C_{LK} = C_{KL} > 0. \tag{6.1}$$

The assumption that production is concave in inputs implies

$$C_{LL}C_{KK} - C_{LK}C_{KL} > 0. \tag{6.2}$$

(There are analogous expressions for the other sector.)

Let W be the nominal wage. The optimality conditions — the value of marginal product equals the price of the input — are

$$p_c \cdot C_L = W \quad \text{and} \quad p_u \cdot U_L = W.$$

It is convenient to work with relative prices. Choose umbrellas as the numeraire good and define $p = p_c/p_u$ and $w = W/p_u$. The wage w has units of umbrellas/labor: w equals the number of umbrellas that exchange in the market for a unit of labor.

Divide the optimality conditions by p_u to rewrite them as

$$p \cdot C_L = w \quad \text{and} \quad U_L = w. \tag{6.3}$$

The total supply of labor is $\bar{L}$, so full employment requires $L_c + L_u = \bar{L}$. Figure 6.1 graphs $p \cdot C_L$ and U_L as functions of the labor allocation. The width of the horizontal axis is $\bar{L}$. Moving left to right increases the stock of labor in umbrellas and decreases the stock of labor in corn. The relative price p is taken as given for the time being. The intersection of the two graphs determines the equilibrium allocation of labor and the equilibrium wage w. The equilibrium umbrella wage is shown in Figure 6.1 as point c.

6.3 Comparative Statics

I consider two types of comparative statics questions. What is the effect of the commodity price on labor allocation and real returns to factors? What is the effect of a change in factor supplies on real returns to factors, holding fixed the commodity price?

6.3.1 *The effect of the commodity price on labor allocation and the wage*

I answer the first comparative statics question using both graphical and mathematical analysis. The graphical analysis may be the easiest way to understand how the model works, but it is worth being able to show the results mathematically. Full employment of labor requires $L_u + L_c = \bar{L}$. Holding the total supply of labor fixed, the differential of this equation implies

$$dL_c = -dL_u, \tag{6.4}$$

which says that labor entering one sector must come from the other.

First consider the effect of an increase in p (the relative price of corn) on the labor allocation. The increase in p causes the curve DE to shift up to the dotted line $D'E'$, causing the allocation of labor to shift from F to F' in Figure 6.1. Labor leaves the umbrella sector and enters the corn sector.

Totally differentiating the equilibrium conditions, equation (6.3), using equation (6.4), gives

$$dw = U_{LL} \cdot dL_u \quad \text{and} \quad dp = \frac{(pC_{LL} + U_{LL})}{C_L} \cdot dL_u. \tag{6.5}$$

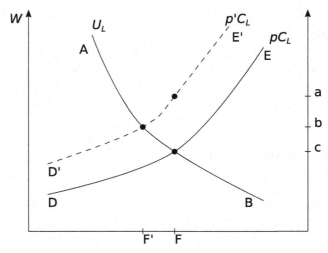

Figure 6.1. Equilibrium wage and labor allocation as a function of the relative commodity price.

The second equality in (6.5) implies that

$$\frac{dL_u}{dp} = \frac{C_L}{(pC_{LL} + U_{LL})} < 0, \qquad (6.6)$$

where the inequality follows from the assumption that the production functions are concave. Thus, an increase in p decreases the amount of labor in the umbrella sector.

To determine the effect of the price on the real return to labor we need to know how a price increase changes both of the ratios W/p_u and W/p_c. An increase in the price p shifts up the curve pC_L in Figure 6.1 to the dashed curve. The relative wage w increases, so W/p_u increases from c to b. We still need to determine how the increase in the relative price changes the ratio

$$\frac{W}{p_c} = \frac{w}{p}.$$

This ratio equals the number of units of corn that a worker can purchase by selling one unit of labor.

I use first a graphical and then a mathematical demonstration to show that an increase in p lowers the ratio $\frac{w}{p}$. In view of the discussion of the real wage in Section 2.7 of Chapter 2, this increase in p implies that the effect of the change in the relative commodity price on the real return to labor is ambiguous.

First consider the graphical approach, using Figure 6.1. For this demonstration I evaluate all of the derivatives at the initial equilibrium allocation, point F. With $p' = p + \Delta p$, the height of the point a is $p'C_L = (p + \Delta p)\, C_L$ and the height of the point c is pC_L. Therefore,

$$\frac{a - c}{c} = \frac{(p + \Delta p)\, C_L - pC_L}{pC_L} = \frac{\Delta p}{p}.$$

Using the same logic,

$$\frac{b - c}{c} = \frac{\Delta w}{w}.$$

By inspection of Figure 6.1,

$$\frac{\Delta p}{p} > \frac{\Delta w}{w}.$$

This inequality implies that

$$\frac{\Delta w}{\Delta p}\frac{p}{w} < 1. \tag{6.7}$$

This inequality states that (for example) a 10% increase in p leads to a less than 10% increase in w. This result implies that an increase in p leads to a fall in $\frac{w}{p}$.

To obtain this result mathematically, divide the first line in equation (6.5) by w and the second line by p, and then divide one equation by the other. We obtain the following expression for the elasticity of the wage with respect to the price:

$$\frac{dw}{dp}\frac{p}{w} = \frac{\frac{dw}{w}}{\frac{dp}{p}} = \frac{\frac{U_{LL}}{pC_L}}{\frac{pC_{LL}+U_{LL}}{pC_L}} = \frac{U_{LL}}{pC_{LL} + U_{LL}} < 1. \qquad (6.8)$$

Again, this inequality implies that a 10% increase in the price causes a less than 10% increase in the wage. Equations (6.7) and (6.8) contain the same information.

6.3.2 *The return to the specific factors*

Thus far I have assumed only that the production function is concave in labor and that labor and capital are technical substitutes, so that the cross partials of the production functions are positive (i.e. more labor increases the marginal product of capital). The fixed factor is the "residual claimant" in this model, meaning that the value of production, minus the wage bill, accrues to the fixed factor. The fixed factor receives rent.

The fact that the fixed factors do not move from one sector to the other means that the rents these factors receive are (typically) different in the two sectors. Thus, it does not make sense to speak of the rental rate of "capital". We have to distinguish whether we mean capital in the umbrella sector, or capital in the corn sector. Subscripts distinguish these two rental rates. We want to know how an exogenous change, e.g. in the relative commodity price, changes both the nominal and the real return to capital in the two sectors.

For concreteness, consider the umbrella sector, where the value of production is $U(K_u, L_u)$; recall that by choice of numeraire, the price of umbrellas is 1, so U is both the quantity and the value of umbrella output. The subscripts to the arguments of the production function emphasize that umbrella production depends on the amount of capital and labor in that sector. The value of umbrella output, less the wage bill is (using equation (6.3)) is

$$U(K_u, L_u) - wL_u = U(K_u, L_u) - U_L L_u.$$

This residual value accrues to umbrella capital, so the rent per unit of capital is simply

$$r_u = \frac{U(K_u, L_u) - wL_u}{K_u}. \tag{6.9}$$

There is a similar relation for the corn sector.

In the interest of simplicity I now assume that in each sector there are constant returns to scale. Euler's Theorem implies that

$$
\begin{aligned}
U_K\left(K, L\right) K + U_L\left(K, L\right) L &= U(K, L) \\
\Rightarrow U_K\left(K, L\right) K + wL &= U(K, L) \\
\Rightarrow \frac{U(K, L) - wL}{K} &= r_u = U_K.
\end{aligned}
\tag{6.10}
$$

The second line of equation (6.3) implies the second line of equation (6.10). Thus, with constant returns to scale, the rent to a factor (equal to its price) is equal to its value of marginal productivity. If I did not assume constant returns to scale, I would use equation (6.9) to determine the price of the sector-specific factor. Alternatively, I could assume that each sector-specific factor earns its value of marginal product; but in that case, I would have to introduce some other factor that is the residual claimant.

With the assumption of constant returns to scale, the equilibrium factor prices in the two sectors equal the value of their marginal product

$$r_c = p \cdot C_K \quad \text{and} \quad r_u = U_K. \tag{6.11}$$

The normalization $p_u = 1$ means that the value of the marginal product of capital in the umbrella sector is equal to the marginal product of capital in that sector. Because capital is immobile across sectors, there is no reason for the return to capital to be equal in the two sectors.

An increase in p increases the real return to capital in the corn sector and decreases the real return to capital in the umbrella sector.

First consider the intuition for this result. We know that the increase in p causes labor to leave the umbrella sector and to enter the corn sector; this reallocation increases C_k and decreases U_K, because the cross-partials are positive (see equation (6.1)). Therefore r_u falls in absolute terms. Because p rises, r_u/p obviously falls, so the real return to capital in the umbrella sector falls. Keep in mind the units: r_u is the number of units of umbrellas that a owner of umbrella capital can purchase by renting one unit of umbrella capital; r_u/p is the number of units of corn the owner obtains by renting one unit of capital. The increase in p means that a person who owns and rents out capital in the umbrella sector is able to buy less of both commodities. The higher p lowers the real return to umbrella-specific capital.

The increased labor in the corn sector caused by the increased price, p, (see equation (6.6)) increases $C_K = r_c/p$. The fact that both this ratio and p increases means that r_c must increase. Thus, the real return to capital in the corn sector increases.

To obtain this result mathematically, rewrite the first line of equation (6.11) as

$$\frac{r_c}{p} = C_K.$$

Differentiate this equation, using equation (6.6) and the assumption that $C_{KL} > 0$ to obtain

$$\frac{d\left(\frac{r_c}{p}\right)}{dp} = \frac{dC_K}{dp} = C_{KL}\frac{dL_c}{dp} = -C_{KL}\frac{dL_u}{dp} > 0.$$

6.3.3   *Changes in the supply of factors*

Now, we consider the effect on the equilibrium real factor returns of a change in factor supplies, holding fixed the commodity price. For example, we represent an increase in labor as an increase in the width of the box in Figure 6.1. This increase leads to a fall in the absolute value of w, and thus a fall in the real wage. Because there is then more labor in both sectors, the marginal product of the fixed factor in each sector rises, as does the real return to capital in each sector.

A higher stock of capital in one sector lowers the real return to capital in both sectors and raises the real return to labor. An increase in the amount of capital in a sector causes the marginal product of capital in that sector to fall and the marginal product of labor in that sector to rise; the curve in Figure 6.1 corresponding to the sector in which capital increases rises, leading to an increase in w. Because p is constant, w/p rises. Therefore, a higher stock of either sector-specific capital raises the real return to labor.

To examine the effect of an increase in capital in a sector on the real returns to capital in both sectors, suppose that the stock of umbrella capital increases. This change increases the marginal productivity of labor in that sector, raising the curve U_L in Figure 6.1, increasing the equilibrium level of labor in the umbrella sector. The change reduces the equilibrium amount of labor in the corn sector and increases the wage. Neither the price nor the stock of capital in the corn sector has changed, so the marginal productivity and thus the real return to capital in the corn sector falls.

The effects are slightly more complicated in the umbrella sector. The increase in the supply of capital in that sector reduces capital's marginal productivity (holding labor constant), but the increase in labor increases capital's marginal productivity. We noted that the increase in umbrella capital also raises the equilibrium wage. The net effect is to reduce the return to capital in the umbrella sector. To help develop intuition for this result, consider the limiting case where the wage does not increase at all (or increases by a negligible amount). In this case, we can write the restricted profit function in the umbrella sector as

$$\pi\left(K, w\right) = \max_L U\left(K, L\right) - wL.$$

By the envelope theorem

$$\pi_K = U_K \equiv r_u.$$

If the restricted profit function is concave in K, we have $\frac{dr_u}{dK_u} = \pi_{KK} < 0$. Thus, given concavity of π, an increase in capital reduces the rent *even in the case where the wage does not change*. Therefore, the increase in capital must also reduce the rent in the case where the wage rises.

The argument above assumes that the restricted profit function is concave. The assumption $U_{KK} < 0$ does not establish concavity of π, because at constant w an increase in K also increases L, and $U_{KL} > 0$ by assumption. Therefore, in order to establish the comparative statics result, we totally differentiate the second equilibrium condition equation in (6.11) (in the case of CRTS) to write

$$dr_u = \left(U_{KK} + U_{KL}\frac{dL_u}{dK}\right)dK.$$

To evaluate this differential we need an expression for $\frac{dL_u}{dK}$. To obtain that derivative, denote $dK > 0$ as the increase in capital in the umbrella sector and take the total differential of the equilibrium condition for labor allocation $U_L = pC_L$ (together with the full employment condition, which implies $dL_u = -dL_c$):

$$U_{LL}\frac{dL_u}{dK} + U_{LK} = -pC_{LL}\frac{dL_u}{dK}$$

$$\Rightarrow \frac{dL_u}{dK} = -\frac{U_{LK}}{U_{LL} + pC_{LL}}.$$

These results imply

$$dr_u = \left(U_{KK} - \frac{U_{KL}U_{LK}}{U_{LL} + pC_{LL}}\right)dK$$

$$\Rightarrow \frac{dr_u}{dK} = \frac{U_{KK}(U_{LL} + pC_{LL}) - U_{KL}U_{LK}}{U_{LL} + pC_{LL}}$$

$$= \frac{U_{KK}U_{LL} - U_{KL}U_{LK}}{U_{LL} + pC_{LL}} + \frac{pU_{KK}C_{LL}}{U_{LL} + pC_{LL}}.$$

The numerator of the first term after the last equality is positive by concavity of the production function, and the numerator of the second term is also positive; because the denominator is negative, both terms are negative. The increase in capital in the umbrella sector lowers the return on capital in that sector.

6.4 Trade

The Ricardo–Viner model is a special case of the model that we studied in Chapter 3, and the trade equilibrium can be studied using the same graphical methods. Figure 6.1 can be used to derive the PPF for this model. Figure 6.1 shows the relation between the relative commodity price and the allocation of labor. If I know the allocation of labor, then I know the amount of each good that is produced, because the other factors are fixed. Figure 6.2 shows the production possibility curve. I know that the slope of the production possibility curve is equal to the relative price, p, in an efficient competitive equilibrium. Picking a particular value of p, we use Figure 6.1 to find the output of each good, obtaining a point on the PPF; at that point the slope of the PPF is p. Repeating this procedure for many values of p, traces out the PPF, shown in Figure 6.2.

Using Figure 6.2 (and indifference curves) we can find the autarchic price, and we can find the level of production, consumption and trade for an open economy. We can also ask the kinds of comparative static policy questions considered in Chapter 3.

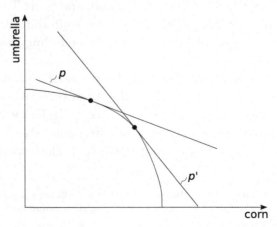

Figure 6.2. As we change the price in Figure 6.1 we generate points on the production possibility frontier and the associated tangencies.

6.5   Imperfect Property Rights

Imperfect property rights have been an important topic in trade economics since at least the 1990s. The Ricardian model and much of the subsequent classical trade theory explains international exchange as arising from cross-country differences associated with endowments and technology.[1] Those differences cause countries to have different relative opportunity costs of production (as in the Ricardian model), creating a basis for gains from trade. Differences in institutions and cultures can also create cross-country differences in relative production costs that lead to trade.

Cultural practices and legal institutions underpin property rights. Many countries that are well-endowed with natural resource also have weak property rights governing those resources. The countries' endowment of natural resources, and their resulting cost advantages in natural resource-intensive sectors, creates a standard, or "real" comparative advantage in these sectors. Their relatively weak property rights to natural resources further lowers — at least temporarily (until the resource is degraded) — production costs in these sectors, creating an "apparent" (but not real) source of comparative advantage. Graciela Chichilnisky's,[2] leading paper in this literature, explains these different types of comparative advantage. A series of papers by James Brander, Brian Copeland, and Scott Taylor (and the book *Trade and the Environment* by Copeland and Taylor) explore many aspects of imperfect property rights, including those related to resource dynamics.

This section uses the Ricardo–Viner model to illustrate and explain some of the basic ideas in this literature. We suppose that there are imperfect property rights to the specific factor in one sector. For example, one sector is natural resource-intensive (e.g. forestry) and the other sector is capital-intensive (e.g. cloth manufacturing).

---

[1] A more recent branch of trade theory studies trade amongs similar countries, in order to explain intra-industry trade — the situation where countries exchange similar commodities.

[2] Garcia Chichilnisky, "North–South Trade and the Global Environment", *American Economic Review*, Vol. 84, (1994).

There are perfect property rights to capital used in the cloth sector but imperfect property rights to the natural capital in the forestry sector. It may be relatively easy to keep unauthorized people from using a factory, but it is difficult to keep people from illegally using a forest. In this case, the competitive equilibrium is not first best. Opening such an economy to trade can lead to a loss in welfare, for now-familiar second-best reasons.

To focus on the role of imperfect property rights in trade it is convenient to consider a situation where two countries (North and South) are identical in every respect except that property rights to forests are weaker in South. In this case, South has an "apparent" comparative advantage in the forestry sector. The advantage is based on an institutional failure (imperfect property right) rather than a "real" comparative advantage. North always gains from trade, but South may either gain or lose. This section considers two types of imperfect property rights. I first consider a common property resource, and then a model with poachers. These two models have similar properties.

6.5.1 *A common property resource*

Suppose that there are n firms in the forestry sector, where n is fixed. All firms can use the forestry resource (natural capital). All labor is equally productive, so each firm's share of total forestry output is equal to their share of the purchased input (labor). This model describes a common property resource, as distinct from an open access resource. Under open access, n is endogenous. With open access and free entry, n changes endogenously to dissipate all rents to the forest resource.

Let $F(L)$ be total output in the forestry sector, where L is aggregate labor in the forestry sector (not aggregate economy-wide labor here). We suppress the sector-specific argument, forestry capital, because that is held fixed for this static model. If firm i hires L_i units of labor, its share of total labor output is $\frac{L_i}{L}$ and its profits are

$$\pi_i = pF(L)\frac{L_i}{L} - wL_i,$$

where p is the relative price of forestry output. Manufacturing is the numeraire good.

At a Nash equilibrium each firm chooses the amount of labor to hire, taking as given prices and other firms' hiring decisions. Firm i chooses L_i taking $\sum_{j \neq i} L_j$ as given. Recall that $L_i + \sum_{j \neq i} L_j = L$. Using this relation, Firm i's first order condition in a Nash equilibrium is

$$p\frac{L_i F'}{L} + p\frac{(L - L_i) F}{L^2} = w.$$

In a symmetric Nash equilibrium $L_i = \frac{L}{n}$, the first order condition can be written as

$$p\left(\frac{1}{n}F' + \frac{n-1}{n}\frac{F}{L}\right) = w. \tag{6.12}$$

(It is important to impose the symmetry condition $L_i = \frac{L}{n}$ after taking the first order condition, not before; otherwise you end up with nonsense.) The function on the left side of equation (6.12) is a convex combination of the value of marginal product and the value of average product. Assuming that $F(L)$ is concave, the average product is greater than the marginal product. The dashed curve in Figure 6.3 is the graph of a particular convex combination of marginal and average products. The equilibrium amount of labor in the sector is shown as L_{cp} (cp for common property), which is less than the open access level, L_{oa}, and more than the level under perfect property rights, L_{ppr}. For $n = 1$ we have perfect property rights, and for $n = \infty$ we obtain the open access equilibrium. With open access, all rents to the forestry resource are dissipated.

6.5.2 *Poachers*

This model of poachers is based on Hotte *et al.*[3] Owners of the forest resource have *de jure* but not *de facto* property rights, because they are not able to keep poachers from using the resource illegally.

---

[3]L. Hotte, N. van Long, and H. Tian's "International Trade with Endogenous Property Rights," *Journal of Development Economics*, Vol. 62, (2000).

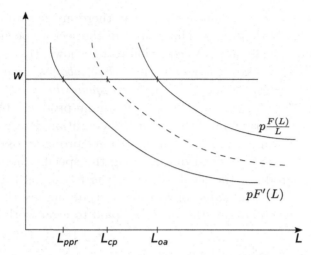

Figure 6.3. The points L_{ppr}, L_{cp}, and L_{oa} are the equilibrium amounts of labor in the forestry sector under, respectively, perfect property rights, common property, and open access.

I first describe the model for fixed relative commodity price p and fixed wage, w. I then show that if property rights are sufficiently weak, owners of the forest resource have a strategic incentive to hire additional workers as a means of discouraging poachers. The next three subsections study the comparative statics of the model, the effect of property rights on real factor returns, and the effect of property rights on the autarchic equilibrium.

6.5.2.1 *Description of the model*

A poacher in forestry has to spend the fraction γ of her time to avoid detection. The amount of *productive* labor in the forestry sector is

$$L = L^e + (1 - \gamma) L^p, \qquad (6.13)$$

where L^e is the number of legal workers (measured in, for example, person-weeks) employed by the legal owner, and L^p is the number of poachers. The average product of all productive labor (L) in the forestry sector is $\frac{F(L)}{L}$. The labor time spent avoiding detection is not productive.

In this section, I again assume that there are constant returns to scale in the both sectors. The owners of the sector-specific factors are the residual claimants. As equation (6.10) shows, the assumption of constant returns to scale means that *when labor is hired up to the point that its value of marginal product equals the wage,* then the sector-specific factor earns its value of marginal product. This "wage equals value of marginal product of labor" condition does not hold in the forestry sector, where there are imperfect property rights to the sector-specific asset. Instead of obtaining the specific factor's value of marginal product, the legal owner of the forest (as the residual claimant) obtains the value of forestry output, minus the amount stolen by poachers, minus the wage bill paid to legal workers.

6.5.2.2 *The equilibrium for given w*

If property rights are very strong (γ is close to 1), then poaching is so unattractive that the forest owner does not have to do anything to discourage poaching. In that case, the fact that property rights are imperfect does not alter the equilibrium. We are interested in the situation where property rights are weak enough (γ is small enough) that the equilibrium differs from the situation with perfect property rights.

The equilibrium to this model has a feature that may seem counter-intuitive (but in fact is not unusual): *the potential entry of poachers affects the equilibrium, even though in equilibrium no poachers are present.* Forest owners are able to make poaching unattractive by strategically hiring a sufficient number of legal workers to drive the return to poaching down to the wage, thereby leaving workers with no incentive to poach.[4] Moreover, it is in the interest of forest owners to do this.

Workers decide whether to work in the cloth sector or in forestry, either as legal employees or poachers. A legal worker in the forestry

---

[4]That is, workers are indifferent between poaching and working as legal employees. If you insist that some workers might nevertheless decide to poach, you can think of a perturbation in which the forest owners drive the return to poaching to a level just below the wage, so that workers strictly prefer not to poach.

sector receives the same wage as workers in the cloth sector, where all workers are legal by definition. While working, instead of avoiding detection, poachers are as productive as legal workers in forestry. Therefore, for each unit of time spent working (as distinct from avoiding detection) a poacher receives the value of average product of labor in Forestry, $\frac{pF(L)}{L}$. A worker who devotes one unit of time to poaching receives no compensation for the γ units of time she spends evading detection, and she receives $(1-\gamma)\frac{pF(L)}{L}$ per unit of time for the remaining time she spends poaching.

Legal workers receive the wage w in both the forestry and the cloth sector. As a poacher, a worker obtains $(1-\gamma)\frac{pF(L)}{L}$ per unit of time. A worker is indifferent between poaching and working legally if and only if

$$(1-\gamma)\frac{pF(L)}{L} = w. \qquad (6.14)$$

Denote $\hat{L}$ as the solution to this equation. The left side of this equation is the "implicit wage" that poachers earn, equal to their income per unit of time. Equation (6.14) states that the implicit wage in the poaching activity equals the explicit wage in either of the legal activities. If the left side were greater than the wage, all workers would want to be poachers; if the left side were smaller than the wage, workers would strictly prefer to be legal employees rather than poachers. If some workers are poachers and others are legal employees, then the left side must equal the wage. Also, the equation holds if workers are indifferent between the two types activities, even if in equilibrium all workers are in one activity or the other.[5]

We assume that in equilibrium, production of cloth is positive. Therefore, workers never strictly prefer to poach rather than to work legally, so the left-hand side of equation (6.14) cannot be greater than

---

[5]In order to understand this possibility, it might help to recall the Ricardian model. There we saw that one possible outcome is for the price at which a country trades to equal its autarchic price, and for the country to nevertheless be specialized in the good for which it has a comparative advantage. If a production in a sector is positive, then price must equal unit costs (profits are zero). The converse is not true: there could be zero profits, and production in the sector still be zero.

the wage. The next step shows that for sufficiently weak property rights, the left side equals the wage.

The parameter γ determines the extent of property rights. If $\gamma = 1$ poachers have to spend all of their time evading detection, so they obtain nothing from poaching. In that case, the potential for poachers has no effect on the equilibrium, because no one would want to poach even if forest owners behaved non-strategically. More generally, if γ is greater than a critical level $\bar{\gamma}$ (defined below) poaching is so unattractive that workers would rather work legally than as poachers even if the Forestry firms are non-strategic. We take γ as exogenous and assume that it is positive but less than the critical level: $0 < \gamma < \bar{\gamma}$. This assumption implies that equation (6.14) holds in equilibrium.

An example with $\gamma = 0.1$ may help. The activity in the forestry sector consists of gathering firewood. An increase in the number of workers in forestry lowers the average and the marginal product of each worker, because with a larger number of workers there is more competition for finding the firewood. A poacher needs to spend 10% of her time avoiding detection, so a full-time poacher can spend 90% of her time collecting firewood. If there are 500 total *productive* person-hours of labor in forestry, producing the total value $pF(500)$, then for each hour in the sector a poacher obtains $0.9\frac{pF(500)}{500}$. The agent is indifferent between working as a poacher or as a legal worker only if this return to poaching equals the legal wage, w.

The legal owners employ workers to produce forestry output — the usual reason for hiring workers. But the owners also may have a strategic incentive to hire workers, as a means of making poaching less attractive by decreasing labor's average product in the sector. We are primarily interested in the situation where property rights are sufficiently weak that the strategic incentive comes into play. To this end, suppose that there would be poachers ($L^p > 0$) if the owner simply hired workers up to the point where their value of marginal product equals the wage.

In that situation, the owner could increase profits by hiring $1 - \gamma$ additional workers. If no poachers left the sector, the average product would fall; in that case, a poacher does better by becoming a legal employee and earning the wage w. By hiring the additional $1 - \gamma$ workers, the owner drives one poacher out of the sector (so that the equilibrium condition (6.14) is restored) and obtains the departed poacher's average product, w. The owner's cost of this strategic hiring is $(1 - \gamma) w$ and the gain is $w = (1 - \gamma) \frac{pF(L)}{L}$, for a net gain of $\gamma w > 0$. Therefore, when $L^p > 0$ the owner leaves money on the table. The owner's opportunity to increase profits are exhausted only when L^p has been driven to zero.

Thus, the equilibrium number of poachers is $L^p = 0$ regardless of the magnitude γ. Using this fact, we can find the critical value $\bar{\gamma}$ below which the forest owners behave strategically in equilibrium. Recall that for $\gamma > \bar{\gamma}$ poaching is so unattractive that no one wants to poach, even when forestry owners do not behave strategically. Define L^* as the socially optimal (equal to the profit maximizing) level of labor in forestry in the absence of poaching, i.e. the value that solves

$$pF'(L^*) = w. \tag{6.15}$$

The critical level $\bar{\gamma}$ is the solution to[6]

$$(1 - \bar{\gamma}) \frac{pF(L^*)}{L^*} = w. \tag{6.16}$$

When $\gamma < \bar{\gamma}$, poaching is sufficiently attractive (i.e. property rights are sufficiently weak) that the forest owner wants to hire labor strategically, as a means of discouraging poachers from entering.

Figure 6.4 provide a graphical representation of the results above, with $\hat{L}$ the solution to equation (6.14) and L^* the solution to equation (6.15). The dashed curves are the graphs of $pF(L^e) - wL^e$ and the solid curves (defined only for $L^e \leq \hat{L}$) are the graphs of $\frac{L^e}{\hat{L}} pF(\hat{L}) - wL^e = L^e \gamma w$. The owner's profits, as a function of L^e, equal the lower envelope of the two curves. For $L^e < \hat{L}$, the total amount of labor in the sector is fixed at $\hat{L}$; the owner can decide how much of that fixed

---

[6]Define $h(\gamma) \equiv (1 - \gamma) \frac{pF(L^*)}{L^*}$; $h(\gamma)$ is a decreasing function of γ. In addition $h(0) = \frac{pF(L^*)}{L^*} > pF'(L^*) = w$, because average product is greater than marginal product for a concave function. Also, $h(1) = 0 < w$. Thus, by the mean value theorem there exists $0 < \bar{\gamma} < 1$ which satisifes equation (6.16).

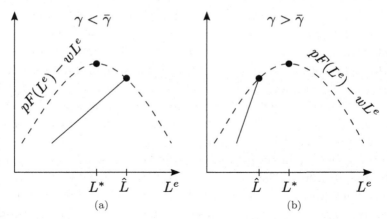

Figure 6.4. (a) Weak property rights: the possibility of poachers affects the forest owner's hiring decision. (b) Strong property rights; the possibility of poachers has no effect on the equilibrium.

stock is legally employed. The solid line increases at a constant rate, γw, because (as shown above) when $L^e < \hat{L}$ each additional unit of legal employment increases the owners profits by γw.

Figure 6.4(a) shows the case where $L^* < \hat{L}$; here, the forestry owner maximizes profits by hiring $L^e = \hat{L} > L^*$ units of labor. Figure 6.4(b) shows the case where $L^* > \hat{L}$; here, property rights are sufficiently strong that no poachers enter even when the owner hires the first best level, L^*.

6.5.2.3 *Comparative statics of poaching model*

The two models of imperfect property rights differ in their particulars, but in each model, for any commodity price, too much labor is attracted to the forestry sector, relative to the first best where there are perfect property rights. This section considers the poaching model. Above I suppressed the sector-specific factors in order not to encumber the notation. I reintroduce them here to show the distributional effects, on the different factor owners, of property rights. Denote these factors as K and f, the factors that are specific to the cloth and forestry sectors, respectively. Normalize the amount of labor to 1 and let L be the amount of labor in forestry, so that

$1 - L$ is the amount of labor in the cloth sector. The economy is incompletely specialized, so $0 < L < 1$.

The assumption of constant returns to scale in both sectors allows us to normalize the number of firms in each sector to 1. If the total amount of forest land is f, it does not matter if there is a single price-taking firm that owns the entire stock, or a number of price-taking firms who own possibly different amounts of the stock.

There are two equivalent ways to express the rate of return to capital in the cloth sector, r_c: either as the amount that a firm would pay to rent a unit of that capital, equal to its value of marginal product, or as the share, per unit of capital, of the residual value in the sector. The residual value is the value of cloth production minus the wage bill. We have

$$r_c \equiv C_K(K, 1 - L) = \frac{C(K, 1 - L) - w(1 - L)}{K}. \qquad (6.17)$$

The rental price of each unit of the forestry asset is

$$r_f \equiv \frac{pF(f, L) - wL}{f}. \qquad (6.18)$$

The rental value of the forestry asset is less than the value of marginal product of this asset, because the additional labor hired (to make poaching unattractive) means that labor is paid more than its value of marginal product. In contrast, labor earns its value of marginal product in the cloth sector. The equilibrium conditions for labor employment in the cloth sector and for labor employment in the forestry sector (equation (6.14)), together with the fact that $L^p = 0$, imply

$$w = C_L(K, 1 - L) = (1 - \gamma)p\frac{F(f, L)}{L}. \qquad (6.19)$$

These two equations determine the labor allocation and the wage, given p.

6.5.2.4 *The effect of property rights on real returns to factors*

We continue to assume that $\gamma < \bar{\gamma}$. At a constant price, p, stronger property rights (larger γ): lowers the wage and the real return to

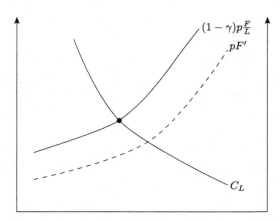

Figure 6.5. The width of the graph equals the stock of labor. Moving from right
to left on the horizontal axis increases labor in the forestry sector, and decreases
labor in the cloth sector. Equilibrium under perfect property rights occurs at
the intersection of dashed curve and C_L, where the value of marginal product
of labor is the same in the two sectors. Equilibrium under poaching occurs at
the intersection of the two solid curves. At this allocation of labor, the value of
marginal product of labor is lower in forestry than in the cloth sector.

labor, and increases the returns and the real returns to the sector-
specific factors in both sectors.

Figure 6.5 graphs the equilibrium condition (6.19). As we move
right to left on the horizontal axis, the amount of labor in forestry
increases. The dashed line shows pF'. The fact that $w = (1 - \gamma)\, p\frac{F}{L} >$
pF' (because $\gamma < \bar{\gamma}$) means that the amount of labor in the forestry
sector (L) is greater than the amount under perfect property rights.
From Figure 6.5, we see that decreasing γ (weakening property
rights) shifts up the solid curve $(1 - \gamma)\, p\frac{F}{L}$, increasing the amount of
labor in forestry. Using either Figure 6.5 or the equilibrium conditions
(6.19), we have

$$\frac{dL}{d\gamma} < 0; \quad \frac{dw}{d\gamma} < 0. \tag{6.20}$$

Now consider the effect of property rights on the return to
the sector-specific factors. Again, Figure 6.5 shows that the larger
amount of labor in cloth $(1 - L)$ caused by stronger property rights
(and lower w) increases the marginal productivity of capital in the

cloth sector, $C_K(K, 1 - L)$, leading to a higher r_c (using equation (6.17)). Formally, we have

$$\frac{dr_c}{d\gamma} = -\frac{\partial C_K(K, 1 - L)}{\partial L_c}\frac{dL}{d\gamma} > 0.$$

For the forest sector we have

$$\frac{dr_f}{d\gamma} = \frac{(pF_L(f, L) - w)\frac{dL}{d\gamma} - L\frac{dw}{d\gamma}}{f} > 0.$$

The last inequality uses the fact that in equilibrium $pF_L(f, L) - w < 0$ (see Figure 6.5 and inequality (6.20)).

This experiment holds fixed the relative price of forestry, p. The conclusions

$$\frac{dr_f}{d\gamma} > 0, \frac{dr_c}{d\gamma} > 0 \quad \text{and} \quad \frac{dw}{d\gamma} < 0$$

mean that an increase in property rights lowers the real return to workers and increases the real return to owners of the sector-specific factors, for a given commodity price. Owners of the two specific factors always prefer stronger property rights to the forestry resource, and workers prefer weaker property rights. In this sense, owners of forestry and cloth capital are natural allies against labor. Both this result, and the conclusion that weaker property rights confers a comparative advantage on the forestry sector, can be overturned in a slightly more general setting.

6.5.2.5 *The effect of property rights on the autarchic equilibrium*

Figure 6.6 graphs the production possibility frontier. Because there is a single, fully employed mobile factor, production takes place on the PPF. In a more general model, a competitive equilibrium is consistent with production inside the PPF. Figure 6.6 shows that under perfect property rights, the autarchic equilibrium would be at point A, where the social indifference curve is tangent to the PPF. Under perfect property rights the autarchic price is p^*, the slope of the tangent at point A. The figure shows the IEP associated with p^*.

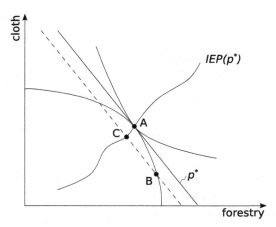

Figure 6.6. Autachic price under perfect property rights: p^*. At that price, with imperfect property rights production is at B and consumption at C: there is excess supply of forestry good, so equilibrium autarchic price must be lower than p^*. (The dashed line shows the budget constraint at price p^* in the economy with poachers.)

To determine the effect of imperfect property rights on the equilibrium autarchic price, we ask: Given imperfect property rights, if the economy were to face the autarchic price p^*, would there be excess supply or excess demand for forestry? (Section 3.6 of Chapter 3, where we discuss the Walrasian auctioneer and the concept of a stable equilibrium, provides the rationale for asking this question.) If the answer is "excess supply", then with imperfect property rights the autarchic price is lower than p^*.

We saw above that weak property rights increases the supply of forestry for any price. In particular, at price p^*, production occurs at a point such as B, i.e. a point associated with more forestry and less cloth production, relative to A. When the price is p^*, production is at B. The dashed line through point B is the consumers' budget constraint; the cost of buying cloth and forestry bundles on this line equals national income, which equals the value of production at B, at domestic prices. The budget constraint intersects the IEP associated with p^* at point C. With production at B and consumption at C, there is excess supply of forestry at price p^*. To equilibrate supply and demand when property rights are imperfect, the relative price of forestry must be lower than p^*, resulting in production between A and B.

6.5.3 *Trade in the poaching model*

In a two-country model, suppose that North has perfect property rights and South has imperfect property rights. The autarchic price in North is p^* and the autarchic price in South is $p^s < p^*$. If the difference in property rights was the only difference between the two countries, South's comparative advantage in forestry would be due entirely to an institutional failure, its weak property rights. In that case, South has only an "apparent", not a "real" comparative advantage in forestry. Given that $p^s < p^*$, when the two countries begin to trade, South increases its forestry production and exports the forestry product. To confirm this claim, use the excess supply and demand curves developed in Section 3.5 of Chapter 3.

The market failure (imperfect property rights) causes South to have too much labor in the forestry sector. At a constant allocation of labor, South would have a pure endowment economy: its PPF would consist of the single point corresponding to this particular allocation of labor. Opening up to trade in an endowment economy generates gains to trade for South, arising from being able to consume at a point other than this endowment. To confirm this claim, pick an endowment point in the forest-cloth plane and draw the indifference curve through this point and draw the associated tangency. This tangency is the autarchic price that equates fixed supply with demand. If production remains at this endowment, any line through this point with slope different than the tangency lies somewhere above the original indifference curve. Any such line is the BOP constraint for the country that faces a world price different than its autarchic price. Thus, holding production fixed, the ability to trade at any price different than the autarchic price raises the country's welfare.

However, in the economy under study, the production point is endogenous, not fixed. A higher relative price of forestry attracts more labor to the forestry sector, exacerbating the market failure, tending to reduce South's welfare. Thus, the net welfare effect (for

South) of opening up to trade is ambiguous. If initially the price difference between the two countries is small, then opening up to trade causes only a small increase in the relative price of forestry for South. In that case, trade is unambiguously harmful to South.

To proceed formally, denote $V(y,p)$ as the indirect utility function for the representative agent in South; here $y = pF + C$ is South's income, evaluated at the world price p. The differential of income is

$$dy = Fdp + pdF + dC. \tag{6.21}$$

In the absence of trade restrictions or tax policies, world price equals domestic prices. By Roy's equation (or identity), consumption of the forestry product in South is

$$F^{con} = -\frac{V_p}{V_y}. \tag{6.22}$$

The superscript "con" denotes consumption; F and C denote South's production of forestry and cloth. From Figure 6.6, production occurs at a point where the PPF is steeper than the relative price that producers face, p. Therefore, at the equilibrium production point

$$\frac{dC}{dF} < -p. \tag{6.23}$$

When the North and the South trade, the equilibrium price must be between their two autarchic prices. Therefore, trade increases the price of forestry in South: we consider the welfare effect when $dp > 0$ Totally differentiate the indirect utility function to obtain

$$dV = V_p dp + V_y dy.$$

Now divide by V_y and use equations (6.21) and (6.22) to obtain

$$\frac{dV}{V_y} = \frac{V_p}{V_y}dp + dy$$
$$= -F^{con}dp + Fdp + pdF + dC = A + B. \tag{6.24}$$

The last equality uses the definitions

$$A \equiv \left(F - F^{\text{con}}\right) dp \geq 0 \quad \text{and} \quad B \equiv \left(\frac{dC}{dF} + p\right) \frac{dF}{dp} dp < 0.$$

Recall that that $\frac{dV}{V_y}$ measures the change in real income, measured in units of money; review Section 2.8 of Chapter 2.

The change in real income equals the sum of A and B in equation (6.24). These two terms capture South's benefit and cost of liberalizing trade, respectively. The term A is positive because South exports forestry $(F - F^{\text{con}} > 0)$ and because $dp > 0$. Trade liberalization increases the relative price of forestry in South, as South's price moves toward North's (higher) forestry price. Term A measures the gains from trade arising from the ability to separate production from consumption, as discussed above in the context of an endowment economy.

We know that $B < 0$ because equation (6.23) implies that $\frac{dC}{dF} + p < 0$, and we know that an increase in the price of forestry goods increases forestry production, i.e. $\frac{dF}{dp} > 0$. (Confirm this inequality using the equilibrium condition (6.19).) Term B is the welfare loss arising from trade liberalization under weak property rights in the forestry sector. These weak property rights cause excessive production in the forestry sector; a higher price of forestry due to trade liberalization exacerbates that imperfection. The function B measures this additional cost.

We obtain a first-order Taylor approximation of the gains from trade by taking the first derivative of welfare with respect to the commodity price $(\frac{\frac{dV}{dp}}{V_y})$ and evaluating this derivative at the autarchic price $p = p^*$. Here $F - F^{\text{con}} = 0$, so $A = 0$. However, $B < 0$. Thus, the first-order Taylor approximation of the South's welfare change due to liberalizing trade is negative. The first-order approximation is valid for small levels of trade liberalization. A small liberalization, beginning at autarchy, lowers South's welfare. The effect of larger degrees of liberalization is ambiguous, because there $A > 0$.

6.6   Minimum Wage

Here, we use the specific-factors model to study the role of trade when there is a distortion in the labor market.[7] In view of the theory of the second best, we know that opening an economy to trade in the presence of such a distortion might either increase or decrease welfare. The analysis provides practice working with the specific-factors model and it shows the relation between the labor market distortion and the welfare effect of opening a closed economy. (We are back to umbrellas and corn.)

Suppose that for some institutional reason, the "umbrella wage", $w = \frac{W}{p_u}$, is not allowed to fall below a constant w^*. We want to find the competitive equilibrium in the presence of the constraint $w \geq w^*$. The reason for this constraint is not important — we take it as exogenous. A more plausible model would define the minimum wage in terms of a bundle of commodities. However, we use models of this sort to improve our intuition — not to describe accurately the real world.

Absent the minimum wage constraint, the ability of labor to move across sectors insures that there is full employment and that the value of marginal product of labor in the corn sector, pC_L, equals the value of marginal product of labor in the umbrella sector (U_L). This equality determines the equilibrium wage. Refer to Figure 6.1 and the discussion there.

Figure 6.7 shows the effect of a change in p on w, and illustrates the consequence of this particular minimum wage constraint. The width of the box equals the total stock of labor; a movement from right to left on the horizontal axis means that labor leaves the umbrella sector and enters the corn sector. As the relative price of corn (p) falls (i.e. the relative price of umbrellas rises), the figure shows that w falls. If p falls to the level p^* in Figure 6.7, the

---

[7]Years ago I used a monograph on minimum wage economies as a basis for lecture notes on the topic; those notes became the present and the next sections. I have long since lost the monograph and forgotten the author(s) names, so I am not able to credit them as my original source for this material.

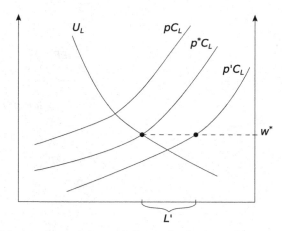

Figure 6.7. Moving from right to left on the horizontal axis reduces labor in the umbrella sector increasing labor in the corn sector. A fall in the relative commodity price p lowers the equilibrium nominal wage w. The minimum wage constraint is not binding at price p and there is full employment The lowest price at which there is full employment is p^*. At lower price such as p' the wage constraint is binding and the amount of unemployment is shown as L'.

constraint becomes binding with full employment of labor. Further decreases in p, below p^*, (e.g. to p') make it impossible to satisfy the wage constraint and also maintain full employment. The result is unemployment and a constant wage at the floor, w^*. The amount of labor in corn manufacturing must fall with the decrease in p, to maintain the minimum wage.

Here is a slightly different perspective. Suppose that the wage constraint is exactly binding, and suppose that the nominal price of umbrellas remains constant while the nominal price of corn falls, so p (the ratio of the price of corn to the price of umbrellas) falls. In order to maintain the wage constraint, the nominal wage must remain the same. Nothing has changed in the umbrella sector, so that sector continues to employ the same number of workers. However, the lower price of corn reduces the value of marginal product in the corn sector; at a constant wage, corn producers are willing to hire fewer workers. As the corn sector sheds workers with the falling p, the amount of unemployment rises, and corn production falls. At relative price p' in Figure 6.7 the amount of unemployment is L'.

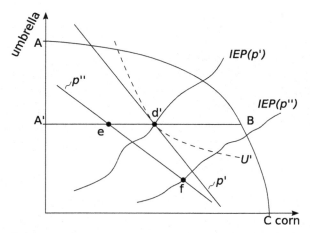

Figure 6.8. Autarchic production and consumption occur on line AB if the minimum wage constraint is binding.

Figure 6.8 shows the PPF in a minimum wage economy ($A'BC$ rather than ABC). For the moment ignore all of the lines and curves in the figure with the exception of the "unconstrained" PPF ABC and the "constrained" PPF $A'BC$. Given the minimum wage, an economy in a competitive equilibrium (without some kind of intervention such as a subsidy or a tax) cannot produce at a point above B. At such points the minimum wage constraint is violated. However, any point between A' and B is feasible; such points involve a constant level of umbrella production and different levels of unemployment and corn production.

6.6.1 *Autarchy with a binding minimum wage*

Now we consider the autarchic equilibrium in the presence of the minimum wage. Price p^* is the price — not necessarily an equilibrium price — that induces full employment and satisfies $w = w^*$. That is, p^* supports production at point B in Figure 6.8. Define p^{af} as the autarchic price in the absence of the minimum wage constraint. We consider two cases: first where the wage constraint is not binding, then where it is binding.

If the autarchic equilibrium lies at a point on BC, then the autarchic price in the absence of the constraint, satisfies $p^{af} > p^*$.

In this case, the minimum wage constraint is not binding, and the constraint is therefore not interesting. The interesting situation arises when the minimum wage constraint is binding in the autarchic equilibrium. For the remainder of this chapter we assume that this case holds. That is, we assume that the autarchic equilibrium in the absence of the minimum wage constraint is at a point such as E on the PPF in Figure 6.9. The tangency at this point is $p^{af} < p^*$. At this point, the minimum wage constraint is not satisfied under full employment. (Refer to Figure 6.7 and the discussion there.) Any point above B on the PPF is therefore not feasible in the presence of the minimum wage constraint.

Given our assumption that the minimum wage constraint is violated under full employment, there is a unique autarchic equilibrium $p^{af} < p^*$, where the minimum wage constraint is satisfied and there is unemployment. This equilibrium occurs on the flat segment $A'B$ in Figure 6.9.

To establish that this equilibrium exists, note that by construction, at price p^* production occurs at point B and consumption occurs at a point such as D, to the left of B (Figure 6.9). Point

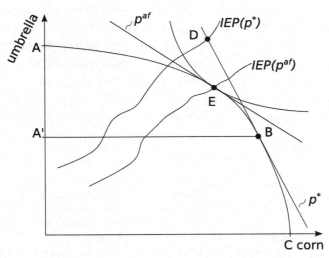

Figure 6.9.   An autarchic price of p^{af} that induces production and consumption at point E violates the minimum constraint.

D is the intersection of $IEP(p^*)$ and the consumers' budget line.[8] Recall that $p^* > p^{af}$. A higher relative price of corn shifts the IEP away from the corn axis. Thus, at p^* there is excess supply of corn.

As p decreases, production of corn falls, so the supply curve is monotonic in price. At a very low p, supply of corn is close to 0, but the demand for corn remains positive. Therefore, at a low price there is excess demand for corn. The supply and demand graphs are continuous, so excess demand is also continuous. Because excess demand is positive for sufficiently low price and negative at p^*, there is an autarchic equilibrium price between the two at which excess demand is zero.

To confirm that this price is unique, define p' as the *highest* autarchic equilibrium price. Figure 6.8 identifies the production and consumption point in this equilibrium as d. We need only show that there are no lower autarchic equilibrium prices.[9] Consider any relative price less than p', e.g. p'' shown in the figure. At this lower price, the IEP shifts toward the corn axis, as $IEP(p'')$ illustrates. Moreover, this lower price causes the production point to shift from d to e in the figure, as unemployment increases. The economy's budget constraint is shown as a line through e with slope p''; at every point on this line, the value of consumption equal the value of production, evaluated at the autarchic price. This budget constraint intersects $IEP(p'')$ at point f. The production and consumption points, e and f, imply that there is excess demand for corn at p''. Thus, at any price below the highest autarchic price p', there is excess demand. Consequently, p' is the unique autarchic price under the wage constraint.

---

[8]Remember that the commodity bundles on the line through B and D have the same value as at B, given the relative price p^*. The value of of B at this relative price is the level of national income. Thus, the line through points B and D is the country's budget constraint when the relative price is p^*.

[9]We do not have to consider prices above p' because this price is defined as the highest autarchic equilibrium price.

6.6.2 *Trade can lower welfare*

Trade can lower welfare in the presence of a binding wage constraint, e.g. a wage constraint that leads to unemployment. To construct an example of this outcome, suppose that the autarchic equilibrium is at d' in Figure 6.8 with autarchic equilibrium price p'. The country begins to trade, and the world relative price of corn is $p'' < p'$ (= the autarchic price). When the country begins to trade (and the domestic price of corn falls) production shifts toward e, and the income expansion path shifts down, as shown. Consumption occurs at f, resulting in a loss of welfare (for this particular case).

Two things have happened here. Consumers face a world price different from the autarchic price. If production had remained at the autarchic level (i.e. if this was a pure endowment economy) welfare would have increased.[10] However, the lower world price exacerbates the unemployment problem, leading to a production loss. For the example shown, the production loss more than offsets the consumption gain, leading to a loss in welfare. Of course, this is just one possibility. It is easy to construct other examples where the world price is less than the autarchic price but opening up to trade raises the country's welfare.

If the world price is greater than the autarchic price, the gains from trade are certainly positive. In this case, trade increases employment and also confers the usual gain arising from being able to produce and consume at different points.

6.7 Adjustment of the Specific Factors

The Ricardo–Viner model can be viewed as a short run model: labor adjusts, but the sector-specific factors do not move at all. Now we consider the long-run, when the sector-specific factors also adjust. In this setting, the sector-specific factors are fixed only in the short

---

[10]For this pure endowment economy, draw a line through d with slope $p'' < p'$. Consumption occurs on $IEP\,(p'')$ above the autarchic indifference curve, U'.

term. These kinds of factors are sometimes called "quasi-fixed". In the long run, they are flexible.

There are a number of ways that we can view adjustment of the quasi-fixed factors. For our purposes, the particular adjustment process does not matter — I just want to compare a short run equilibrium in which capital earns a different return in the two sectors, and a long run equilibrium in which the return to capital is the same in both sectors. The point of this extension is to show that an increase in economic flexibility may increase the welfare loss resulting from trade (in the presence of a minimum wage constraint).

In a "putty-clay" model, capital can be allocated to either sector while it is putty. However, once invested in a particular sector (e.g. as an irrigation system in the corn sector or an umbrella machine in the umbrella sector) it becomes clay — it cannot be transformed back into putty. The flow of new capital (putty) is exogenous. This flow is allocated between the two sectors by investors who seek to maximize their present discounted value of returns. All capital within a sector (i.e. capital of all "vintages") obtain the same rental price Capital depreciates in both sectors. In a steady state (i.e. a long-run equilibrium), the amount of new investment in a sector equals the depreciation in that sector. The putty-clay structure means that the allocation of capital between the two sectors changes gradually.

Suppose that we begin at a long run autarchic steady state equilibrium, where capital earns the same return in the two sectors. The assumption that capital decays and the assumption that the capital stocks in the two sectors are unchanging means that both sectors must be receiving new investment. Consequently, the return to the specific factors in the two sectors must be the same. It would not pay to invest in a sector if the other sector offers a higher rate of return. Remember that capital's rental price equals its value of marginal product.

The minimum wage constraint is binding, so there is unemployment in this long run equilibrium. In the minimum wage economy, unemployment is consistent with long run equilibrium in the capital market. In the long run, capital adjusts to achieve equality of rental rates in the two sectors; there is no reason that this equality eliminates unemployment, which is caused by the minimum wage constraint. Assume also that the world relative price of corn is lower than the autarchic relative price. When trade begins, the domestic relative price of corn falls to the world price. As we have seen, this fall causes the corn sector to shed labor. The production point moves from d' to e and the consumption point moves from d' to f in Figure 6.8.

The price change and the resulting change in labor allocation both reduce the value of marginal product (which equals the rental price) of the corn-specific factor. The fall in the price of corn causes the value of marginal product to the corn-specific factor to fall, holding constant the amount of labor in the sector. As labor leaves the sector during the short-run labor adjustment process, there are fewer workers per machine in the sector, causing a further fall in the value of marginal product of the corn-specific factor. Consequently, the return on capital in the corn sector falls. No one invests new capital in the corn sector because the return is higher in the umbrella sector.

Because there is no investment in the corn sector, depreciation causes the stock of capital in the sector falls. The increased flow of investment in the umbrella sector causes the stock of capital in that sector to increase. Prior to beginning trade, the flow of new investment into the umbrella sector was just enough to offset depreciation. Because (by assumption) the aggregate flow of new capital is exogenous, the decreased investment in corn means that investment in umbrellas increases. As more capital moves to the umbrella sector, the flow of investment is greater than depreciation, so the stock of capital grows. With this putty-clay model, it is as if capital were leaving the corn sector and moving to the umbrella sector, although that is not literally occurring.

Capital flows to the sector where its marginal return is higher. In a first best setting, that allocation is efficient, but it need not be efficient in a distorted economy, courtesy of the Theory of the Second Best. As capital leaves the corn sector, that sector sheds labor, worsening the unemployment problem. As capital moves into the umbrella sector, that sector hires more labor. The net

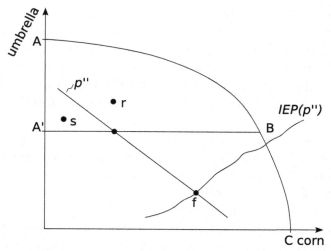

Figure 6.10. Adjsutment of capital moves production above AB to point s (with lower income) or to point r (with higher income).

effect on employment depends on whether the dying sector (corn) is labor intensive, relative to the umbrella sector. If the dying sector is relatively labor intensive, the welfare effect of the readjustment of capital is ambiguous. The increase in unemployment tends to offset the efficiency-increasing effect of having capital move to a sector where its marginal product is higher. If the growing sector is relatively labor intensive, then the adjustment of capital improves welfare, because both effects increase welfare.

Figure 6.10 shows two possibilities. After opening to trade, but before capital adjusts, the economy consumes at point f. Its BOP constraint is the line through f with slope equal to the world price p''. (Production occurs at the intersection of the BOP constraint and the line $A'B$.) The adjustment of capital draws capital into the umbrella sector, and the price of the mobile factor, labor, is constant at w^*, because the minimum wage constraint continues to bind. With more capital and more labor in the umbrella sector, umbrella production increases. The economy moves to a point above the line $A'B$. It might move to a point such as r, where national income (and therefore welfare) has increased, or to a point such as s, where national income and welfare are lower.[11]

6.7.1 *An algebraic treatment*

I specialize to constant returns to scale, to demonstrate that adjustment of the quasi-fixed factor might lower welfare. With constant returns to scale we can write the production function in each sector as the product of the capital in that sector times a function that contains a single argument, the labor/capital ratio in that sector. The production functions are

$$C = H\left(L_c, K_c\right) = K_c h\left(n_c\right),$$
$$U = G(L_u, K_u) = K_u g(n_u),$$
$$\tag{6.25}$$

where labor/capital ratios in the two sectors are

$$n_c \equiv \frac{L_c}{K_c}, \quad n_u \equiv \frac{L_u}{K_u}.$$

Equality of wages fixes the two labor/capital ratios:

$$w^* = ph'\left(n_c\right) = g'\left(n_u\right). \tag{6.26}$$

After the economy opens to trade, p and w^* remain constant. Therefore, the capital labor ratios in the two sectors remain constant, as equation (6.26) shows. However, as capital adjusts from one sector to another (i.e. as the levels of K_c and K_u change), the production in the two sectors change. The change in output resulting from the reallocation of capital is

$$dC = h\left(n_c\right) \cdot dK_c \quad dU = g(n_u) \cdot dK_u. \tag{6.27}$$

Consistent with the scenario in the previous subsection, we assume that following trade liberalization the rental rate in the corn

---

[11]If in doubt about this claim, students should draw the BOP contraints through points s and r, and obtain the intersections of these lines with $IEP\left(p''\right)$. At production point s, welfare is lower than the original level at f; at production point r, welfare is higher.

sector is below the rental rate in the umbrella sector, so that over time capital in the umbrella sector increases and capital in the corn sector decreases. That is

$$r_c = p\left(h\left(n_c\right) - n_c h'\left(n_c\right)\right) < r_u = g\left(n_u\right) - n_u g'\left(n_u\right). \qquad (6.28)$$

The total demand for labor is

$$L = K_c n_c + K_u n_u. \qquad (6.29)$$

Suppose that dK units of capital move from umbrellas into corn, i.e. $0 < dK = -dK_c = dK_u$. Differentiate equation (6.29) to obtain the effect of capital reallocation on the total demand for labor:

$$dL = \left(n_u - n_c\right) dK.$$

Recall that the capital labor ratios are fixed, because these are determined by equation (6.26).

As capital moves from one sector to another, commodity prices do not change, because this is a small country. Therefore, welfare increases if and only if nominal income increases. Total (nominal) income in this economy is

$$y = pC + U. \qquad (6.30)$$

Differentiating equation (6.30), and then using equations (6.27), (6.28), and (6.26), we can write the change in income as

$$
\begin{aligned}
dy &= p\,dC + dU \\
&= \left(-ph + g\right) dK = \left[-\left(r_c + p n_c h'\left(n_c\right)\right) + r_u + n_u g'\left(n_u\right)\right] dK \\
&= \left[r_u - r_c + n_u g' - p n_c h'\right] dK \\
&= \left[\left(r_u - r_c\right) + \left(n_u - n_c\right) w^*\right] dK. \qquad (6.31)
\end{aligned}
$$

The last line decomposes the income effect into two terms. The first term $(r_u - r_c)\,dK$, is positive, because both $(r_u - r_c)$ and dK are positive. This positive term reflects the fact that moving a factor into a sector where it obtains a higher return, increases national income.

The second term, $(n_u - n_c)\,w^*$, is the employment effect. There is unemployment in this economy, so one additional unit of employment increases national income by w^*. As one unit of capital moves into the umbrella sector it employs n_u additional workers; however, as that unit of capital leaves the corn sector, it releases n_c workers. If the corn sector is relatively labor intensive, total employment falls, so the employment effect of the capital reallocation is $(n_u - n_c)\, w^* < 0$. In that case, the net welfare-effect of the capital reallocation can be positive or negative.

6.7.2 *A different interpretation*

A slightly different interpretation of the results above uses the concept of "shadow value". We noted above that in this small country model, a change in the allocation of capital increases welfare if and only if the change increases national income, which equals the value of production evaluated at world prices. The shadow value of capital in the umbrella sector (denoted λ_u) equals the change in the value of income due to a change in the stock of capital in the umbrella sector; the shadow value of capital in the corn sector (denoted λ_c) equals the change in the value of income due to a change in the stock of capital in the corn sector.

Section 3.4 of Chapter 3 shows that in the social planner's optimization problem (given in equation (3.5)), the Lagrange multiplier associated with the full employment constraint for capital equals the competitive rental rate of capital. The Lagrange multiplier for capital, also called the "shadow value" of capital, equals the marginal change in the social planner's objective due to a marginal change in the amount of capital. In that setting — with no distortions — the private value of capital (the return to capital, it's price) equals the social value of capital (the shadow value). A distortion in the economy drives a wedge between the private and social values of capital (and also of many other things).

In the current context, define the shadow value of capital in a particular sector as the change in national income due to a change in the amount of capital in that sector. Here, a unit of capital in one sector may have a different social value than a unit of capital in the other sector; we have two stocks of capital, so there are two shadow values. Repeating the steps used to obtain the last line of equation

(6.31), we can write these shadow values as

$$\lambda_c \equiv \frac{\partial y}{\partial K_c} = r_c + n_c w^* \quad \text{and} \quad \lambda_u \equiv \frac{\partial y}{\partial K_u} = r_u + n_u w^*.$$

A social planner would like to choose the allocation of capital to maximize social welfare. Because the planner takes the world price as given, maximizing national welfare is equivalent to maximizing national income, evaluated a world prices. The social planner takes as given: (i) the world price (because this is a small country); (ii) the minimum wage constraint (because we treat this as exogenous); and (iii) the requirement that labor earn the same wage in both sectors (because labor is mobile across sectors). If this planner can allocate capital across the two sectors, she does so by equating the two shadow values of capital. If one shadow value were higher than the other, the planner would send capital to the sector with the higher shadow value. The planner could decentralize the optimum by means of a capital tax/subsidy in one sector.

In the competitive equilibrium, in contrast, capital moves to the sector where its *private value*, the rental price of capital r_u or r_c, is higher. The minimum wage creates a distortion in the labor market. This distortion drives a wedge between the private value of capital in a sector (its value of marginal product) and the social (shadow) value of capital in the sector. The social shadow value includes the employment-increasing effect of capital. The reallocation of capital causes the private value of the capital in the two sectors to approach each other (and eventually become equal); but as the difference in the private value of capital in the two sectors diminishes, the difference between the social value in the two sectors *might* actually increase. If the reallocation does cause a greater divergence in the shadow values of capital, then the reallocation decreases national income.

The general point of this example is that a distortion in one part of the economy (here, the labor market) creates a wedge between private values and social values in other markets (here, the capital market). The intuition we develop from studying perfect markets may be misleading in a distorted market. Of course, this is just another application of the Theory of the Second Best.

Chapter 7

The Heckscher–Ohlin–Samuelson Model

7.1 Introduction

This chapter presents the four basic theorems of the Heckscher–Ohlin–Samuelson (HOS) model: (i) the Factor Price Equalization theorem, (ii) the Stolper–Samuelson theorem, (iii) the Rybczynski theorem, and (iv) the Heckscher–Ohlin theorem. The factor price equalization theorem gives conditions under which trade in commodities is a perfect substitute for the international mobility of factors. The Stolper–Samuelson theorem gives conditions under which a change in relative commodity prices has an unambiguous effect on real factor returns. The Rybczynski theorem shows how a change in factor supply alters production, holding fixed all prices. Finally, the Heckscher–Ohlin theorem shows the relation between relative factor endowments and comparative advantage.

Recall from Chapter 2 that comparative advantage, and thus the direction of trade, depends on a comparison of relative autarchic prices in the two countries. In the Ricardian model, autarchic prices are completely determined by technology; there, a difference in technology between two countries is the basis for trade. The HOS model provides an explanation for trade based on a cross-country difference in *relative* factor endowments — rather than on differences in technology, tastes, or something else.

There is a single factor of production in the Ricardian model, and a single mobile factor together with sector-specific factors in the Ricardo–Viner model. In the HOS setting there are two or more mobile factors. We consider the $2 \times 2 \times 2$ model: two countries, two goods, and two factors of production, capital and labor. These factors move freely across sectors, so the wage rate and the rental rate must be the same in both sectors, within a country.

We emphasize the case where factors do not move from one country to another, i.e. where there is no international labor migration or international investment. This lack of international factor mobility is irrelevant when the Factor Price Equalization theorem holds. However, we also consider a situation where the price of capital is higher in Home than in Foreign. In our example, Home imposes a tariff and also restricts international investment. Absent the tariff, liberalization of the capital market, increasing foreign investment, raises Home's welfare because the value of marginal product of capital in Home exceeds the international price of capital. The tariff, together with the restriction on capital imports means that Home is in a second-best world, so it will come as no surprise that liberalization of the capital market might either increase or decrease Home's welfare. Our objective is not to establish this now-familiar possibility, but to make sure that students can understand the forces that determine the welfare effect. We also use this setting as the final example of immizerizing growth.

We first discuss the assumptions about technology in the HOS model, and then present the four theorems.

7.2 Technology

We assume that the technology is convex and that each sector has constant returns to scale (CRTS).[1] Convexity implies that the PPF is concave, i.e. that the line segment joining any two points on the PPF lies (weakly) below the PPF. To verify this claim, consider any

---

[1]Within-sector CRTS in the presence of cross-sectoral spillovers is consistent with a non-convex technology.

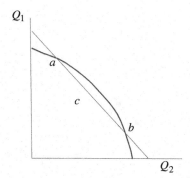

Figure 7.1. Points a and b lie on the PPF. The assumption that the technology is convex means that any convex combination of these points, e.g. point c, is also feasible. Provided that there is some substitutability between capital and labor in both sectors, there exist points above c that are also feasible. In this case, the PPF is strictly concave, as shown by the curve through points a and b. If the technology in both sectors is Leontieff, the PPF is a straight line through point a and b.

two points on the PPF, e.g. a and b in Figure 7.1. Convexity of the technology implies that any convex combination of these two points, such as point c in the figure, is feasible: c lies (weakly) below the PPF. Therefore, the PPF is concave. Provided that there is some substitutability between capital and labor in both sectors (i.e. provided that the technology in each sector is not Leontief), point c is feasible but not efficient: it lies strictly below the PPF. In this case, the PPF is strictly concave, as shown by the curve in Figure 7.1. If technology in both sectors is Leontief, then point c lies on the PPF. In this case, the PPF is a line: it is weakly concave.

The output expansion path for a sector is the locus of tangencies between isoquants and lines whose slope is the negative of the relative factor price, as shown in Figure 7.2. In general these expansion paths are curves, but for CRTS they are lines through the origin, as the figure shows.[2] To verify this claim, consider a firm's cost

---

[2]Constant returns to scale is sufficient, not necessary for the conclusion that the capital/labor ratio in a sector depends on relative factor prices, not on the scale of output (and thus, the expansion paths are straight lines). The result also holds if the production function is homothetic, i.e. if output can be written as

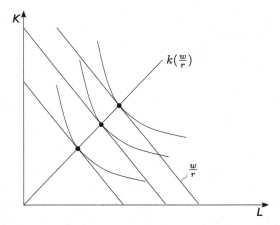

Figure 7.2. The output expansion path is the locus of tangencies between isoquants representing different levels of production (for a particular good), with lines having slope $-\frac{w}{r}$, the relative factor price. For homothetic production functions, the output expansion path is a line through the origin: the optimal capital/labor ratio in the sector producing this good depends on the relative prices, not on the scale of output. CRTS is a special case of homotheticity.

minimization problem:

$$C(w, r, Q) = \min_{L,K} (wL + rK)$$
$$\text{subject to} \quad F(K, L) \geq Q,$$

(7.1)

where w and r are the prices of capital and labor, K and L, and $F(K, L)$ is the production function for the sector under consideration. The assumption of CRTS means that we can write

$$F(K, L) = LF\left(\frac{K}{L}, \frac{L}{L}\right) \equiv Lf(k),$$

(7.2)

where $k = \frac{K}{L}$ is the capital/labor ratio in the sector. Use equation (7.2) to rewrite the constraint in the minimization problem as

$$L \geq \frac{Q}{f(k)}.$$

$G(F(K, L))$, where G is an increasing monotonic function and $F()$ is a CRTS function. If G is concave, there are decreasing returns to scale, and if G is convex there are increasing returns to scale.

This constraint is binding, because the price of labor is positive and the firm wants to minimize costs. Therefore we can rewrite the firm's cost minimization problem (7.1) as

$$C\left(w, r, Q\right) = \min_{L,k} L\left(w + rk\right) \text{ subject to } L = \frac{Q}{f(k)}$$

$$= \min_{k} \frac{Q}{f(k)}\left(w + rk\right)$$

$$= Qw \min_{k} \frac{\left(1 + k/\frac{w}{r}\right)}{f(k)}. \tag{7.3}$$

This series of steps shows that with CRTS, *the optimal capital/labor ratio k depends only on relative factor prices, $\frac{w}{r}$, not on the scale of output, Q.* We will use this result repeatedly. Hereafter we use $\omega = \frac{w}{r}$ to denote the relative factor price, the price of labor relative to the price of capital.

CRTS also implies that the average cost of production is independent of the scale of output. To confirm this claim, define

$$c\left(w, r\right) = w \min_{k} \frac{\left(1 + k/\frac{w}{r}\right)}{f(k)},$$

the minimum cost of producing one unit of output (set $Q = 1$ in problem (7.3)). Using problem (7.3), the cost of producing Q units is $Qc\left(w, r\right)$, so the average cost of producing Q units is $c\left(w, r\right)$, which is independent of the scale of output, Q. CRTS is necessary (as well as sufficient) for average costs to be independent of the scale of output. This independence is important, because it means that the condition for 0 profits in a sector, $P = c\left(w, r\right)$ does not depend on the scale of output.

7.3 Factor Price Equalization

Here, we consider the relation between relative commodity prices, $p = \frac{p_2}{p_1}$ and relative factor prices ω. This relation is key to determining whether the equality of relative factor prices, under free trade without transportation costs, implies that countries' real factor returns are also equal. If, for example, the real return to labor is the same in the two countries, there is no incentive for international migration of labor. This incentive arises if real factor returns are not equal in the two countries. Recall that in the Ricardian model, free trade typically does not imply the equality of real returns to labor. Thus, in general there is no reason to suppose that trade in commodities causes real factor returns to be equal across countries.

However, in the HOS model, the factor price equalization theorem gives conditions under which trade equates these returns, for both factors of production. When these conditions hold, trade in commodities is a perfect substitute for trade in factors. The first step in proving this theorem requires the relation between relative commodity prices p and relative factor prices, ω. This relation is monotonic if and only if one sector is relatively capital intensive for all relative factor prices.

Denote k_i as the capital/labor ratio in sector $i = 1, 2$. Sector 1 is relatively capital intensive if $k_1 > k_2$. We showed above that under the assumption of CRTS, the value of k_i depends only on the value of ω, the relative factor price. If the inequality $k_1 > k_2$ (or the opposite inequality) holds for *all* values of ω, then we say that there are no factor intensity reversals. If, however, $k_1 - k_2$ is sometimes positive and sometimes negative, depending on ω, then there are factor intensity reversals. We first consider the situation where there are no factor intensity reversals, and then the opposite situation.

7.3.1 *No factor intensity reversals*

The relative price of commodity 2 is $p = \frac{p_2}{p_1}$. We begin with fixed commodity prices, p_1 and p_2, and thus with a fixed value of the relative price, which we denote as p'. Define the one-dollar isoquant for good i as the isoquant showing the combination of capital and labor needed to produce $\frac{1}{p_i}$ units of good i. The locations of these one-dollar isoquants depend on prices as well as technology. Figure 7.3 shows the one-dollar isoquants for two goods, for particular values of p_1, p_2, and technology.

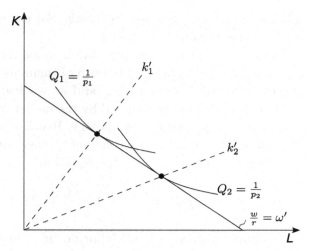

Figure 7.3. The "one-dollar" isoquants for two goods, and the relative factor price that supports zero profits in both sectors.

With factors freely mobile across sectors, profits must be zero in both sectors in a competitive equilibrium. Profits are zero in a sector if the sector closes down or if it operates and the price of output in that sector equals the average cost of production. We saw above that with CRTS, the cost-minimizing average cost of production does not depend on the scale of output. Therefore, we can check the "price = average cost" condition at an arbitrary level of output. It is convenient to use the level of output needed to produce one dollar's worth of output.

Figure 7.3 depicts a pair of relative commodity and factor prices, (p, ω) that supports an equilibrium with positive production in both sectors. (Not every pair of relative prices supports such an equilibrium.) We explain the construction of this figure and then show how it is used to determine the relation between p and ω when both sectors operate. We begin with an arbitrary pair of output prices p_1 and p_2 (and their ratio $p' = \frac{p_2}{p_1}$). Using these prices, we construct the one-dollar isoquants for the two sectors. Figure 7.3 embodies the assumption that the one-dollar isoquants have a single intersection. Later we will see that this single crossing of isoquants is equivalent to the assumption of no factor intensity reversals. For the time being we maintain the single crossing assumption.

Because (in this figure) the isoquants have a single intersection, there is exactly one line that is tangent to both of them, as the figure shows. Denote the slope of this line as $-\omega'$ and its vertical intercept as I. The values of ω' and I are determined by the model "data": the commodity prices p_1 and p_2 and the technology. Recall now that for any factor prices w and r and a positive constant C, the combinations of capital and labor that cost C satisfy the equation

$$wL + rK = C \Rightarrow K = \frac{C}{r} - \frac{w}{r}L = \frac{C}{r} - \omega L.$$

Thus, every combination of capital and labor on the line with slope $-\omega$ costs \$$C$, when evaluated at factor prices w and r (with $\omega = \frac{w}{r}$). Setting $C = 1$ and using the relations $\frac{w}{r} = \omega'$ and $\frac{C}{r} = \frac{1}{r} = I$ we can solve for factor prices w and r that support production of both goods in a competitive equilibrium, where profits are zero, i.e. where price = average cost. The choice $C = 1$ mean that the cost of producing at each tangency points equals \$1, the revenue obtained from selling the amount of the good that is produced at that point.

To summarize, we began with arbitrary commodity prices and used the single crossing assumption to compute the factor prices that support a competitive equilibrium where both sectors operate and have zero profits. Only the ratio of prices, not their levels, matter. For example, if we had doubled the two commodity prices we began with, this would have resulted in doubling the factor prices, but there would have been no change in either the relative commodity price or the corresponding equilibrium relative factor pice.

The points a', b', and c' in Figure 7.4 summarize the pertinent information contained in Figure 7.3. For the time being, ignore the curves in Figure 7.4. We saw that when the relative commodity price is p', the only relative factor price that is consistent with production of both goods is ω'. The bottom panel of Figure 7.4 shows this information. The point a' is the combination (p', ω').

Now return to Figure 7.3. At the relative commodity price p' and the corresponding relative factor price ω', producers minimize costs

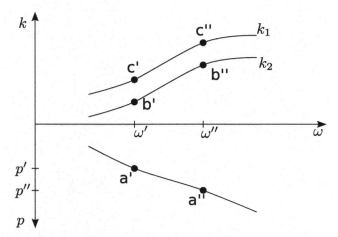

Figure 7.4. Relation between relative commodity and relative factor prices (the bottom orthant) and between relative factor prices and capital labor ratios (the top orthant). The figure assumes that sector 1 is relatively capital intensive and that there are no factor intensity reversals.

by producing at the point where the isocost line is tangent to the isoquant. The slope of the ray from the origin through each point of tangency is the cost-minimizing capital/labor ratio. The slopes of these two rays are denoted k_1' and k_2' in Figure 7.3.

The top panel of Figure 7.4 repeats this information. The points $b' = (\omega', k_2')$ and $c' = (\omega', k_1')$ show the capital/labor ratios at the relative commodity price p' and the associated relative factor price ω'. For this example, sector 1 is relatively capital intensive ($k_1' > k_2'$) at the relative factor price ω'.

We began with a specific but arbitrary relative commodity price and found the relative factor price and the capital/labor ratio in each sector that are consistent with positive production of both goods. This procedure relies on the assumption of CRTS and on the assumption that the one-dollar isoquants cross only once. Absent the first assumption, the capital/labor ratios depend on the scale of output. The fact that these ratios are independent of the scale of output under CRTS allows us to begin the derivation by using the one-dollar isoquants. Absent the second assumption, there would, in

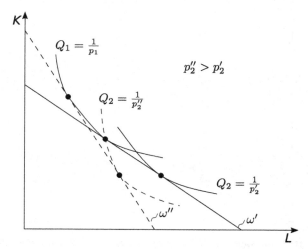

Figure 7.5.   An increase in the price of good 2 shifts in the "one-dollar" isoquant for good 2 and increases the equilibrium $\frac{w}{r}$ needed to support zero profits in both sectors.

general, be two relative factor prices that support positive production in both sectors in a competitive equilibrium.

Now we show how a change in relative commodity price changes the relative factor price and the capital/labor ratios. Figure 7.5 repeats the information in Figure 7.3, but excludes the rays that show the capital/labor ratios in order to avoid clutter. Suppose that we hold the price of commodity 1 constant and increase the price of commodity 2, thus increasing the relative commodity price to a level $p'' > p'$. This increase in the price of commodity 2 causes the one dollar isoquant for that sector to shift in to the dashed isoquant: it now takes less capital and labor to produce a dollar's worth of commodity 2 because the commodity sells for a higher price. The slope of the line tangent to the one dollar isoquant for commodity 1 and the (new) one dollar isoquant for commodity 2 is $\omega'' > \omega'$.

Point a'' in the bottom panel of Figure 7.4 is the combination (p'', ω''). To avoid clutter, Figure 7.5 does not show the ray through the origin and the points of tangency associated with ω''. However, it is easy to see from the figure that at the higher relative wage, both sectors have become more capital intensive, and that sector 1 is still more capital intensive than sector 2. Points a'', b'' and c'' show the relative factor price and the capital intensity in each sector, at the factor price p''.

The two curves in the top panel of Figure 7.4 show the capital/labor ratio in each sector, as a function of the relative commodity price. The curve in the bottom panel shows the relative factor price as a function of the relative commodity price. The procedure above has identified two points on each of the three curves in Figure 7.3. We can imagine choosing many relative commodity prices and for each of these obtaining the relative factor price (consistent with production in both sectors), and also the corresponding capital/labor ratios in the two sectors. "Connecting the dots" generates the three curves in the figure.

The curves in Figure 7.4 show a monotonic relation between the relative factor price and the relative commodity price; and for each relative factor price, sector 1 is always more capital intensive than sector 2. There are no factor intensity reversals. These two features are consequences of our assumption that the one-dollar isoquants intersect only once.

7.3.2 *Factor intensity reversals*

Here, we explore the consequence of dropping the single crossing assumption. Without this assumption, there are factor intensity reversals and the relation between relative commodity and factor prices is not monotonic. Figure 7.6 shows the one dollar isoquants for the two sectors. The notable feature is there is much more substitutability between factors in sector 1, compared to sector 2. The isoquant for sector 1 is relatively flat, and the isoquant for sector 2 resembles the isoquant for a Leontief production function. Consequently, there is a relative commodity price, say p', for which the one dollar isoquants are tangent, as shown in Figure 7.6. At this relative commodity price, there is a single relative factor price, shown as ω', that is consistent with production of both goods. At this factor price, the capital/labor ratios in the two sectors are equal.

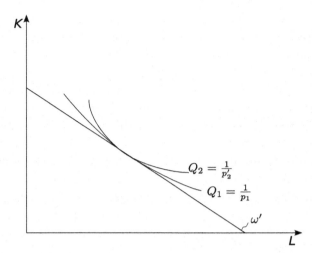

Figure 7.6. The elasticitity of substitution between factors is much greater in sector 1 than in sector 2. Here there are factor intensity reversals.

However, if for example we increase the price of good 2, the one-dollar isoquant for the second good shifts down; in that case there would be two intersections between the two isoquants. Figure 7.7 shows the effect of increasing the price of commodity 2, and the resulting downward shift (the dashed curve) in the one dollar isoquant for sector 2. In Figure 7.7, there are two relative factor prices consistent with zero profits in both sectors; these two prices are shown as $\omega'' > \omega'''$. To avoid clutter, the figure does not show the capital/labor ratios associated with these two relative factor prices. It is clear that at ω'' sector 1 is relatively capital intensive, and the relation is reversed at ω'''.

Figure 7.8 is analogous to Figure 7.4, but it corresponds to the case where for a range of relative commodity prices there are two intersections between the one dollar isoquants. A factor intensity reversal occurs as the relative factor prices passes through the point ω'. For relative commodity prices greater than p' there are two relative factor prices consistent with production of both commodities; the mapping from commodity prices to factor prices is a correspondence, not a function. Either sector might be relatively more capital intensive, depending on the actual relative factor price.

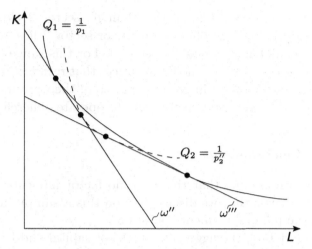

Figure 7.7. As the price of good 2 increases, the "one-dollar isoquant" for good 2 shifts in, and there are now two relative factor prices that support zero profits in both sectors. The sectors' relative factor intensity switches between these two relative factor prices.

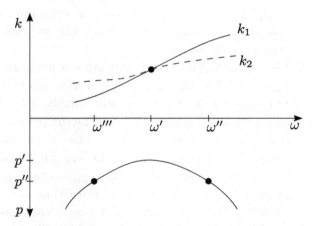

Figure 7.8. With factor intensity reversals, the relation between relative factor and relative product prices is a correspondence, and the graphs of the relative capital intensity in the two sectors cross.

At a relative commodity price less than p', sector 2 closes down: at such a price, the one dollar isoquant for sector 2 lies everywhere above the one dollar isoquant for sector 1. For this range of relative commodity prices, there are no factor prices that result in zero profits in both sectors. If profits in sector 1 are zero, then profits in sector 2 would be negative if that sector were to operate. Therefore, sector 2 shuts down.

7.3.3 *Full employment*

Henceforth, we assume that there are no factor intensity reversals; all of the theorems that we discuss rely on this assumption. We now introduce the full employment condition.

Let K and L be the aggregate stocks of capital and labor in the economy. Full employment requires

$$\frac{K}{L} = \frac{K_1 + K_2}{L} = \left(\frac{K_1}{L_1} L_1 + \frac{K_2}{L_2} L_2 \right) \frac{1}{L} = k_1 \frac{L_1}{L} + k_2 \frac{L_2}{L}. \quad (7.4)$$

Because $L_i \geq 0$ and $\frac{L_1}{L} + \frac{L_2}{L} = 1$, equation (7.4) states that the aggregate capital/labor ratio $\frac{K}{L}$ is a convex combination of the capital/labor ratios in the two sectors, with the weights equal to the share of labor in each sector.

Figure 7.9 reproduces Figure 7.4, but adds a horizontal dashed line at the aggregate capital/labor ratio in the top panel. If we ignored the full employment constraint, and naively used Figure 7.4 to find the relation between commodity and factor prices, we would conclude that at the commodity price $\hat{p}$, the equilibrium factor price is $\hat{\omega}$ (Figure 7.9). However, at $\hat{\omega}$ the capital/labor ratio in both sectors is strictly greater than the aggregate capital/labor ratio. Consequently, the price $\hat{\omega}$ would require that some labor is unemployed, violating the full-employment condition. Therefore, $\hat{\omega}$ cannot be an equilibrium factor price when commodity prices are $\hat{p}$.

To see how the full employment constraint alters the relation between commodity and factor prices, suppose that we begin at the relative price p_2. (Here, p_2 denotes a particular value of the relative commodity price p, not the price of commodity 2.) At this price the relative factor price is ω_2; here the capital/labor ratio in sector 2

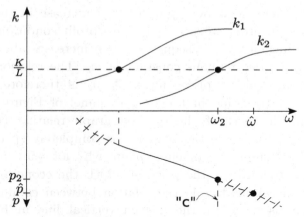

Figure 7.9. The full employment condition limits the responsiveness of the relative factor price to changes in the relative commodity price.

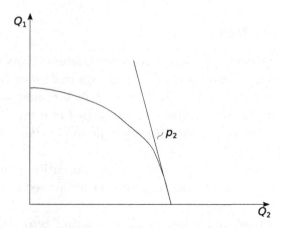

Figure 7.10. The price that induces the economy to specialize in sector 2.

intersects the horizontal line at $\frac{K}{L}$ in the top panel of Figure 7.9. At this price all of the labor is in sector 2; sector 1 has closed down. The economy is specialized in sector 2, as shown using the PPF in Figure 7.10.

Suppose that the price of commodity 2 increases, thereby increasing the relative price to a value above p_2. The economy remains specialized in sector 2. The increase in the price of commodity 2 means that there must be a proportional increase in the price of both factors (in order to satisfy the zero profit condition), leaving their ratio unchanged. Consequently, as p increases above p_2, the relative factor price remains constant at ω_2. The relation between commodity and factor prices for $p \geq p_2$ is therefore given by the dashed vertical line in the bottom panel of Figure 7.9. (For this reason, the part of the original graph relating commodity and factor prices, where the economy is completely specialized, is crossed out.) A similar argument explains why, for commodity prices less than p_1 (defined as the price at which the economy becomes specialized in commodity 1) the relation between commodity and factor prices is given by the dashed vertical line in Figure 7.9, rather than the crossed out portion of the downward sloping curve.

7.3.4 *The theorem*

We are now in a position to state the theorem: *Suppose that two countries have free trade, perfect competition and no distortions; they have the same CRTS technology without factor intensity reversals, and both countries are incompletely specialized in a trade equilibrium. In this case, the real return to each factor is the same in both countries.*
The theorem implies that trade in commodities eliminates any motivation for trade in factors. Figure 7.9 can be used to demonstrate the theorem.

First note that under free trade (assuming zero transportation costs, as always) relative commodity prices in two trading countries are equal. The *levels* of the two commodity prices (as distinct from their ratios) are related by the exchange rate, e, defined as the number of Home units of currency (e.g. dollars per unit of Foreign currency (e.g. pesos). Chapter 2 explains why there is no loss in generality in setting the exchange rate equal to 1; this amounts to a choice of units, i.e. a normalization.

There are two steps to the argument: (i) First show that the assumptions of the theorem imply that *relative* factor prices are equal in the two countries. (ii) Then show that equality of relative factor prices implies equality of *real* factor returns.

Part (i) Because the two countries have the same technology, the graph of the relation between relative commodity prices and relative factor prices, shown as the downward sloping curve in the bottom panel of Figure 7.9, is the same for both countries. Because both are incompletely specialized, they are both on the downward sloping portion of this curve (not on a vertical segment in Figure 7.9). Therefore, because the countries face the same relative commodity prices, they also face the same relative factor prices.

Part (ii) Because both countries have the same relative factor prices and the same CRTS technology (with no factor intensity reversals) they both choose the same unit input requirements in sector i. Denote these input requirements as a_{iL} and a_{iK}, the amount of labor and the amount of capital per unit of output in sector i. The zero profit conditions in each country are

$$P_1 = wa_{1L} + ra_{1K} \quad \text{and} \quad P_2 = wa_{2L} + ra_{2K}.$$

Because the commodity prices and the unit input requirements are the same in the two countries, the equilibrium factor prices are also the same. Therefore the ratios

$$\frac{r}{p_1}, \quad \frac{r}{p_2}, \quad \frac{w}{p_1}, \quad \text{and} \quad \frac{w}{p_2}$$

are the same in both countries. Consequently, the real factor returns are the same in the two countries (see Section 2.7 of Chapter 2).

7.3.4.1 *Some implications*

If any of the assumptions of the theorem are dropped, equality of relative commodity prices does not imply equality of real factor returns. The assumptions of the theorem are restrictive.

The theorem is usually interpreted as providing an indication that as trade liberalization moves relative commodity prices in different countries closer together, it also causes real factor returns to move closer together. In other words, trade tends to increase equality between owners of capital in two countries, and between workers in two countries. This tendency is precisely what many people fear from increased globalization: that wages in the rich countries will be move towards poor country wages. This movement would lower rich country wages and increase poor country wages, decreasing the pressure for migration from poor to rich countries.

Copeland and Taylor[3] note that the theorem has implications for the Kyoto Agreement, which attempted to restrict signatories' carbon emissions, but without allowing international trade in emissions permits. To the extent that the theorem holds, it implies that trade in commodities renders trade in factors unnecessary.

Many economists stress the importance of allowing international trade in greenhouse gas (GHG) emissions permits, to reduce the aggregate cost of abating emissions. For example, if marginal abatement costs are higher in the US than in Europe, then Europe could sell to the US its right to emit one unit of emission. The resulting increase in Europe's abatement costs (resulting from the need to reduce emissions by one unit) is less than the decrease in the US abatement costs (resulting from the right to increase emissions by one unit). Therefore, by choosing a price between the two countries' marginal emissions cost, both countries benefit from the sale; trade reduces worldwide abatement cost without changing the overall level of emissions.

However, if the factor price equalization theorem holds, then trade in commodities makes it unnecessary to trade emissions permits. Output adjusts so that the marginal cost of achieving a particular level of emissions is equal in all countries, even without international emissions trade. We assume throughout that there are no transportation costs, or other kinds of trade cost (except possibly tariffs). In reality, of course, there are transportation costs. It is cheaper to ship an emissions permit than a car, so the factor price equalization theorem cannot be taken literally in this context. It

---

[3] Copeland and Taylor ("Free Trade and Global Warming: A Trade Theory View of the Kyoto Protocol," *Journal of Environmental Economics and Management*, Vol. 49, (March 2005).

merely suggests that trade in permits may be less important than often thought.

This application of the theorem might not be obvious, because GHG emissions are not literally a factor of production. However, there is (almost) no loss in generality in viewing them as such. Section 4.4 of Chapter 4 notes that if a sector produces an output, Q, and GHG emissions, x, using factors of production K, L, then (Q, x) are joint outputs. Under mild conditions we can invert the joint output production function to write the production function $Q = g(K, L, x)$. That is, we can treat x as if it were a factor of production.

7.4 The Stolper–Samuelson Theorem

The Stolper–Samuelson theorem states: *Suppose that there are constant returns to scale in both sectors, no factor intensity reversals, and incomplete specialization. In this case an increase the relative price of a good increases the real return to the factor that is used intensively in the production of that good, and decreases the real return to the other factor.*

7.4.1 *Intuition*

In the example in Figures 7.4 and 7.9, sector 1 is relatively capital intensive, an assumption that is maintained throughout this chapter. (It is easier to speak of "sector 1" than to speak of "the sector that is relatively capital intensive".) The theorem states that if $p = \frac{p_2}{p_1}$ increases then $\frac{w}{p_1}$ and $\frac{w}{p_2}$ increase and $\frac{r}{p_1}$ and $\frac{r}{p_2}$ fall. (Recall the discussion of real factor returns in Section 2.7 of Chapter 2.) From Figure 7.9, we see that an increase in p increases $\omega = \frac{w}{r}$.

We want to know how an increase in p affects real factor returns. In these general equilibrium models there is always one degree of freedom; we can choose one price (*any price*) as the numeraire. Only relative commodity prices matter. There are uncountably many ways to double p, for example. This being the case, there is no loss in generality in thinking of an increase in p being caused by an increase in p_2, holding p_1 constant. This convention simplifies the exposition.

Suppose, then, that the increase in p is due to an increase in p_2, holding fixed p_1. With p_1 fixed, it is not possible that both w and r increase or that both fall; in those cases there would be negative or positive profits in sector 1. Therefore, the increase in p and ω must cause w to increase and r to fall. Therefore the ratios $\frac{r}{p_2}$ and $\frac{r}{p_1}$ both decrease, lowering the real return to capital; and $\frac{w}{p_1}$ strictly increases. To complete the argument, we need only show that $\frac{w}{p_2}$ weakly increases.

We establish this fact using the zero profit condition

$$p_2 = w \cdot a_{2L}(\omega) + r \cdot a_{2K}(\omega),$$

where $a_{2L}(\omega)$ and $a_{2K}(\omega)$ are the unit labor and capital inputs. The argument ω emphasizes that these are functions of the relative factor price. If, for example, p_2 increases by 10%, and w were to increase by less than 10% (so that $\frac{w}{p_2}$ falls), there would be positive profits in sector 1. The original unit factor inputs remain feasible, but are (in general) no longer optimal after the change in ω. With a 10% increase in p_2, a fall in r, and a less than 10% increase in w, the original unit factor inputs lead to positive profits. Because positive profits are not consistent with equilibrium, we conclude that w must have increased by more than 10%, so $\frac{w}{p_2}$ increases.

7.4.2 *A formal demonstration*

Although the formal demonstration of the theorem does not add to the intuition, it provides an opportunity to practice derivations and also to introduce machinery used later in this chapter.

7.4.2.1 *The machinery*

Equation (7.1) defines the cost function. We work with the unit cost function, obtained by setting output $Q = 1$. The unit cost function is

$$c(w, r) = \min_{a_L, a_k} (w a_L + r a_K),$$
$$\text{subject to } F(a_L, a_K) \geq 1,$$

using the previously defined unit input requirements a_K, a_L. By the envelope theorem

$$\frac{\partial c}{\partial w} = a_L, \quad \frac{\partial c}{\partial r} = a_k. \tag{7.5}$$

The set of points in w, r space on which c is constant, i.e. the isocost curve, satisfy

$$dc = \frac{\partial c}{\partial w} dw + \frac{\partial c}{\partial r} dr = 0.$$

Solving this relation gives the slope of an isocost curve

$$\frac{dw}{dr}\Big|_{dc=0} = -\frac{\frac{\partial c}{\partial r}}{\frac{\partial c}{\partial w}} = -\frac{a_k}{a_L}.$$

The slope of the isocost curve equals the negative of the capital/labor ratio, as shown in Figure 7.11. Factor prices to the Northeast of an isocost curve entail higher costs of production. I restate these facts as

Property 1: The (negative of the) slope of the tangent of an iso-cost curve equals the optimal capital-labor ratio at the factor prices associated with the tangency point.

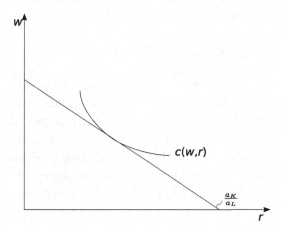

Figure 7.11. The slope of the unit isocost curve equals the capital/labor ratio. The slope of the line (not shown) from the origen to a point on the curve equals the wage/rental rate.

Property 2: Higher costs are associated with higher iso-cost curves.

7.4.2.2 *Digression*

We confirm that the isocost curve is convex. Pick two price pairs (w_1, r_1) and (w_2, r_2) on the same isocost curve, and then choose a convex combination of those pairs $(w_\lambda, r_\lambda) = \lambda (w_1, r_1) + (1 - \lambda) (w_2, r_2)$, with $0 \leq \lambda \leq 1$. The factor mix that is optimal at (w_λ, r_λ) is feasible but not in general optimal at (w_1, r_1) and (w_2, r_2). Therefore, the two points (w_1, r_1) and (w_2, r_2) lie on a lower isocost curve than (w_λ, r_λ).

With $a_{K\lambda}$ and $a_{L\lambda}$ the optimal unit inputs at factor prices equal to (w_λ, r_λ), we have

$$
\begin{aligned}
c(w_\lambda, r_\lambda) &= w_\lambda a_{L\lambda} + r_\lambda a_{K\lambda} \\
&= \lambda (w_1 a_{L\lambda} + r_1 a_{K\lambda}) + (1 - \lambda)(w_2 a_{L\lambda} + r_2 a_{K\lambda}) \\
&\geq \lambda c(w_1, r_1) + (1 - \lambda) c(w_2, r_2).
\end{aligned}
\tag{7.6}
$$

The first equality follows from the definition of the cost function, the second equality follows from the definition of (w_λ, r_λ), and the inequality follows from the fact that the input mix $a_{K\lambda}$ and $a_{L\lambda}$ does not (in general) minimize costs at factor prices (w_1, r_1) and (w_2, r_2).[4] Thus, the isocost curve is convex.

7.4.2.3 *Back to the demonstration*

Subscripts identify the two sectors. If unit costs are greater than prices, the sector shuts down (production equals zero). Profits can never be positive in equilibrium, because firms would compete for additional factors in order to increase their output, thereby increasing their positive profits. Given the fixed aggregate supply of factors, the increased demand for factors would increase their price, until profits fall to zero. Equilibrium requires that profits are non-positive,

---

[4]For Leontieff technology, the input mix is independent of factor prices, i.e. there is no substitutability. In that case the weak inequality in equation (7.6) is an equality. Here, the isocost curves are straight lines.

i.e. that

$$c_i(w, r) \geq p_i, \quad i = 1, 2 \tag{7.7}$$

for each sector. If the sector operates, then profits equal 0. Figure 7.12 graphs the isocost curves that satisfy this relation as an equality, for the two sectors, given the output prices. Factor prices in the shaded area are feasible, because those prices satisfy the inequality constraints in equation (7.7). The envelope of this set is called the factor price frontier. It is the set of points that is consistent with 0 profits in both sectors, with at least one sector operating.

Figure 7.12 incorporates the assumption that there are no factor intensity reversals. Therefore, the curves intersect at only one point, denoted A in the figure. At the commodity prices corresponding to A, there is a single factor price pair that is consistent with positive production and zero profits in both sectors. If the curves intersected in two points, then there would be two pairs of factor prices consistent with operation of both sectors, as in the lower panel of Figure 7.8, where there are factor intensity reversals.

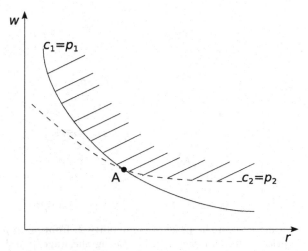

Figure 7.12. The set in (r, w) space bounded below by the upper envelope of the "isocost = price" curves give combinations of the rental rate and wage leading to non-positive profits. Profits are zero only on the envelope.

Property 1 above notes that the slope of the isocost curve gives the capital/labor ratio in a sector. If both sectors operate, then the factor prices are at point A in Figure 7.12. At this point, the capital/labor ratio in sector 1 equals the slope of the sector 1 isocost curve, and the capital/labor ratio in sector 2 equals the slope of the sector 2 isocost curve. (As noted above, absent factor intensity reversals, we assume that sector 1 is more capital intensive.) The aggregate capital/labor ratio in the economy is a convex combination of the capital/labor ratios in the two sectors (see equation (7.4)). Therefore, if the economy is at point A, the aggregate capital/labor ratio equals the slope of a line that lies in the cone formed by the tangencies (not shown) to the two curves at point A.

Figures 7.12 and 7.13 provide another way to visualize the relation between commodity and factor prices. An increase in the price of commodity 2 causes the curve labelled $c_2 = p_2$ to shift out, as shown in Figure 7.13, because higher factor prices are now consistent with zero profits. Therefore, if the economy is incompletely specialized, w increases and r falls with the increase in the sector 2 commodity price. The equilibrium factor prices move from point A to point B in Figure 7.13.

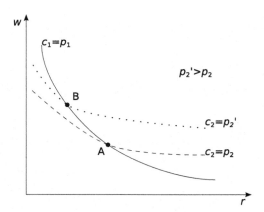

Figure 7.13.   An increase in the price of commodity 2, from p_2 to p_2', shifts out the "isocost = price" curve for sector 2, increasing the wage/rental rate that is consistent with zero profits in both sectors. The curve corresponding to sector 1 is steeper than the curve corresponding to sector 2, because sector 1 is relatively capital intensive by assumption.

7.4.3 *The algebra*

Using upper case P_i to denote the price of commodity 1 (not a relative price), we differentiate the equilibrium conditions $P_i = c_i(w, r)$, using the envelope result in equation (7.5). The result is

$$dP_i = a_{iL} \cdot dw + a_{ik} \cdot dr, \quad i = 1, 2. \tag{7.8}$$

Define the matrix

$$H = \begin{bmatrix} a_{1L} & a_{1K} \\ a_{2L} & a_{2k} \end{bmatrix},$$

and the determinate as

$$|H| = a_{1K} a_{2K} \left(\frac{a_{1L}}{a_{1K}} - \frac{a_{2L}}{a_{2K}} \right) < 0,$$

where the inequality is due to the assumption that sector 1 is relatively capital intensive. To simplify notation define

$$g = \left(\frac{a_{1L}}{a_{1K}} - \frac{a_{2L}}{a_{2K}} \right).$$

Using matrix notation, we rewrite the system (7.8) as

$$H \begin{pmatrix} dw \\ dr \end{pmatrix} = \begin{pmatrix} dP_1 \\ dP_2 \end{pmatrix}. \tag{7.9}$$

Because we care only about relative prices, there is no loss in generality in setting $dP_1 = 0$, and letting the price of the second commodity vary. With this convention, we can solve the system (7.9) to obtain

$$\begin{pmatrix} \dfrac{dw}{dP_2} \\ \dfrac{dr}{dP_2} \end{pmatrix} = H^{-1} \begin{pmatrix} 0 \\ 1 \end{pmatrix} \Rightarrow \frac{dw}{dP_2}$$

$$= \frac{\begin{vmatrix} 0 & a_{1K} \\ 1 & a_{2K} \end{vmatrix}}{|H|} = -\frac{a_{1K}}{a_{1K} a_{2K} g} > 0. \tag{7.10}$$

Now use the zero profit condition to write

$$P_2 = wa_{2L} + ra_{2K} > wa_{2L}. \tag{7.11}$$

Convert the derivative in equation (7.10) to an elasticity and use inequality (7.11) to write

$$\frac{P_2}{w}\frac{dw}{dP_2} > \frac{wa_{2L}}{w}\frac{dw}{dP_2} = \frac{1}{1-h} > 1, \tag{7.12}$$

where

$$h = \frac{\frac{a_{1L}}{a_{1K}}}{\frac{a_{2L}}{a_{2K}}} < 1.$$

The second inequality in equation (7.12) follows from the fact that $h < 1$, because sector 1 is (by our convention) relatively capital intensive. We conclude that the elasticity is strictly greater than 1. That is, an increase in P_2 causes a more than proportional increase w, the price of the factor that is used intensively in the sector. The other parts of the theorem can be shown using even simpler arguments, because the convention that $dP_2 = 0$ means that we need only find the sign of the derivatives (not the magnitude of the elasticities) in equation (7.10).

7.4.4 *Some implications*

The Stolper–Samuelson theorem describes the effect on real factor returns of a change in relative commodity prices, regardless of the source of that change. Suppose, for example, that a rich and a poor country trade, and the rich country imports a commodity that uses low-skilled labor intensively. (This statement means that the ratio of low-skilled labor to other inputs is higher for this import good compared to for other goods.) The relaxation of trade restrictions between the rich and poor country reduces the import good's relative price in the rich country. If the assumptions of the theorem hold, the real return to low-skilled workers in the rich country falls.

People sometimes mistakenly claim that trade makes everyone better off. The Stolper–Samuelson theorem shows why that claim is false. Any change in relative prices is likely to make some agents worse off. In the absence of distortions, trade liberalization increases national income, so it would be possible to use transfers to make all agents better off. However, absent transfers and given that some agents own mostly capital or mostly labor, there is no reason to think that trade makes all agents better off. The Ricardian model, in which there is a single factor of production, obscures this point. We need two or more factors of production to determine the effect of a price change on the distribution of income.

As as second example of the implications of the Stolper–Samuelson theorem, consider the effect of a price change on the demand for environmental services. We can interpret increased emissions to mean an increased demand for environmental services, because higher emissions make greater use of the environment as a dumping ground. We can also think of increased use of a renewable resource, e.g. increased fishing or increased logging, as representing an increased demand for environmental services.

Up to this point we have taken the supply of factors as exogenous; the equilibrium conditions determine their price. However, it is a short step to view the supply of a factor as endogenous, i.e. responsive to its price. In many (but not all) applications, it is reasonable to assume that an increase in the real return to a factor increases the available supply: the supply function has a positive slope.

Suppose that a country uses the environment (either as a dumping ground for emissions, or a source of a natural resource) to provide services — i.e. factors — for production. More concretely, let $f(K, L, x)$ be the production function for a sector that creates emissions x, and suppose that firms face an emissions tax τ. From firms' standpoint, it is as if they face a perfectly elastic supply function for emissions at the price τ. If the tax is indeed fixed, then society's supply function for emissions is perfectly elastic at this price. Given the tax, firms in this sector have a unit cost function $c(w, r, \tau)$. The firm views the tax as the cost per unit of emissions, just as the wage is the cost per unit of labor. Under the assumption of CRTS, the emissions per unit of output is $\frac{\partial c}{\partial t}$ (see equation (7.5)). The aggregate level of emissions depends on the tax.

Now suppose that the country opens up to trade, or relaxes trade restrictions. If this liberalization has any effect, it must change commodity prices. Suppose that the liberalization increases the relative price of the commodity that uses intensively the environmental services. If the level of emissions were to remain constant (just as the aggregate stock of labor and capital remain constant), then the Stolper Samuelson theorem implies that there would have to be a more than proportional increase in the price of emissions. That is, τ would have to increase more than proportionally to the price increase to maintain the same level of aggregate emissions.

If the tax does not increase (or if it does not increase by enough to offset the commodity price increase), then emissions increase, because the higher output price raises the firm's value of the marginal product of emissions. In this case, when a country that has a comparative advantage in the environment-intensive commodity opens up to trade, firms' demand for environmental services — here, the level of emissions — increases.

If the tax is set optimally before and after the trade liberalization, liberalization increases welfare.[5] However, if the tax was optimal before liberalization, but it does not adjust optimally, then the economy has moved from a situation with one distortion (the trade restriction) to a situation where that distortion has been reduced (by moving toward free trade) but an environmental distortion has been created. In view of the theory of the second best, trade liberalization has an ambiguous effect on the country's welfare.

7.5   The Rybczynski Theorem

The theorem states:

Suppose that an economy produces with CRTS and there are no factor intensity reversals, and the economy is incompletely specialized. Holding commodity prices constant, an increase in a factor of

---

[5]In this setting, higher emissions lower welfare. The optimal emissions tax balances the benefit of being able to produce more because of raising emissions, with the direct welfare cost of those emissions.

production leads to a more than proportional increase in output in the sector that uses that factor intensively, and a decrease in output of the other sector.

The intuition for the theorem is straightforward. Under the assumptions of the theorem, there is a one-to-one relation between commodity and factor prices. Because commodity prices are held fixed, factor prices are fixed. Therefore, the unit labor requirements in each sector are fixed. Suppose, for example, that the stock of capital increases. Because unit input requirements are unchanged, it is not possible for output in both sectors to increase, as that would require additional labor. In equilibrium, the output of both sector cannot fall, as that would lead to unemployment of both factors. Therefore, output in one sector increases and output in the other sector falls.

For this example, capital flows into sector 1 (the capital intensive sector) requiring sector 2 to release labor to maintain a constant capital/labor ratio in sector 1. As sector 2 releases labor, it must also release some capital, to maintain its own constant capital/labor ratio. Output in sector 2 falls because that sector is now using less labor and less capital. Therefore, sector 1 obtains all of the initial increase in capital, plus the amount of capital and labor that sector 2 releases. Consequently, the output of sector 1 increases more than proportionally to the increase in the aggregate stock of capital.

Demonstration

I provide a geometric and then an algebraic demonstration. The geometric argument uses the Rybczynski lines, or "full employment lines". Denoting Q_i as the output in sector i, the full employment conditions for capital and labor are

$$a_{1L}Q_1 + a_{2L}Q_2 = L \quad \text{and} \quad a_{1K}Q_1 + a_{2k}Q_2 = K. \qquad (7.13)$$

Figure 7.14 graphs these two full employment lines. The assumption that sector 1 is relatively capital intensive implies that the slope of the full employment line for labor (FEL) is steeper than the

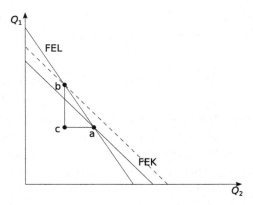

Figure 7.14.   The full employment lines for capital and labor in (Q_2, Q_1) space. The relative slope of the curves is due to the assumption that sector 1 is relatively capital intensive. An increase in capital shifts out the full employment line for capital, changing equilibrium production from point a to b.

full employment line for capital (FEK). The economy is initially incompletely specialized at point a.

Suppose that the stock of capital increases. Because prices have not changed, the unit input requirements have not changed, so the slopes of the two lines are unchanged. The stock of labor is unchanged, so the FEL line is unchanged. The increase in the stock of capital causes the FEK line to shift up to the dashed curve, causing production to move to point b. The supply of commodity 1 increases and the supply of commodity 2 decreases. The increase in the output of sector 1 is the vertical distance bc in Figure 7.14 and the increase in the stock of capital equals the vertical distance between the original and the new intercept, divided by a_{1k}. The increase in output of sector 1 is more than proportional to the increase in the stock of capital.

The algebraic proof proceeds by first solving the system (7.13) to obtain and expression for Q_1, and then converting to an elasticity:

$$Q_1 = \frac{a_{2L}K - a_{2K}L}{-a_{1L}a_{2K} + a_{2L}a_{1K}} \Rightarrow \frac{dQ_1}{dK}\frac{K}{Q_1} = \frac{1}{1 - \frac{L}{K}\frac{a_{2k}}{a_{2L}}} > 1.$$

The inequality follows from the assumption that sector 1 is relatively capital intensive. This assumption implies that the capital/labor ratio in sector 2 is lower than the capital labor ratio in the economy, i.e. $\frac{a_{2k}}{a_{2L}} < \frac{K}{L}$, so the denominator, $1 - \frac{L}{K}\frac{a_{2k}}{a_{2L}}$, is less than 1. An analogous argument shows that an increase in K lowers Q_2.

7.5.1 *Incomplete vs. complete specialization*

To appreciate the importance of the assumption that the economy is incompletely specialized, suppose instead that the economy is initially specialized in good 2. To determine the effect of an increase in the endowment of labor, return to Figure 7.9. Recall that for any relative price greater or equal to p_2, the economy is specialized in commodity 2. Figure 7.3 shows p_2 as the slope of the PPF at the corner where the economy is specialized in commodity 2. Suppose that the economy is specialized in good 2, so the relative factor price is w_2, and suppose that the relative commodity price is strictly greater than p_2. The economy is on the vertical portion labelled C in Figure 7.9. The aggregate capital/labor ratio determines the location of both of the vertical portions, as shown in the figure.

An increase in the labor endowment causes the line at $\frac{K}{L}$ in the upper panel of Figure 7.9 to shift down, causing both vertical portions in the lower panel to shift to the left. Holding the commodity price fixed, the relative factor price w falls, and the economy remains specialized in commodity 2. There is no change in production of commodity 1 (which remains at 0) and the increase in production of commodity 2 is less than proportional to the increase in the stock of labor.

The economic explanation is that if the economy is specialized in good 2, an increase in the endowment of labor makes capital relatively more scarce, causing it's relative price is bid up. The relative price of labor falls. The zero profit condition for sector 2 provides an easy way to demonstrate this result.

7.5.2 *Trade implications*

For the sake of concreteness, suppose that the import good is relatively capital intensive and that the stock of labor increases. For example, the population may become more educated, leading to an increase in "effective units" of labor. Alternatively, immigration may increase the stock of labor.

At constant prices, the increase in the amount of labor increases national income. If both goods are normal, increased income leads to an increase in demand for both goods. Because the production of the capital intensive import-competing good has fallen, the increased demand for this good requires increased imports. Because the prices have not changed, the increased imports must be paid for by increasing exports.

7.5.2.1 *Immizerizing growth: Another example*

Chapter 3 provides two examples of immizerizing growth. In the first, growth causes a deterioration in the country's term's of trade; in the second, growth causes an endogenous increase in the tariff used to achieve a targeted level of production of one commodity. Here we assume that the country is small and that there is a fixed tariff. Therefore, neither of the reasons for the loss in welfare in the previous examples occur here.

The current example is valuable both because it provides practice using the tools developed above, and because it sheds light on a practical question: How does liberalization of capital markets affect welfare in the presence of restrictions on commodity trade? I first describe the setting and show that growth can be immizerizing. The next sections develop the intuition for the result, and explain its importance.

7.5.2.2 *Statement and demonstration*

The intersection of the full employment lines for labor and capital identify a point on the production possibility frontier, as shown in Figure 7.15. If we pick the relative commodity price p we know that production (in a competitive equilibrium) occurs where the PPF is tangent to a line with slope $-p$, as shown at point A in Figure 7.15. We have also seen that (under the assumptions of CRTS, no factor intensity reversals, and incomplete specialization), the relative commodity price determines the relative factor price,

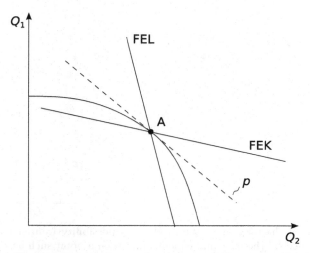

Figure 7.15. The tangent to the production possibility curve lies in the cones formed by the full employment lines.

and this determines the unit input requirements. These unit input requirements, together with the stocks of factors, determine the full employment lines. The intersection of these two lines must also be at point A.

The tangent at point A lies in the cone spanned by the two full employment lines. To verify this fact, suppose to the contrary that the tangent lies outside the cone, as illustrated in Figure 7.16. To see that this situation is not possible, notice that at point B in Figure 7.16, capital is fully employed but there is unemployed labor. Therefore, point B is feasible. However, point B lies outside the PPF, so it cannot be feasible. Therefore, the situation illustrated in Figure 7.16 is impossible.

We are now in a position to consider the effect of growth in a small open economy with a fixed tariff. For this example, we assume that growth arises from an increase in the supply of one or more factor — not, for example, an improvement in technology. Suppose that the economy imports commodity 1 and imposes an *ad valorem* tariff τ. If the world relative price of commodity 2 is $p^w = \frac{P_2}{P_1}$, then the domestic relative price is $p^d = \frac{P_2}{(1+\tau)P_1} = \frac{p^w}{1+\tau} < p^w$. With a

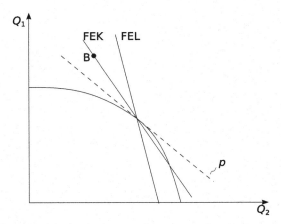

Figure 7.16. If the tangent to the production possibility frontier did not lie in the cone formed by the full employment lines, then a point such as B is feasible, because it involves full employment of capital but some unemployed labor. But B lies outside the production possibility frontier and therefore is not feasible. Therefore, the tangent to the PPF must lie in the cone spanned by the full employment lines.

tariff, domestic producer and consumer relative prices are equal to each other, but different than the world price.

The production point on the PPF depends on the *domestic* relative producer price, p^d; this is the price that determines factor prices and unit input requirements. Prior to growth, the production point is A in Figure 7.17. As noted above, the tangent of the PPF (not shown to reduce clutter) at A equals the domestic producer price. However, because of the tariff, the domestic relative price is less than the world relative price: $p^d < p^w$. Therefore, the slope of the county's BOP constraint is steeper than the tangent to the PPF at point A. Recall that the BOP constraint intersects point A.

If the tariff was small, i.e. if $p^d \approx p^w$, then the BOP constraint would lie close to the tangent to the PPF at A. In that case, the BOP (like the tangent) would lie inside the cone created by the two full employment lines. If, however, the tariff is large, then the domestic relative price of commodity 2 is much smaller than the world price. In that case, the BOP can lie outside the cone, as illustrated in

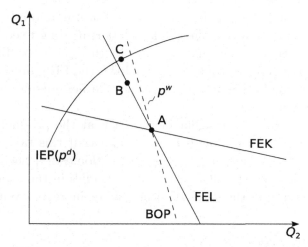

Figure 7.17. With a tariff, the world relative price of the export good, Q_2, is higher than the domestic relative price. The BOP constraint therefore might lie outside the cone formed by the full employment lines. If an increase in capital causes production to move from A to B, welfare falls.

Figure 7.17. This figure shows the case where a country imposes a large tariff on its imports.

An increase in the stock of capital shifts out the FEK line; the production point moves up the FEL line, because the stock of labor has not changed, to a point such as B. To reduce clutter, the figure does not show the new FEK line or the new BOP constraint, which contains B, has the slope $-p^w$, and is parallel to and lies below the original BOP constraint. Because the tariff has not changed, the domestic consumer price has not changed, so the IEP has not moved. The new BOP constraint intersects the IEP at a point such as C, where utility is lower than at the pre-growth consumption point. Growth is immizerizing.

We can use this figure to examine the effects of other changes in the stocks of factors. Maintaining the same assumptions used to produce the figure, we see that a decrease in the stock of capital increases national income and welfare. The decrease in the stock of capital, and the inward shift in the FEK line, causes the production point to move down the FEL, leading to equilibrium consumption on the IEP north east of the original equilibrium, and a higher level of welfare. An increase in the stock of labor, holding fixed the stock of capital, increases national income. In this case, the FEL shifts out, and the production point travels down the FEK line. The BOP constraint through this new production point lies outside the original BOP constraint.

We know that the tangent of the PPF at the production point has slope equal to the domestic price, and that this tangent lies in the cone. If the world price is close to the domestic price, i.e. if the tariff is small, then the BOP constraint also lies in the cone. In that case, an increase in the stock of either factor increases welfare.

7.5.2.3 *Interpretation*

There are a number of ways to interpret the result above. First, it is just another example of the theory of the second best. An apparently beneficial change occurs (the stock of a factor increases) in a second-best setting. The theory of the second best tells us that in this circumstance, we cannot be certain that the change improves welfare.

In order for the change to lower welfare, it must increase the existing distortion. We hold the tariff fixed, so in that sense the distortion is fixed. However, the effect of the tariff does change with growth. The tariff causes excessive production of good 1, relative to the first best, free trade optimum. Increased production of commodity 1 does not in itself make the economy poorer. However, increased production of commodity 1 draws factors away from sector 2, reducing production there.

The tariff causes production of commodity 2 to be too low, relative to the first best level. When growth occurs due to an increase in the capital stock, resources are drawn out of sector 2, in accordance with the Rybczynski Theorem. Growth makes the distortion "too little production of commodity 2" worse; therefore growth can reduce welfare.

An alternative interpretation proceeds along the lines suggested in Section 6.7 of Chapter 6, which notes that a distortion in one market creates distortions in other markets. Here the "immediate" distortion is that domestic commodity prices differ from world prices; world prices determine the slope of the BOP constraint, while the domestic producer price determines the production point. We saw (throughout these lectures) that commodity and factor prices are inextricably linked via general equilibrium relations. Therefore, the "wrong" (i.e. distorted) commodity price is translated into a distorted relative factor price. Producers make their decisions about factor mix based on the "wrong" factor prices.

In what sense are these prices "wrong"? Section 6.7 of Chapter 6 discusses the idea of the shadow value of capital, defined as the increase in real national income due to an increase in capital, or equivalently the social marginal value of capital. In that setting we had two stocks of capital, because there capital is sector-specific in the short run. We pointed out that in the presence of a distortion (there, the minimum wage constraint), the private return to capital differs from the shadow value of capital. Agents make their decisions based on the private return to capital, not its shadow value. In this sense, agents respond to the "wrong" prices (from society's perspective). The firm's individually optimal behavior — the behavior that maximizes its profits — is not socially optimal.

The setting is similar here, except that here capital is freely mobile across sectors, so there is a single stock of capital, and thus a single shadow value and private return (r) to capital. However, here we also have a distortion (the tariff) that causes agents to face the "wrong" commodity prices. Because commodity and factor prices are tied together via general equilibrium relations, agents also face a return on capital that does not equal the shadow value of of capital.

The example in this section is extreme, because an increase in capital lowers national income: the shadow value of capital is negative. The general point, however, is that when there is a tariff and the import-competing good is relatively capital intensive, the shadow value of capital is less than the private value, r. If we had changed the assumption so that the import-competing good is relatively labor intensive, the shadow value of capital would exceed its private value.

7.5.3 *Application*

Consider an economy that restricts both trade in commodities and in factors. For concreteness, suppose that the economy uses a tariff to restrict trade and a quantity restriction on foreign investment (capital). The economy is small, so it takes both the relative commodity price and the world price of capital as given. The quantity restriction on capital imports is binding; if the restriction were relaxed, firms would want to import more capital. Therefore, the domestic price of capital (equal to its value of marginal product) exceeds the world price of capital.

The economy now allows increased capital imports. This liberalization of the capital market increases foreign investment (equivalently, domestic borrowing for the purpose of investment). Because the domestic value of the marginal product of capital exceeds the world price, it might appear that liberalization of the capital market would raise national income. By this time, students are on guard against that kind of easy surmise. We have seen that the tariff drives a wedge between the private and the social shadow value of capital. Firms make their decisions based on the private value of capital: they respond to the wrong price, from the perspective of society.

The example of immizerizing growth showed that *even if capital was free*, an increase in the amount of capital might lower welfare. Therefore, if the economy has to pay for capital, it is even more likely that capital inflows lower welfare. If an increase in the stock of capital lowers welfare, then by definition the social shadow value of capital is negative.

Because nations must in fact pay for capital imports, the relaxation in capital import restrictions might lower welfare even if the social shadow value of capital is positive. Increased capital imports lower welfare whenever the social shadow value of capital is less than the world price of capital.

Many nations imposed tariffs in part to increase foreign investment; this was sometimes a component of the import substitution policy discussed in Section 4.2 of Chapter 4. The high tariff was sometimes used to encourage foreign investment in domestic import-competing industries. This type of investment is known as "tariff jumping", because the point of it is to circumvent the tariff wall. If the import-competing industry is capital intensive, capital inflows draw resources away from the export sector. That sector is already "too small" (relative to the first best) because of the tariff. Thus, the foreign investment can lower welfare in the presence of a tariff.

This kind of example does not, by itself, provide an argument against liberalized investment rules. Greater investment might either increase or decrease national income. The tariff might make capital imports more valuable than they would have been in the absence of the tariff. The point of the example is to make students cautious about facile policy recommendations in a second best world: our world.

7.6 The Heckscher–Ohlin–Samuelson Theorem

The HOS theorem has a "price version" and a "quantity version"; the latter requires an assumption about preferences, introduced below. The two versions differ in their definition of what it means for a country to be "relatively well endowed" in a factor. Remember our convention in this chapter that sector 1 is relatively capital intensive, so a larger relative price $p = \frac{P_2}{P_1}$ implies a larger relative factor price, $\omega = \frac{w}{r}$, as shown in the lower panel in Figure 7.9.

The theorem states

Suppose that trading partners have the same constant returns to scale technology with no factor intensity reversals. (For the quantity version of the theorem we introduce an additional assumption on preferences at this point.) Then a country has a comparative advantage in, and therefore exports the commodity that uses intensively the factor in which the country is relatively well endowed.

7.6.1 *The price version*

In this version of the theorem, a country is said to be relatively well endowed in labor (for example) if its autarchic relative price of labor is lower than its partner's. That is, if $\omega^a < \omega^{a*}$, home is relatively well endowed in labor. (The superscript a denotes "autarchy" and the $*$ denotes the foreign country.)

This version of the theorem is almost immediate from Figure 7.9. If $\omega^a < \omega^{a*}$ then from Figure 7.9, $p^a < p^{a*}$. Therefore, Home has a comparative advantage in commodity 2, and exports that commodity when trade begins. (Here review the import demand and export supply curves from Chapter 3.)

This version of the theorem provides limited insight, because it requires knowing the autarchic relative prices – something that would be hard to measure, even in principle.

7.6.2 *The quantity version*

This version of the theorem, which states that home is relatively well endowed in labor if $\frac{K}{L} < \frac{K^*}{L^*}$, depends on physical quantities, rather that autarchic prices. There are two cases, depending on whether one country is specialized.

7.6.2.1 *Trade involves complete specialization by at least one country*

Figure 7.18 illustrates the situation where Foreign is completely specialized in sector 1; it has autarchic factor prices at point B. Home is incompletely specialized, with autarchic factor prices at point A. Because Foreign produces only commodity 1, it exports commodity 1. Section 7.4.2 explains the relation between factor intensity and a point on an isocost curve. Because Foreign is specialized in sector 1, its capital/labor ratio in sector 1 equals the country's aggregate capital/labor ratio $\frac{K^*}{L^*} = k^*$. This ratio equals the (negative of) the slope of the isocost curve at point B. Home produces both goods, so its capital/labor ratio is a convex combination of the factor intensities in the two sectors, denoted k_1 and k_2. These values equal the slope of the tangencies of the isocost curves at point A. Both of these slopes are clearly smaller than k^*, the tangency at point B. (This statement is evident from Figure 7.18. It can be confirmed using the convexity of the

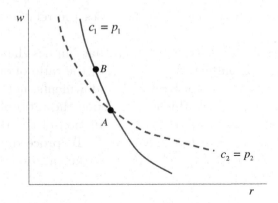

Figure 7.18. If Home is incompletely specialized with factor prices at A, its capital/labor ratio lies between the slopes of the tangents of the two curves at A. If Foreign is completely specialized in good 1, with factor prices at B, its capital/labor ratio equals the slope of the tangent at B. Foreign must have a higher capital/labor ratio than Home.

isocost curve, established in Section 7.4.2 of Chapter 7.) Therefore we have

$$\frac{K^*}{L^*} = k^* > k_1 > \lambda k_1 + (1 - \lambda) k_2 = \frac{K}{L} = k,$$

Foreign is relatively well endowed in capital in the "quantity sense". Foreign exports commodity 1, the good that uses capital intensively.

7.6.2.2 *Trade involves incomplete specialization by both countries*

The case where both countries are incompletely specialized requires the additional assumption alluded to above: the two countries have identical homothetic preferences. With homothetic preferences, a country's IEP is a ray from the origin. Consequently, the ratio of a country's demand for the two goods, $d = \frac{D_1}{D_2}$ depends on prices but not on income. Because Foreign has the same homothetic preferences (by assumption), its ratio of demand for the two commodities is the same as Home's. From Section 3.2 of Chapter 3, an increase in the relative price of a commodity causes the IEP to move away from the axis of the commodity that has become more expensive.

Therefore, an increase in $p = \frac{p_1}{p_2}$ decreases the relative demand for commodity 1, d.

Now we exploit a feature of CRTS that implies that (at a given price and under incomplete specialization) the ratio of output in the two sectors depends on relative factor endowments, not on the scale of the economy. To verify this claim, define the ratio of outputs as $q = \frac{Q_1}{Q_2}$. We want to show that q is a function of the ratio $k = \frac{K}{L}$, but not on the absolute levels K and L. To proceed, divide both equations in (7.13) by Q_2 and then take the ratio of the resulting two equations to write

$$\frac{a_{1K}q + a_{2k}}{a_{iL}q + a_{2L}} = k. \tag{7.14}$$

This equation shows that q is a function of k, but does not depend on the levels K and L. For subsequent use we note that

$$\frac{dq}{dk} = \frac{(q \cdot a_{1L} + a_{2L})^2}{(a_{1K}a_{2L} - a_{1L}a_{2K})} > 0. \tag{7.15}$$

The inequality follows from the assumption that sector 1 is relatively capital intensive, so the denominator on the right side of equation (7.15) is positive.

We use equation (7.15) to construct a geometric argument for the HOS theorem. Define p as the relative price of commodity 1. Chapter 3 shows that an increase in p increases the equilibrium output of sector 1 and decreases the output of sector 2, so $\frac{dq}{dp} > 0$. The relative supply curve (the ratio of commodity 1 to commodity 2) increases in the relative price (the ratio of the price of commodity 1 to commodity 2).

Figure 7.19 shows the relative demand curve for Home and Foreign, $d(p)$, which is the same by virtue of the assumption that the two countries have the same homothetic preferences. The relative supply curves are $q(p, k)$ for Home and $q(p, k^*)$ for Foreign, drawn under the assumption that Foreign is relatively capital intensive. Inequality (7.15) implies that for a given price, $q(p, k^*) > q(p, k)$, as the figure shows. The autarchic prices in the two countries, shown as p^a and p^{a*}, equate relative supply and relative demand. Because

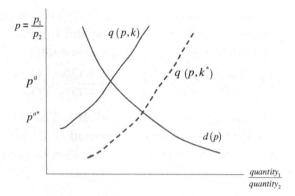

Figure 7.19. The trading partners have the same relative demand curve because of the assumption of identical homothetic preferences. Foreign has a greater relative supply curve of commodity 1 because of the assumption that Foreign is relatively well endowed in capital, the input that is used intensively in commodity 1. Therefore, Foreign has a lower autarchy relative price for commodity 1.

$p^a > p^{a*}$, Foreign (the country relatively well-endowed in capital) has the comparative advantage in commodity 1 (the commodity that uses capital relatively intensively).

We conclude by providing the algebraic argument, again under the assumption that Foreign is relatively well endowed in capital, i.e. that $k^* > k$. This assumption and equation (7.15) imply that for any price

$$q^* = \frac{Q_1^*}{Q_2^*} > \frac{Q_1}{Q_2} = q$$

$$\Rightarrow \frac{Q_1^*}{Q_1} > \frac{Q_2^*}{Q_2}$$

$$\Longrightarrow \frac{Q_1^* + Q_1}{Q_1} > \frac{Q_2^* + Q_2}{Q_2}$$

$$\Rightarrow \frac{Q_2}{Q_1} > \frac{Q_2^* + Q_2}{Q_1^* + Q_1}. \tag{7.16}$$

Home's ratio of supply of commodity 2 to commodity 1 exceeds the ratio for the world. The assumption of identical homothetic preferences and the requirement that aggregate supply equals aggregate demand for both commodities means that in a free trade equilibrium (where countries face the same relative price, and aggregate supply equals aggregate demand), the ratio of demand in each country and in the world must equal the ratio of aggregate supply. That is

$$\frac{D_2}{D_1} = \frac{D_2^*}{D_1^*} = \frac{D_2 + D_2^*}{D_1 + D_1^*} = \frac{Q_2 + Q_2^*}{Q_1 + Q_1^*} < \frac{Q_2}{Q_1}, \qquad (7.17)$$

where the last inequality uses inequality (7.16). The conclusion that $\frac{Q_2}{Q_1} > \frac{D_2}{D_1}$ implies that Home exports commodity 2, the commodity that uses intensively labor, the factor with which Home is relatively well endowed.

Appendix A

Derivation of Equation (4.11)

Denote $S^x(t;p)$ and $S^y(t;p)$ as the equilibrium supply of the dirty and the clean good, respectively. Consumers' budget constraint requires $pD^x + D^y = I$, where $D^x(t)$, $D^y(t)$, $I(t)$ are demand for the dirty and the clean good and income, respectively; these are all functions of t. By homotheticity, $D^y = \alpha(p)D^x$, where α depends only on p, a constant. The budget constraint therefore implies $(p+\alpha)D^x(t) = I(t)$, or $\frac{dD^x(t)}{dt} = \frac{1}{p+\alpha}\frac{dI}{dt}$. National income is $I(t) = pS^x + S^y$ so $\frac{dI}{dt} = p\frac{dS^x}{dt} + \frac{dS^y}{dt}$. Putting these two results together gives

$$\frac{dD^x(t)}{dt} = \frac{1}{p+\alpha}\left(p\frac{dS^x}{dt} + \frac{dS^y}{dt}\right). \tag{A.1}$$

Imports of the dirty good equal $m(t;p) = S^x - D^x$. Differentiating this identity and using equation (A.1) gives

$$
\begin{aligned}
\frac{dm}{dt} &= \frac{dD^x}{dt} - \frac{dS^x}{dt} = \frac{1}{p+\alpha}\left(p\frac{dS^x}{dt} + \frac{dS^y}{dt}\right) - \frac{dS^x}{dt} \\
&= \frac{1}{p+\alpha}\left((p-p-\alpha)\frac{dS^x}{dt} + \frac{dS^y}{dt}\right) \\
&= \frac{1}{t(p+\alpha)}\left(-\alpha\frac{dS^x}{dt}\frac{t}{S^x}S^x + \frac{dS^y}{dt}\frac{t}{S^y}S^y\right)
\end{aligned}
$$

$$= \frac{1}{t\left(p+\alpha\right)}\left(-\alpha\varepsilon^{x,t}S^x + \varepsilon^y \beta S^x\right) = \frac{S^x}{\alpha t\left(p+\alpha\right)}\left(\varepsilon^y \frac{\beta}{\alpha} - \varepsilon^{x,t}\right)$$

$$\implies \frac{dm}{dt} = \frac{S^x}{\alpha t\left(p+\alpha\right)}\left(\varepsilon^y \frac{\beta}{\alpha} - \varepsilon^{x,t}\right).$$

where the penultimate line uses the fact that at the initial equilibrium, $S^y = \beta S^x$. The last equality implies equation (4.11).

Appendix B

Problem Sets

The first problem set asks students to verify the two remarks in Chapter 2. The second problem set has students work through examples using the Ricardian model. The third problem set also uses the Ricardian model, but this exercise encourages students to use the concept of stability and also illustrates one source of immizerizing growth. It builds on ideas developed in Section 3.6 of Chapter 3. It provides an example of the possibility discussed in Section 5.6 of Chapter 5, but it can be assigned before covering that material.

Problem set 4 begins with a question that asks students to use a partial equilibrium model to show how a "target price" policy affects the gains from trade. Many agricultural programs have used this kind of a policy; similar to a tax, it drives a wedge between the producer and consumer prices, but differs from the tax in important respects. This question is preceded by a warm-up problem to make sure that students can use a partial equilibrium model to measure the gains from trade. The remaining questions in problem set 4 use a general equilibrium setting.

Problem set 5 also uses a partial equilibrium setting. This problem asks students to work through the consequences of an environmental externality under both autarchy and trade. The question requires both graphical and mathematical analysis. The graphs are similar to those used in Problem set 4; the calculus requires using an integral.

Problem set 6 contains a number of problems similar to the material in Sections 5.6 and 5.7 of Chapter 5. These problems provide additional practice in using the graphical methods introduced in Chapter 3 and they provide other examples of the Principle of Targeting and the possibility of immizerizing growth. They also illustrate some important differences between conclusions reached in general and partial equilibrium models.

B.1 Problem Set 1

1. Prove Remark 1 from Section 2.7 of Chapter 2.

   Hint: The budget constraint is $w = n\,(p_1 a + p_2 b)$, where w is the wage (equal to the income of a person who sells one unit of labor), and n is the number of consumption bundles, (a, b). Solve the budget constraint for n, the equilibrium number of consumption bundles that the person buys, and rewrite the expression as a function of the relative prices $\frac{w}{p_i}$. Totally differentiate the resulting equation to obtain the differential for dn. Use this equation to prove the claim.

2. Prove Remark 2 from Section 2.7 of Chapter 2, using the indirect utility function, defined as

$$V(p_1, p_2, y) = \max U(x_1, x_2)$$

subject to $p_1 x_1 + p_2 x_2 \le y$,

where y is the individual's income and U is the utility function. The Lagrangian is

$$\mathcal{L} = U(x_1, x_2) + \lambda\,(y - p_1 x_1 - p_2 x_2)$$

where the constraint multiplier λ is the shadow value of income. The indirect utility function is

$$V(p_1, p_2, y) = \mathcal{L}^*(p_1, p_2, y) = \max_{x_i} \min_{\lambda} \mathcal{L},$$

where a superscript $*$ denotes the value of a function evaluated at the optimum.

3. Suppose that the agent's utility function is $U(x_1, x_2) = x_1^\alpha x_2^{1-\alpha}$. The agent's sole source of income is her wage, w; she works for one unit of time per period and consumes everything she earns.

   (a) Write the person's indirect utility as a function of α, $W = \frac{w}{p_2}$ and $p = \frac{p_1}{p_2}$. (Choose good 2 as the numeraire.)

   (b) Prices and the wage may change. Following such a change, what is the necessary and sufficient condition (a function of α) for the change to have increased her utility? Write this as an inequality involving $\frac{dW}{W}$, $\frac{dp}{p}$, and α

   (c) Suppose that you do not know the value of α. What is a sufficient condition for the change to have increased her utility?

   (d) Suppose that the population contains a continuum of people. Their individual values of α range over the interval $(0, 1)$. What is a necessary and sufficient condition for the change to have increased the utility of everyone in the population?

B.2 Problem Set 2

1. Suppose that in Bolivia four labor hours are required to produce a bottle of llama milk and six labor hours are required to produce a salteña. In Chile, ten labor hours are required to produce a bottle of llama milk and "A" labor hours are required to produce a salteña.

   (a) Find a necessary and sufficient condition for Bolivia to have a comparative advantage in llama milk (an inequality involving A) and a necessary condition for the post-trade wages to possibly be equal in the two countries (a different inequality involving A). When do both of these conditions hold?

   (b) Chile and Bolivia have decided to also trade with Peru, which can produce a bottle of llama milk with six labor hours and a salteña with six labor hours. Suppose $A = 8$, and each country has 240 units of labor. Draw the world PPF with salteñas on the vertical axis. For each region on the frontier, describe the pattern of the trade.

(c) Consider again only Bolivia and Chile, and let $A = 8$. Suppose Bolivia experiences a technological improvement so it can now produce a bottle of llama milk in two labor hours. How will this alter trade?

2. Everyone in the world has Leontief preferences, and for all price ratios each person consumes 2 beers for each slice of pizza. The world price of a slice of pizza is $4.00 and the world price of beer is $1.00. Venezuela, a small country, produces 3 slices of pizza per hour and 6 beers per hour of labor.

   (a) If Venezuela has 5000 hours of labor, how much beer and pizza does it produce, import, and export?
   (b) What is Venezuela's wage under free trade?
   (c) In autarky what does Venezuela produce?
   (d) How do the answers to a, b, and c change if a technological innovation doubles productivity in the beer sector?

3. The following table gives the number of units of labor required to produce one ipod (remember those?) or one milk shake in a Ricardian world with two commodities and three countries:

Commodity\Country	Vietnam	Paraguay	Chad
iPod	1	0.5	1
Milk shake	1	2	4

Assume that in equilibrium both commodities are consumed. There is free trade. Fill in the blanks.

(a) (Fill in the blank with the commodity name) Vietnam has a comparative advantage in_____, compared to Paraguay. Vietnam has a comparative advantage in _____ compared to Chad.
Paraguay has a comparative advantage in _____ compared to Vietnam. Paraguay has a comparative advantage in _____compared to Chad.

(b) For what (if any) pattern(s) of production are the wages in Vietnam and Paraguay possibly equal?

(c) For the pattern(s) of production in part (b), are the wages necessarily equal? [Yes/No]

(d) For what (if any) pattern(s) of production are the wages in Vietnam and Chad possibly equal?

(e) For what (if any) pattern(s) of production are the wages in Paraguay and Chad possibly equal?

B.3 Problem Set 3

This question is raised in Section 2.10 of Chapter 10. In a two country Ricardian model, Canada has a comparative advantage in the production of corn, and the US in umbrellas. The two countries trade, and there is a small improvement in US umbrella technology. (The amount of labor required to produce one umbrella decreases in the US.) Assume that the exogenous change in technology is small enough that the equilibrium regime does not change; that is, a country produces a product after the change if and only if it also produced the product before the change. Show what happens to world price and to the countries' welfare under the three possibilities for the trade equilibrium: (a) only the US is specialized; (b) both countries are specialized; and (c) only Canada is specialized.

Begin by drawing a figure that shows how the technological improvement changes the world production possibilities frontier. Then explain the effect of the change on the world price and welfare in the two countries. Use the 0 profit conditions to determine equilibrium prices and real wages under the three possibilities (only one or both countries are specialized).

The only (slightly) tricky part of this question concerns the situation where both countries are specialized in equilibrium. In this case, you need to know how the technological change alters the equilibrium relative price of umbrellas. The answer to this question is unambiguous. Begin with a common sense answer. (Think: improving the technology will cause supply to increase/decrease, and that change will cause the price of the commodity to increase/decrease.)

Now convince yourself that this common-sense answer is correct. You can do this by using the world excess demand curve for umbrellas (or corn) studied in Chapters 2 and 3. Find out how the technological change alters this excess demand curve. Using the assumption that the initial equilibrium was stable (see Chapter 3), you then know the direction of change in the equilibrium relative price of umbrellas. Once you have determined how the initial change in technology changes the equilibrium relative world price, you are in a position to say something about the change in welfare, using the definition of "real return to labor".

If you identify a circumstance in which the effect of the technological change on welfare is ambiguous, construct a graphical example to illustrate this ambiguity.

B.4 Problem Set 4

The purpose of the first two problems is to accustom students to using graphical methods to analyze economic problems. You need to know how to identify producer and consumer surplus on a graph, and you need to be able to graph an excess supply (or demand) function — i.e. you have to be able to graph the difference between two functions. That part should be straightforward. The trickier part is in using these simple tools.

The third problem makes sure that you know how taxes affect relative prices. The fourth problem makes sure that you know the relation between a social planner's problem and a competitive equilibrium. The fifth problem makes sure that you can use graphical methods to identify the effect of returning tax revenues to consumers (rather than throwing them away).

1. (Background) Use a two-panel diagram.

    (a) In panel *a* of the two-panel (side-by-side) figure, draw a linear supply and demand curve for the US, and identify the consumer and producer surplus in an autarkic equilibrium.

    (b) In panel *b* draw the excess supply function that corresponds to the functions you drew in panel *a*.

    (c) In panel *b* draw a perfectly elastic rest-of-world (ROW) excess demand curve at a price higher than the US autarky price.

Use this figure to identify the world equilibrium price and the level of US exports.

(d) In both panels identify the increase in the sum of US producer and consumer welfare that results in moving from autarky to free trade. This increase is the partial equilibrium representation of the gains from trade, for the US. The point of this exercise is to illustrate that you can identify the gains from trade (in this partial equilibrium model) either by (i) using the domestic supply and demand curves and looking at the changes in producer and consumer surplus associated with these two curves, or by (ii) using the excess supply (or excess demand) curve, and finding the surplus associated with this curve. To emphasize the analogy with the domestic supply and demand functions, I refer to the surplus corresponding to the export supply function as the "producer surplus", and the surplus corresponding to the import demand function as the "consumer surplus".

2. As in the previous question, draw (linear) US supply and demand curves (in the left panel) and the corresponding US excess supply in the right panel. Now I want you to figure out how a particular policy changes one or both of the supply and/or demand curves, and the resulting change in equilibrium.

Suppose that the US institutes a "target price" of p^* for US producers. With this policy, markets are allowed to clear. (Private Supply = Private demand, i.e. the government does not purchase any of the commodity). If the market clearing price, $\hat{p}$, is less than p^*, then producers receive a "deficiency payment" of $p^* - \hat{p}$ from the government for each unit sold; consumers pay the market clearing price $\hat{p}$.

You can imagine the government buying from producers at a the target price p^* and then selling the total amount to consumers at a price that clears the market. This transaction does not literally occur. The actual transaction is between producers and consumers, but the government steps in to make up the "deficiency", by paying producers an amount equal to the difference in the target price and the price that clears the market. If the market clearing price is above p^*, then the government does not intervene.

(a) Consider the autarchic economy. Using the left panel, show how the policy changes the demand and or supply function. Identify the market clearing price under autarchy (with the policy), and label it $\hat{p}^a$. (The market clearing price is the price that consumers pay; the price that producers receive equals the fixed target price, providing that the target price exceeds the market clearing price. Assume that it does exceed the market price.) Identify (on the graph) the change in consumer surplus, the change in producer surplus, and the cost of the policy to taxpayers (the deficiency payment times supply). Identify the "deadweight cost" of the policy, defined as the sum of the change in consumer, producer and taxpayer welfare.

Note that in the previous paragraph you are asked about the welfare effect of the policy. You hold the trade regime fixed (autarchy) and compare the (autarchic) equilibria with and without the target price policy.

In the adjacent figure draw the US excess supply curve under the policy. Remember, the excess supply curve is just the difference between the domestic supply and demand curves. If you know how the target price policy affects one or both of these curves, you can figure out how the policy affects the excess supply curve.

Now allow for trade. Suppose that ROW excess demand is perfectly elastic at a price p^w higher than the US autarchic price with the policy, and lower than the US target price. Identify US exports and US gains from trade in the two panels. Remember, the gains from trade measure the difference in welfare under trade and under autarky. Welfare (as before) is the sum of producer and consumer welfare, minus the cost to the treasury. (Look at part (d) of Question 1 for a clue.)

Note that you are asked to identify the welfare effects of trade under an existing target price policy. You are not asked to identify the welfare effects of the target price policy. You hold the target price policy fixed, and compare the equilibria with and without trade.

(b) Now draw a downward sloping linear ROW excess demand curve, with the property that the US would be an exporter with or without the target price policy. Identify the equilibrium world price with and without the US policy. How does the US policy affect the world price?

(c) Maintain the assumption of part (b): the US would be an exporter with or without the target price policy. Also assume that the equilibrium world price is lower than the target price. Does the presence of the target price policy increase or decrease the gains from trade for the US? Explain your conclusion. Remember, the gains from trade is the difference in welfare with and without trade. Look at part (a) again. There are gains from trade without the policy, and gains from trade with the policy. You are asked to compare the size of these two gains. In some cases — but not in this problem — the gains from trade might be negative.

Hint: You might think that your answer depends on the slope of the ROW excess demand curve relative to the US excess supply curves (with and without the policy). To help in discovering the correct answer, it may be useful to experiment with "limiting (i.e. extreme) cases" for the ROW demand curve. It is up to you to think of what these cases might be. It's nothing subtle! By considering these cases you can form a conjecture about the answer. Then construct a graph with a downward sloping ROW excess demand that satisfies the assumption of the question. With the help of this graph and geometry, determine whether the policy increases or decreases the US gains from trade.

(d) What does your answer to (c) say about the effect of the policy on US welfare? Remember (again!) the gains from trade is the difference in welfare with and without trade.

(e) How would your answers to (c) and (d) have changed if you were not told to assume that the US would be an exporter with or without the target price policy?

3. There are two commodities, food and cloth. Food is the numeraire. The relative world price of cloth is p. Home, a small country, imports food.

   (a) Home uses (only) an *ad valorem* import tariff of τ. The relative price of cloth for domestic consumers is _____and the relative price for producers is _____ .

   (b) Home uses (only) an *ad valorem* export subsidy of s, The relative price of cloth for domestic consumers is_____ and the relative price of cloth for domestic producers is_____ .

   (c) Home uses (only) an *ad valorem* production tax of t on cloth. The relative price of cloth for consumers is _____ and the relative price of cloth for producers is _____ .

   (d) How would your answer to part (a) have changed if Home is a large country rather than a small country? (Explain briefly)

4. Draw a strictly concave production possibility frontier with food on the vertical axis and cloth on the horizontal axis. Food is the numeraire good. Find the no-tax equilibrium autarchic consumption point; label this point A. Assume that production of both goods remains positive under the taxes considered here.

   (a) Use this figure to identify the autarchic relative price of cloth, p^a

   (b) Now suppose that the (closed) country imposes an *ad valorem* tax of t on cloth *production* and returns all revenue to consumers in a lump sum; there are no other taxes and no market failures. Denote the autarchic relative price facing consumers p^{ct} and denote the relative price facing producers as p^{pt}. Write the producer price as a function of the consumer price and the tax: $p^{pt} =$??? (Compete the equation; the tax and p^{ct} are on the right-hand side). What is the ranking of the magnitude of p^a, p^{ct} and p^{pt}? On the figure illustrate the production and consumption point under the tax as point B and draw the representative consumer's indifference curve through this point.

(c) Find the magnitude of the *consumer* tax or subsidy on cloth that leads to the same autarchic outcome. Is this policy a tax or a subsidy on consumption of cloth?

(d) Holding fixed the production tax in part (b), discuss the effect on welfare of opening the economy to trade. Do this by deriving the first order approximation of the change in welfare of the representative consumer due to the change in price (resulting from trade. Write this approximation as a function of the producer tax.

B.5 Problem Set 5

The problem set asks students to work through questions about trade and the environment using a partial equilibrium setting. Although the course emphasizes general equilibrium models, students should be able to use the simpler partial equilibrium models.

Domestic supply and demand are given by the curves $S(p)$ and $D(p)$. Domestic consumption of the quantity D results in social environmental cost γD. This cost is external to consumers and producers. The country is small, and is able to trade on the world market at price p^w, which might be either greater of less than the autarchy price absent regulation, $\bar{p}$. The social welfare function is the sum of consumer and producer surplus, minus environmental damage plus any tax revenues (minus any program costs) that arise from government intervention. Where you are asked to use graphs, label the areas carefully. Where you are asked for an explanation, you should be brief (no more than a couple of sentences).

Draw a figure with linear supply and demand curves $S(p)$ and $D(p)$, and social marginal value of consumption, $p^{-1}(D) - \gamma$, where $p^{-1}(D)$ is the inverse demand function. For this figure, assume that $p^w < \bar{p}$.

1. What is the first best policy (i.e. the policy that maximizes the sum of producer and consumer surplus minus environmental cost plus tax revenue) if there is no trade? In Figure 1 label the consumer price without trade, under the first best policy, as p^a. What is the first best policy if there is trade? (Remember, the country is small, and absent regulation it imports the good.)

2. Using your figure, identify social welfare in autarchy, absent any policy intervention.

3. Assume no policy intervention. Give a (simple!) sufficient condition for free trade to lead to higher social welfare than autarky, and briefly explain this sufficient condition.

4. Assume no policy intervention. Define $\Delta_1\left(p^w,\bar{p}\right)$ as the increase in the sum of consumer and producer surplus resulting from trade when world price is p^w and define $\Delta_2\left(p^w,\bar{p}\right)$ as the increase in environmental damages resulting from trade. The gains from trade is therefore $\Delta_1\left(p^w,\bar{p}\right) - \Delta_2\left(p^w,\bar{p}\right)$. (The function $\Delta_1\left(p^w,\bar{p}\right)$ is an integral and $\Delta_2\left(p^w,\bar{p}\right)$ equals γ times a change in quantity.) Graph $\Delta_1\left(p^w,\bar{p}\right)$ and $\Delta_2\left(p^w,\bar{p}\right)$ as functions of p^w on the same figure (to make them easily comparable). Based on this graph, state a sufficient condition for trade to lower welfare; use the graph to also confirm your answer to question 3.

5. Suppose that the (small) country is able to import at price $p^w < \bar{p}$, and that the only policy instrument is a tariff. Is the optimal tariff greater or less than the level of the first-best policy you identified in question 1? Explain briefly. (Think about the economic intuition and try to come up with a plausible conjecture — not a random guess — before you approach the problem formally.)

6. Create a new figure with the domestic supply and demand and the social marginal benefit of consumption in the left panel. In the right panel graph the import demand function (the private marginal benefit of imports) and the *smb*, the social marginal benefit of imports (equal to the private benefit minus the increased externality cost due to greater consumption.) Graph $M(p)$ and $smb(p)$ in the right panel. Pick a world price lower than the

vertical intercept of $smb(p)$. Using this figure, find the optimal tariff.

Next, derive the optimal tariff using algebra. Define $p = p^w + t$. For given p^w, welfare under the tariff equals

$$W(t) = \Delta_1 (p^w, \bar{p}) - \Delta_2 (p^w, \bar{p}) + t (D(p) - S(p)). \qquad \text{(B.1)}$$

The first two terms equal the increase in consumer + producer surplus minus the higher environmental damage when the domestic price is p. The last term is tariff revenue. Use the first order condition to the problem of maximizing $W(t)$ to find the formula for the optimal tariff. Then specialize to linear supply and demand functions to find an explicit expression for the optimal tariff.

7. Suppose that our country is a large importer, i.e. it faces an upward sloping world excess supply curve for the good. Provide a very brief verbal explanation for whether this monopsony power increases or decreases the optimal tariff in part 6. Describe how you would use the graphical method from question 6 to find the optimal tariff for a large importer.

8. Now suppose (as in question 7) that the country is large, and also that the environmental damage it suffers depends on aggregate world consumption of the good — not just on domestic consumption. (A unit of consumption in ROW might cause less damage to Home compared to a unit of consumption at Home, because — for example — some of the pollution generated by ROW's consumption dissipates before reaching Home.) Explain whether this change increases or decreases the optimal tariff from part 7.

B.6 Problem Set 6

This exercise has three objectives. The first is to help make the Principle of Targeting (Section 5.7 of Chapter 5) second nature. Ask yourself "What is the quantity that I want to influence? What is the price (or set of prices) that I need to change in order to influence this quantity?" The second is to give students practice identifying equilibria and making comparisons using the by now familiar graphical construction. The third is to improve students' understanding of the comparison between general and partial equilibrium models.

If (as is likely) students can guess the answer before using the graphs, the graphs are still important as a means of confirming a guess. Sometimes the graphs may help you to find the answer. In either case, you should be sure to work on the economic intuition for the answer. Don't be satisfied with a mechanical answer.

Under free trade a small country imports food and exports cloth. The government has three possible policy levers:

  (i) A consumption tax/subsidy
 (ii) A production tax/subsidy
(iii) A tariff/export tax

Case I. There is a non-economic constraint that consumption of food be less than or equal to F*.

Case II. There is a non-economic constraint that the import of food be less than M*.

Use the geometric two-good general equilibrium model with a production possibility frontier, indifference curves, and a balance of payments constraint. For your graphs, put food on the vertical axis. For questions 2–4 provide a couple of sentences of explanation to go with your graphs.

For each of the two cases:

1. Illustrate a free trade equilibrium in which the constraint is violated in the absence of policy intervention.
2. What is the optimal policy (i.e. which of the three instruments above should be used to achieve the objective)? Show how the optimal policy affects consumption, production, trade and welfare. Find the level of the optimal policy.
3. Show the welfare effects when the constraint is achieved using a sub-optimal policy.

4. If growth can be immizerizing when the constraint is achieved using a sub-optimal policy, provide an example. If you conclude that growth cannot be immizerizing for a particular second best policy, demonstrate your conclusion and explain it.

5. Answer all of the previous problems in a partial equilibrium setting, i.e. using a supply and demand model in which income is held constant. Compare the answers you get, and comment on the difference between the general and partial equilibrium setting. This exercise shows the role of the assumption — in the partial equilibrium setting — that income remains constant. In the partial equilibrium setting, "growth" corresponds to a downward shift in the supply curve, making it possible to produce the same amount at a lower cost.

Appendix C

Answer Key

C.1 Problem Set 1

(1) Given prices p_1, p_2 one consumption bundle (a, b) costs $p_1 a + p_2 b$. Given wage w, a person who sells one unit of labor can afford to buy n consumption bundles, where n solves

$$w = n \left(p_1 a + p_2 b \right) \Rightarrow$$

$$n = \frac{w}{(p_1 a + p_2 b)} = \frac{1}{\dfrac{a}{\left(\frac{w}{p_1}\right)} + \dfrac{b}{\left(\frac{w}{p_2}\right)}} \cdot \Longrightarrow$$

$$dn = \frac{1}{\left(\dfrac{a}{\left(\frac{w}{p_1}\right)} + \dfrac{b}{\left(\frac{w}{p_2}\right)} \right)^2} \left(\frac{a}{\left(\frac{w}{p_1}\right)^2} \left(d\left(\frac{w}{p_1}\right) \right) + \frac{b}{\left(\frac{w}{p_2}\right)^2} \left(d\left(\frac{w}{p_2}\right) \right) \right).$$

I used the quotient rule twice to obtain the last equality. If $d\left(\frac{w}{p_1}\right)$ and $d\left(\frac{w}{p_2}\right)$ are of the same sign, then dn (the change in the number of consumption bundles) is also of the same sign. However, if $d\left(\frac{w}{p_1}\right)$ and $d\left(\frac{w}{p_2}\right)$ are of opposite signs, then dn can be either positive or negative, depending on the magnitude of a and b.

(2) Using the envelope theorem,

$$\frac{\partial V}{\partial p_i} = -\lambda x_i^*. \tag{C.1}$$

Assuming non-satiation (all of income is consumed), $\lambda > 0$; assuming that the commodity is consumed ($x_i^* > 0$) equation (C.1) implies that an increase in the price of a commodity decreases the level of utility — an obvious result.

Suppose that each worker owns one unit of labor. The only source of income in this model is labor income, as noted above, so $y = w$; we can write $V(p_1, p_2, y) = V(p_1, p_2, w)$. The indirect utility function is homogenous of degree 0 in prices and income, i.e. doubling all prices and income leaves the individual no better or worse off. Therefore we can write

$$V(p_1, p_2, y) = V(p_1, p_2, w) = V\left(\frac{p_1}{w}, \frac{p_2}{w}, \frac{w}{w}\right) \equiv v\left(\frac{p_1}{w}, \frac{p_2}{w}\right).$$

Equation (C.1) implies (under the assumptions of non-satiation and positive consumption) that

$$v_i \equiv \frac{\partial v}{\partial \left(\frac{p_i}{w}\right)} < 0.$$

(Here, and in (some) other contexts a subscript on a function denotes a partial derivative.) The change in v following an exogenous change in $\frac{p_i}{w}$ is

$$dv = v_1 d\left(\frac{p_1}{w}\right) + v_2 d\left(\frac{p_2}{w}\right).$$

If $d\left(\frac{p_i}{w}\right) < 0$ and $d\left(\frac{p_j}{w}\right) \leq 0$ (so that $d\left(\frac{w}{p_i}\right) > 0$ and $d\left(\frac{w}{p_i}\right) \geq 0$), then $dv > 0$, i.e. utility increases. If we reverse the inequalities, utility falls. However, if $d\left(\frac{w}{p_i}\right) > 0$ and $d\left(\frac{w}{p_i}\right) < 0$ we have one positive and one negative effect. We cannot determine the sign of the change in utility, dv, without putting more structure on the problem, i.e. without putting additional restrictions on the utility function.

(3) (a) The first order conditions for utility maximization are

$$\alpha x_1^{\alpha-1} x_2^{1-\alpha} = \lambda p_1$$

$$(1-\alpha) x_1^{\alpha} x_2^{-\alpha} = \lambda p_2$$

$$p_1 x_1 + p_2 x_2 = w$$

Dividing the second equation by the first gives

$$\frac{(1-\alpha) x_1^{\alpha} x_2^{-\alpha}}{\alpha x_1^{\alpha-1} x_2^{1-\alpha}} = \frac{\lambda p_2}{\lambda p_1} \Longrightarrow$$

$$\frac{(1-\alpha) x_1}{\alpha x_2} = \frac{p_2}{p_1} \Longrightarrow$$

$$\frac{(1-\alpha)}{\alpha} = \frac{p_2 x_2}{p_1 x_1} \Longrightarrow$$

$$\frac{(1-\alpha)}{\alpha} p_1 x_1 = p_2 x_2$$

Using the last equation in the budget constraint gives

$$p_1 x_1 + \frac{(1-\alpha)}{\alpha} p_1 x_1 = w \Longrightarrow$$

$$p_1 x_1 = \alpha w \Longrightarrow$$

$$p_2 x_2 = (1-\alpha) w.$$

Using these relations in the utility function gives the indirect utility

$$V(p_1, p_2, w) = x_1^{\alpha} x_2^{1-\alpha} = \left(\frac{\alpha w}{p_1}\right)^{\alpha} \left(\frac{(1-\alpha) w}{p_2}\right)^{1-\alpha}$$

$$= \alpha^{\alpha} (1-\alpha)^{1-\alpha} \left(\frac{w}{p_1}\right)^{\alpha} \left(\frac{w}{p_2}\right)^{1-\alpha}$$

$$= \alpha^{\alpha} (1-\alpha)^{1-\alpha} w \left(\frac{1}{p_1}\right)^{\alpha} \left(\frac{1}{p_2}\right)^{1-\alpha}. \qquad \text{(C.2)}$$

If we choose good 2 as the numeraire, $p_2 = 1$, so $p = \frac{p_1}{p_2}$ and $W = \frac{w}{p_2}$ and we can write indirect utility as

$$v(p, W) = \alpha^{\alpha} (1-\alpha)^{1-\alpha} W p^{-\alpha}$$

For this utility function, indirect utility is linear in income, i.e. the shadow value of income is a constant. Here, α is a price index.

(b) The necessary and sufficient increase for utility to increase is

$$dv = dW p^{-\alpha} - \alpha p^{-\alpha-1} dp W > 0 \Longrightarrow$$

$$dW p^{-\alpha} > \alpha p^{-\alpha-1} dp W \Longrightarrow$$

$$dW p > \alpha dp W \Longrightarrow$$

$$\frac{dW}{W} > \alpha \frac{dp}{p}.$$

This condition states that the percent increase in W is greater than α times the percent increase in p. Using expression (C.2), we could alternatively have written the necessary and sufficient condition as

$$0 < \frac{d\left[\left(\frac{w}{p_1}\right)^{\alpha}\left(\frac{w}{p_2}\right)^{1-\alpha}\right]}{\left(\frac{w}{p_1}\right)^{\alpha}\left(\frac{w}{p_2}\right)^{1-\alpha}} = \alpha \frac{d\left(\frac{w}{p_1}\right)}{\left(\frac{w}{p_1}\right)} + (1-\alpha)\frac{d\left(\frac{w}{p_2}\right)}{\left(\frac{w}{p_2}\right)}. \qquad \text{(C.3)}$$

This condition states that the convex combination (with weights α and $1-\alpha$) of the percent change in $\frac{w}{p_1}$ and in $\frac{w}{p_2}$ is positive.

(c) If we do not know the value of α, the only way to guarantee that inequality (C.3) is satisfied (i.e. the weakest sufficient condition) is to require

$$\frac{d\left(\frac{w}{p_1}\right)}{\left(\frac{w}{p_1}\right)} \geq 0 \quad \text{and} \quad \frac{d\left(\frac{w}{p_2}\right)}{\left(\frac{w}{p_2}\right)} \geq 0, \qquad \text{(C.4)}$$

with one of the inequalities being strict.

(d) If we know that some member of the population has a value of α close to zero and another member has a value close to 1, the necessary condition for both to benefit is that equalities (C.4) hold, with at least one holding strictly.

C.2 Problem Set 2

(1a) (i) Bolivia has a comparative advantage in milk production iff $A < 15$.

(ii) A necessary condition for post-trade wages to be equal is that neither county has an absolute advantage in both commodities. This condition requires $A < 6$.

If both (i) and (ii) hold, it must be the case that $A < 6$.

(1b) The PPF contains three flat regions. The highest of these (label it B) has slope $\frac{2}{3}$. The next highest (label it P) has slope 1. The lowest segment has slope $\frac{5}{4}$. Bolivia always produces milk and Chile always produces salteña. A country can be nonspecialized only if the world equilibrium price equals its autarkic price. On the two kinks all countries are specialized. On segment B, Peru and Chile are specialized. On segment P, Bolivia and Chile are specialized. On segment C, Bolivia and Peru are specialized.

(1c) The improvement in Bolivia's technology in the commodity for which Bolivia has a comparative advantage causes Bolivia's export supply function to shift out. If this curve intersects the flat portion of Chile's import demand function (before and after the technology change), then world price does not change, but the volume of imports and exports increase. (In this scenario, Chile is incompletely specialized before and after the technology change.)

In any other scenario, the shift out of Bolivia's export supply function must cause the world price of milk to fall, increasing Chile's import of milk — so the *volume* of milk trade increases. The *volume* of salteña trade might either increase or decrease.

(2) (a) Venezuela's autarky (relative) price of beer is $\frac{1}{6}/\frac{1}{3} = \frac{1}{2}$. This autarkic relative price is greater than the world relative price of beer $= 1/4$. Therefore when Venezuela trades, it specializes in pizza. Consequently, Venezuela produces $(3)5000 = 15,000$ units of pizza. It total revenue (national income) is $4(15,000) = 60,000$.

By assumption, when it consumes x pizzas, it consumes $2x$ beers. The budget constraint is

$$4x + 2x = 6x = 60{,}000$$

so it consumes 10,000 pizzas and 20,000 beers. It imports 20,000 beers and exports 5,000 pizzas.

(b) The zero profit condition in the pizza sector requires

$$4 = \frac{w}{3}$$

so the wage is 12.

(c) Denote y as pizza production (and consumption) under autarky, so $2y$ equals beer production (because of the assumption on preferences). The total supply of labor is 5000 units. The requirement of full employment implies

$$\frac{y}{3} + \frac{2y}{6} = 5000,$$

which implies $y = 7500$.

(d) In this case Venezuela's autarky price equals world price. Now Venezuela has no gains from trade. Starting from free trade, the technological improvement does not alter Venezuela's wage or its consumption. However, the change in technology means that Venezuelan production is indeterminate.

3 (a) (Fill in the blank with the commodity name) Vietnam has a comparative advantage in <u>milk shake</u>, compared to Paraguay. Vietnam has a comparative advantage in <u>milk shake</u> compared to Chad.

Paraguay has a comparative advantage in <u>ipod</u> compared to Vietnam. Paraguay has a comparative advantage in <u>neither good</u> compared to Chad.

(b) For what (if any) pattern(s) of production are the wages in Vietnam and Paraguay possibly equal?

Answer: [Vietnam specialized in milk shake, Paraguay and Chad both specialized in ipods].

(c) For the pattern(s) of production in part (b), are the wages necessarily equal?

Answer: NO.

(d) For what (if any) pattern(s) of production are the wages in Vietnam and Chad possibly equal?

Answer: Wages in the two countries can be equal iff the equilibrium relative price of milk shakes, $\frac{p_M}{p_I} = 1$. In this case, Chad is specialized in ipods and Vietnam is either incompletely specialized, or in the "knife-edge case" completely specialized in milk shakes. The answer "both countries completely specialized in the good for which they have comparative advantage" is not correct, because this complete specialization is neither necessary nor sufficient for equality of wages.

(e) For what (if any) pattern(s) of production are the wages in Paraguay and Chad possibly equal?

Answer: No pattern of production.

C.3 Problem Set 3

Begin with the type of PPF shown in Chapter 2. As a result of the productivity increase, the world production possibility frontier shifts to the dashed line in Figure C.1. Remember that we can think of the "real wage" either as the number of consumption bundles that a worker can exchange for one unit of labor, or it is the number of utils that a worker can exchange for one unit of labor. We know that the real wage unambiguously increases if and only if the worker can buy more of everything with one unit of labor. That possibility requires that w/p_1 and w/p_2 weakly increase.

(A) If the initial equilibrium is in region A, where the US is completely specialized and Canada is non-specialized, the US welfare increases and Canadian welfare is unchanged. The world relative commodity price $(\frac{p_2}{p_1})$ is given by the Canadian autarkic price, which is unchanged by technological change in US umbrella manufacturing. Canada receives no benefits from trade — before or after the technological improvement. We can normalize by setting

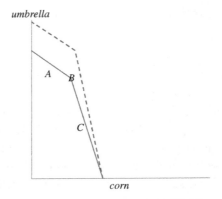

Figure C.1.   The solid graph shows the initial world PPF, and the dashed graph shows the world PPF after the change in technology.

$p_1 = 1$ (any other normalization is OK). The free trade equilibrium relative price $\frac{p_2}{p_1}$ (and therefore p_2) is unchanged by the change in US technology. Therefore the nominal wage in Canada, w^c, is unchanged, as is the Canadian real wage. The nominal wage in US is given by the 0 profit condition $p_2 = w^u a_2^u$. Since a_2^u has decreased, the nominal US wage must have increased. Since nominal commodity prices are unchanged, real US wage has increased. (Both w^u/p_1 and w^u/p_2 increase.)

   (C) If the initial equilibrium is in region C, where only Canada is specialized, the world price under trade equals the autarkic US price. The world relative price of corn increases (i.e. the relative price of umbrellas falls) as a result of technological improvement in umbrella sector). If I normalize by setting p_2, the nominal price of umbrellas, equal to 1, this means that p_1, the nominal price of corn, must have increased. Zero profits in the Canadian corn sector requires $p_1 = w^c a_1^c$, so the nominal Canadian wage increases. Since w^c/p_1 is unchanged, but w^c/p_2 increases, the real Canadian wage (and therefore Canadian welfare) increases. Given my normalization $p_2 = 1$, the 0 profit condition in US umbrella sector implies that the nominal US wage, w^u, has increased, as has w^u/p_2. The 0 profit condition in US corn sector requires $p_1 = w^u a_c^u$, or $1/a_c^u = w^u/p_1$, which is unchanged. Therefore, US real wage (and US welfare) has increased.

Note that US does not gain from trade. The welfare increase it obtains is due to the improvement in technology. The US would obtain that welfare increase under autarky or free trade. Canada does benefit from trade. Canada benefits from the improvement in technology only because it trades. Under autarky Canada would obviously not be affected by a change in US technology.

(B) If the initial equilibrium is at point B, both countries are specialized and both gain from trade. However, it is not necessarily the case that both benefit from the technological improvement in US umbrella manufacturing. The increased supply of umbrellas means that p_2/p_1 must have decreased. (This claim requires the assumption that the original equilibrium is stable. See the hint to the problem.) Therefore, the improved US umbrella technology turns the terms of trade against the US. Canada is certainly better off. Normalize by setting $p_1 = 1$, so the 0 profit condition in Canadian corn sector implies that nominal Canadian wage is unchanged. Therefore, w^c/p_1 is unchanged, but w^c/p_2 increases; conclude that the real Canadian wage increases. The 0 profit condition in US umbrella sector requires $w^u/p_2 = 1/a_2^u$, which has increased. However, we do not know what has happened to w^u/p_1, so we do not know whether US real wage has increased or decreased.

Figure C.2 shows an example where the US welfare falls as a consequence of the improvement in umbrella technology when the initial equilibrium is at point B. I now discuss this possibility.

Initially, if the US is specialized, it can produce A units of umbrellas. The solid line through this point, with slope p^w is the US's BOP constraint in the initial equilibrium.

After the improvement in umbrella technology, the US can produce A' umbrellas. If world relative price was unchanged, the US BOP constraint would shift out in a parallel fashion, and its welfare would certainly increase. However, the improvement in the US umbrella technology causes the US export supply (of umbrellas) to shift out. See Chapters 2 and 3 to make sure that you understand how to draw the US export supply function in the Ricardian model; make sure you understand why the improvement in US technology causes the function to shift out. This shift causes a decrease in the relative price of umbrellas (equivalently, an increase in the relative price of corn, from p^w to $p^{w'}$. The US BOP constraint under the higher relative corn price is the steep line through point A'. The IEP shifts to the dashed line. For this example, the new consumption point, B', is below the initial level of utility. The improvement in US technology leads to such a large deterioration in its terms of trade, that welfare falls.

For this result to occur, it must be the case that the US consumption of corn is lower at the new equilibrium (after the change in technology) compared to the original equilibrium (point B' lies to the left of point B in Figure C.2). Because world corn production is unchanged, it must be the case that, after the increase in the relative price of corn, Canada exports less corn. Therefore, the equilibrium must occur on the negatively sloped portion of Canada's export supply function.

Figure C.3 shows the US import demand for corn, the curve labeled M_1^{US}, and the Canadian export supply for corn, labeled X^{CAN}. The initial equilibrium is at point C. The improvement in the US technology causes the US import demand function to shift out, as shown by the dashed curve. This change occurs because, at every

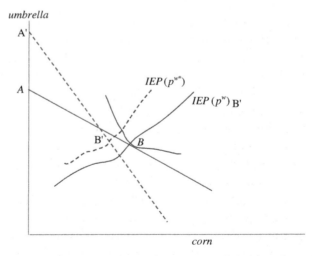

Figure C.2.   An example where the improvement in technology in umbrellas (the good that the US exports) lowers US welfare, due to the deterioration in its terms of trade (the fall in the relative price of its export good).

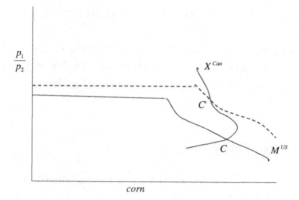

Figure C.3. The improvement in US umbrella technology causes causes its demand function for corn imports to shift out, resulting in a higher equilibrium relative price of corn. Because (for this example) Canada is on the backward bending part of its export supply curve, equilibrium exports of corn falls. Therefore, US corn consumption falls, as shown in Figure C.2.

price, the level of income in the US is higher after the improvement in technology. Because corn is a normal good, at every price the US wants to consume more corn. Because the US produces no corn, it must be the case that at every price the US wants to import more corn. Therefore, the US import demand function shifts out, as a consequence of the improvement in technology. For the example shown here, the new equilibrium is at point C'. At the higher price associated with this equilibrium, Canada exports less corn.

At this point, students should review the discussion of the Marshall–Lerner condition in Chapter 3. There you see that if the export supply elasticity is negative (that is, if the supply curve has a negative slope), then the import demand is inelastic. Figure C.3 shows the situation where the Canadian export supply of corn has a negative slope at the new equilibrium; therefore, the Canadian export supply elasticity is negative. Therefore, the Canadian import demand (for umbrellas) is inelastic. Note that both the original and the new equilibria are stable.

In this example the US is facing an inelastic demand for the good that it exports. When the improvement in umbrella technology causes its export supply function to shift out, the relative price of its exports falls. Because the Canadian demand for this good is inelastic, Canada now spends less on umbrellas. The US therefore has less revenue to buy corn.

This example illustrates the possibility that US welfare falls as a result of an improvement in technology in its export sector. In general, the change in technology might either increase or decrease US welfare.

C.4 Problem Set 4

See the instructor if you have trouble with Question 1.

Question 2

(a) In the absence of the target price policy, consumers and producers both face the same price. Here, there is no ambiguity about the meaning of "price". I can graph both supply and demand as a function of the price — because there is only one price. However, when we introduce the target price policy, there are two relevant prices — the price that consumers pay and the price that producers receive. These prices are not the same; they differ by the amount of the deficiency payment. It is convenient to continue to let the vertical axis represent the *consumer price*. With this convention, the demand curve is unchanged by the policy. However, whenever the market price (i.e. the price that consumers pay) is below the target price, p^*, the relevant price for producers is p^* (because that is the price that they receive). Therefore, because I have the consumer (i.e. "market") price on the vertical axis, and because the producer supply is determined by p^* whenever the market price is less than p^*, the "policy-distorted supply curve" is vertical at p^*, as shown in the left panel of Figure C.4.

The autarchic price, $\hat{p}^a$, is given by the intersection of this vertical line and the demand curve. The right panel shows the exports supply curve without the policy (the solid line). With the policy, the export supply curve is steeper below the target price, as the dashed line shows. The export supply function has a kink at the target price. The statement of the question assumes that the world price, p^w, is between the target price and the autarchic price under the policy; the figure reflects this assumption.

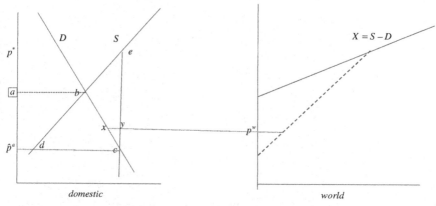

Figure C.4. The autarchic equilibrium in the absence of the target price policy is at point b in the left panel. With the target price, the supply function is vertical for prices below the target price, and is unchanged for higher prices. Therefore, the autarchic equilibrium in the presence of the target price policy is at point c. The target price policy causes the US export supply function to shift to the dashed line in the right panel, for prices below the target price; for higher prices, the US export supply function is unchanged.

The target price policy increases consumer surplus by the area $abc\hat{p}^a$ and it increases producer surplus by the area $abep^*$. The cost of the program is the area $p^*ec\hat{p}^a$, so the deadweight cost is the area bce.

The gains from trade under the policy is the triangle xyc; the area of this triangle equals the area of the "producer surplus" triangle corresponding the excess supply curve, shown in the right panel. Why is this area the correct measure of the gains from trade? When the country begins to trade at p^w, domestic consumers lose some consumer surplus. Producer welfare is unchanged. (Why?) However, the cost to the government (and therefore to taxpayers) decreases by the amount associated with the distorted excess supply curve.

(b) Figure C.5 reproduces the US export supply curve without the policy (the solid upward sloping line) and the export supply function with the policy — the upward sloping kinked curve. ROW excess demand, M^{ROW}, is the downward sloping curve. This excess demand curve intersects the two US excess supply curves — the supply curve without the policy and the supply curve with the

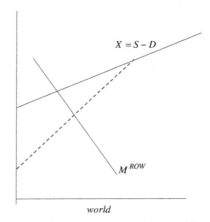

Figure C.5. The figure shows a downward sloping world import demand function. By shifting out the US export supply function, the target price policy causes the price of US exports to fall. The "producer surplus" (= the gains from trade) corresponding to the dashed export supply function is greater than the surplus corresponding to the solid export supply function: the policy increases the gains from trade, even though it lowers US welfare.

policy — at a positive quantity. This construction reflects the assumption that the US exports this commodity with or without the policy.

The target price policy shifts out the total US supply, so it shifts out the US excess supply, and it reduces the equilibrium price. The point of intersection between the ROW excess demand curve and the US excess supply curve without (respectively, with) the policy gives the equilibrium world price without (respectively, with) the policy.

(c) You need to compare the "producer surplus" (corresponding to the US excess supply curve) with and without the policy. The policy has two effects: (1) It shifts out the excess supply curve, and thus at a given world price increases the gains from trade. (2) Unless ROW demand is perfectly elastic, the policy also reduces the world price, which decreases the gains from trade.

These two effects cut in opposite directions, and the trick is to figure out which is larger. We often need to compare offsetting effects, so it is important to develop skills in approaching such problems. Frequently it helps to consider limiting cases, under which

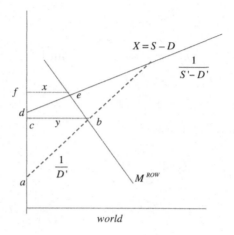

Figure C.6.

a particular effect is as large or as small as possible. The price effect is zero if price does not change, i.e. if ROW demand is flat (perfectly elastic). The price effect is as large as possible if ROW quantity does not change, i.e. its excess demand is completely inelastic (vertical). To get some insight into the answer, it is a good idea to check these two cases first. If you construct the figures corresponding to these two limiting cases, you should be able to convince yourself that in both cases the "producer surplus" corresponding to the export supply function (i.e. the US gains from trade) is larger with the target price policy than without it. These limiting cases should persuade you that (under the assumptions of the question) the target price policy increases the US gains from trade.

To confirm this conjecture, consider Figure C.6, which shows a downward sloping world excess demand and the two US export supply functions, with and without the target price policy. The slope the US exports supply is $\frac{1}{S'-D'}$ without the policy, and $\frac{1}{D'}$ with the policy, where S' and $-D'$ are the (positive) slopes of the US supply and demand functions in the linear model.

The triangle abc measures the gains from trade with the policy, and def measures the gains from trade without the policy. I want to show that area abc > area def. Define x = US exports without policy and y= US exports with the policy. Refer to Figure C.6.

Use the following facts:

$$y > x \implies \frac{y^2}{x^2} > 1 \quad \text{and}$$

$$1 > \frac{-D'}{S' - D'}.$$

These two inequalities imply

$$\frac{y^2}{x^2} > \frac{-D'}{S' - D'} \implies$$

$$abc = \frac{-y^2}{2D'} > \frac{x^2}{2(S' - D')} = def.$$

In establishing the first equality in the last expression I used

$$\frac{-y^2}{2D'} = \frac{y}{2}\frac{\text{rise}}{\text{run}}y$$

$$= \frac{y}{2}\frac{\text{rise}}{x_t}x_t = \frac{1}{2}(\text{run})(\text{rise})$$

$$= \frac{1}{2}(\text{base})(\text{height}) = abc.$$

I have repeatedly used the formula for the area of a triangle. The conclusions can be overturned under more general functional forms.

Under the assumption that the country is an exporter with or without the policy, trade is "more valuable" to society in the presence of the target price policy — i.e. the gains from trade are higher. Trade reduces the social cost of the distortion created by the target price policy.

(d) The answer to (c) does not imply that domestic welfare is higher with the target price policy. The policy reduces domestic welfare with or without trade. You should be able to show graphically the deadweight loss of the policy with and without trade. Regardless of whether the country trades, its welfare is higher without the policy. The gains from trade measure the CHANGE in welfare. The policy, which introduces a distortion, lowers welfare with or without trade, but it lowers welfare more without trade than with trade, and therefore increases the gains from trade.

(e) The answer changes. To see how it changes, pick the simplest case, where ROW demand is perfectly elastic. Fix the world price between the autarchic US prices with and without the policy. At this world price, the US exports the good with the policy, and it imports the good without the policy. In the two cases, the gains from trade equal the "producer surplus" associated with the excess supply curve (when the US is an exporter) and the "consumer surplus" associated with the import demand curve (when the US is an importer. By raising or lowering the world price, you should be able to convince yourself that the gains from trade might be higher in either of the two scenarios (with or without the policy).

Question 3
There are two commodities, food and cloth. Food is the numeraire. The relative world price of cloth is p. Home, a small country, imports food.

(a) Home uses (only) an *ad valorem* import tariff of τ. The relative price of cloth for domestic consumers is $\underline{\frac{p}{1+\tau}}$ and the relative price for producers is $\underline{\frac{p}{1+\tau}}$.

(b) Home uses an *ad valorem* export subsidy of s, The relative price of cloth for domestic consumers is. $\underline{p(1+s)}$ and the relative price of cloth for domestic producers is $\underline{p(1+s)}$.

(c) Home uses (only) an *ad valorem* production tax of t on cloth. The relative price of cloth for consumers is $\underline{p}$ and the relative price of cloth for producers is $\underline{p(1-t)}$.

(d) How would your answer to part (a) have changed if Home is a large country rather than a small country? [The price would have been greater than $\frac{p}{1+\tau}$. The use of the tariff improves the term of trade, i.e. it increases p.]

Question 4
(a) The tangent to the PPF at point A is the autarchic relative price.

(b) The relation between the consumer and producer relative prices is

$$p^{pt} = (1-t)p^{ct},$$

$$p^{pt} < p^a < p^{ct}.$$

Point B should lie on the PPF above A, and the indifference curve through point B should cut the PPF from above; the indifference curve is not tangent to the PPF.

(c) Denote the consumer tax as τ and the equilibrium price received by producers as p. In order for producers and consumers to face the same prices as under the production tax, require:

$$(1+\tau)\,p = p^{ct}$$

$$p = p^{pt} = (1-t)\,p^{ct}.$$

These equalities imply

$$\tau = \frac{t}{1-t} > 0,$$

because $t < 1$. (Production of cloth falls to 0 unless producers receive a positive price.)

(d) The country enjoys the "standard gains from trade" that occur because trade makes it possible to separate production and consumption. However, trade can either exacerbate or ameliorate the distortion. The tax on cloth causes cloth production to be too low, relative to the first best level. If trade causes a further reduction in cloth production, i.e. if the country becomes a cloth importer under trade, $(p^w < p^{ct})$ then trade *might* lower the country's welfare. If the country becomes a cloth exporter, trade definitely increases welfare.

Simplify notation by writing $p^{ct} = p$, denote C, F by cloth and food production, and C^{con} as cloth consumption The value of production plus tax revenue in autarky is

$$y = (1-t)pC + F + tpC = pC + F \Longrightarrow$$

$$dy = dpC + pdC + dF.$$

Indirect utility is $V(y,p)$ and the first approximation (evaluated at the initial price) of the change in utility due to a change in price, resulting from trade (or anything else) is

$$\frac{dV}{V_y} = dy + \frac{V_p}{V_y}dp$$

$$= dpC + pdC + dF - C^{\text{con}}dp$$

$$= pdC + dF \quad (1)$$

$$= \left(p + \frac{dF}{dC}\right)dC$$

$$= (p - (1 - t)\,p)\,dC \quad (2)$$

$$= tpdC,$$

where line (1) follows from the fact that in autarchy production equals consumption, and line (2) follows from the tangency condition that determines production: $-(1 - t)p = \frac{dF}{dC}$.

Therefore, for a small change in price, welfare falls if cloth production falls after trade. Cloth production falls if and only if the producer price falls, i.e. iff $p^w < p$.

C.5 Problem Set 5

(1) The solid downward sloping curve in Figure C.7 is the domestic demand curve. A point on this curve equals the private marginal utility of consumption. The dashed curve that is shifted γ units below the solid curve is the social marginal utility of consumption, equal to the private marginal utility minus the social cost γ. In autarky, without regulation, the price is at $\bar{p}$ (the intersection of Supply and Demand, the two solid lines) and consumption and production occur at point x. At that point, the social marginal value of consumption $\bar{p} - \gamma$, is less than the marginal cost of production, $\bar{p}$. The optimal level of consumption under autarky, at point b, can be achieved with either a consumption or a production tax of γ. In autarchy, consumption = production, so it doesn't matter which group directly pays the tax. The consumer price is $p^a + \gamma$ and the producer price is p^a, regardless whether a production or consumption tax is used.

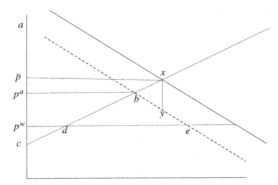

Figure C.7. The solid lines show the domestic supply (upward sloping) and demand (downward sloping) functions in the partial equilibrium setting. The dashed downward sloping curve shows the social marginal utility of consumption, including the environmental cost.

This result illustrates the fact that, in a closed economy (with competitive markets), it does not matter which group (consumers or producers) has the statutory obligation to pay the tax; see Section 3.7 of Chapter 3.

Now consider trade, and suppose that the country is an importer, so the world price p^w is below the autarkic price. With trade, production does not equal consumption. The "distortion" arises from consumption, so the Principle of Targeting implies that consumption should be targeted; consumers rather than producers should be taxed. Domestic producers should face the world price, causing them to produce at point d and consumers should face a consumption tax of γ, so that they pay $p^w + \gamma$, causing consumption to occur at point e.[1]

Confirm that the policy recommendation does not change if the country is an exporter.

For a small country that trades, the price that consumers face is independent of a tax/subsidy applied to domestic producers. When only producers are taxed/subsidized, consumers continue to pay the

---

[1]When I say that production occurs at point "d" I really mean, of course, that production occurs at the horizontal coordinate of the point "d". This is an example of slightly sloppy speech that we frequently use in order to keep the language reasonably simple.

world price. Thus, a tax/subsidy for producers does not affect the level of consumption — which is what the policymaker wants to influence. Therefore, in the partial equilibrium setting (where income and all other prices are held constant), a producer tax is completely ineffective in remedying the distortion. The optimal producer tax is therefore 0.

(2) With price (absent regulation) at $\bar{p}$, the consumer + producer surplus is the larger triangle (using the solid demand function). However, the damage from the externality equals the area between the demand function and the social marginal benefit of consumption. That area equals γ times the level of consumption. Subtracting damages from the consumer + producer triangle leaves the triangle abc minus the triangle bxy.

(3) If the country exports the commodity, i.e. the world price is above the autarkic price, it obtains the usual gains from trade. Trade also reduces the environmental cost because consumption falls as the domestic price rises (when the country begins to trade).

(4) From part 3 you know that a *sufficient* condition for the country to gain from trade is for the world price to be higher than the autarchic price. Therefore, a *necessary* condition for the country to be made worse off from trade is for the world price to be below the autarchic price. Consider the case where, when the country begins to trade, $p^w < \bar{p}$. In moving from autarchy to free trade, the increase in consumer + producer surplus is

$$\Delta_1 \left(p^w, \bar{p}\right) = \int_{p^w}^{\bar{p}} \left(D(p) - S\left(p\right)\right) dp.$$

(If $p^w < \bar{p}$, the country imports the good, so $D - S > 0$. If $p^w > \bar{p}$, the country exports the good, so $D - S < 0$. In both cases, $\Delta_1 \left(p^w, \bar{p}\right)$ gives the increase in consumer + producer surplus.) This integral is the area between the demand and the supply curves, between the two prices. Note that

$$\frac{d\Delta_1 \left(p^w, \bar{p}\right)}{dp^w} = - \left(\left(D(p^w) - S\left(p^w\right)\right)\right), \tag{C.5}$$

$$\frac{d^2\Delta_1 \left(p^w, \bar{p}\right)}{d\left(p^w\right)^2} = - \left(\left(D'(p^w) - S'\left(p^w\right)\right)\right) > 0. \tag{C.6}$$

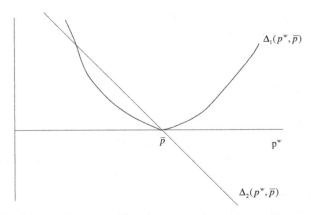

Figure C.8. The U-shaped curve is the graph of the "standard" gains from trade, equal to the change in the sum of producer and consumer surplus. The downward sloping line is the graph of the change in the damage due to the environmental externality.

The inequality holds because the slope of demand is negative and the slope of supply is positive. Therefore, $\Delta_1\left(p^w,\bar{p}\right)$ is convex in p^w and reaches its minimum (where $\Delta_1\left(p^w,\bar{p}\right)=0$) at $p^w=\bar{p}$ as shown in Figure C.8.

The increase in environmental cost due to trade is γ times the increase in consumption

$$\Delta_2\left(p^w,\bar{p}\right)=\gamma\left(D\left(p^w\right)-D\left(\bar{p}\right)\right)\Rightarrow \qquad\qquad \text{(C.7)}$$

$$\frac{d\Delta_2}{dp^w}=\gamma D'\left(p^w\right)<0,$$

so $\Delta_2\left(p^w,\bar{p}\right)=0$ at $p^w=\bar{p}$ and is decreasing in p^w, as shown in Figure C.8. (The figure shows the case where demand is linear, so $\Delta_2\left(p^w,\bar{p}\right)$ is a linear function of p^w. Convince yourself that the following argument does not depend on this linearity assumption.) The gain from trade is $\Delta_1\left(p^w,\bar{p}\right)-\Delta_2\left(p^w,\bar{p}\right)$. This figure shows that if p^w is slightly less than $\bar{p}$ then the increase in environmental damages is greater than the increase in consumer+producer surplus; in this case, trade reduces welfare. If $p^w>\bar{p}$, trade lowers environmental costs and increases the sum of consumer and producer surplus, so trade definitely increases welfare.

(5) We noted above that the optimal ("first best policy") policy is a consumption tax. A tariff of the right magnitude can nevertheless increase welfare. The "optimal tariff" is the optimal level of the tariff — which in this model is not zero. Sometimes we refer to such a policy as a "second best optimal", to emphasize that even though the *level* of the tariff is optimal, there are better types of policies than the tariff.

A tariff increases domestic price and therefore increases both the price that consumers pay and the price that producers receive. The tariff creates a production distortion, in the process of reducing the consumption distortion arising from the environmental externality. What is this production distortion?

The country obtains goods from both domestic production and from trade (imports). For a small country, the marginal cost of obtaining a unit of the good from the world market is the world price. The marginal cost of obtaining a unit of the good from domestic production is the marginal domestic production cost, which equals the (vertical coordinate corresponding to the) point on the supply curve. The optimal way to achieve *any* level of domestic consumption is to produce up to the point where domestic marginal production costs equals the world price. This production point occurs only when domestic producers face the world price. A tariff, however, increases the price that domestic producers face, and therefore causes them to produce above the optimal level.

In short, the tariff reduces the consumption distortion (arising from the environmental externality) but it does so at a cost of creating a (secondary) production distortion. The tariff is an expensive (in terms of the secondary distortion) way to correct the consumption distortion. Therefore, if society is forced to use the tariff, the optimal tariff is lower than γ.

(6) You are asked to find the optimal tariff both graphically and algebraically. Here is how to proceed graphically. The left panel in Figure C.9 shows the demand and supply functions, D and S, and the social marginal benefit of consumption, $D^{-1}(p) - \gamma$. The vertical distance between this curve and the demand curve is the constant unit externality cost, γ. The right panel shows the import demand function, $M = D - S$, and the social marginal benefit of imports,

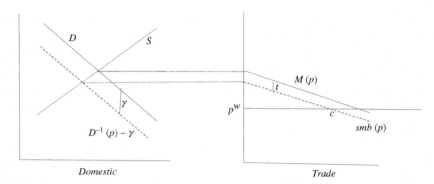

Figure C.9.   The solid curves in the left panel show domestic supply and demand. The dashed curve is the social marginal benefit of consumption (taking into account the environmental cost of consumption). The solid curve in the right panel is the import demand function. The dashed curve in the right panel is the social marginal benefit of imports.

$smb\,(p) = D^{-1}\,(p) - \gamma - S\,(p)$. The horizontal lines between the two panels make it easy to see the intercepts of the curves in the right panel (the prices at which $M\,(p) = 0$ or $smb\,(p) = 0$). Notice that the vertical difference between these two curves — equal to the vertical difference between their intercepts — is strictly less than γ. Denote this vertical difference as t.

An earlier problem set showed that you can calculate the gains from trade by calculating the "consumer surplus" corresponding to the curve $M(p)$. You can think of $M(p)$ as representing the private marginal benefit of imports. In the problem here, the social marginal benefit of imports is less than the private marginal benefit. The optimal level of imports occurs where the social marginal benefit equals the world price. This occurs at point c in the right panel. In order to induce (by means of a tariff) the country to import at the level point c, it must face the tariff t, which we noted above is less than γ.

Now find the optimal tariff using calculus, when the fixed world price is p^w. With a unit tariff, the domestic price is $p = p^w + t$. With the domestic price p, the increase in the sum of producer plus consumer surplus is $\Delta_1\,(p, \bar{p})$ and the increase in environmental cost is $\Delta_2\,(p, \bar{p})$. (Both of these functions are defined above.) For a tariff of

t, tariff revenues equal $t\left(D\left(p\right)-S\left(p\right)\right)$. Thus, total welfare increase (relative to autarchy), as a function of the tariff, is

$$W\left(t\right)=\Delta_1\left(p,\bar{p}\right)-\Delta_2\left(p,\bar{p}\right)+t\left(D\left(p\right)-S\left(p\right)\right).$$

Remember, world price is fixed. Using the derivatives from part 4 we have

$$\frac{dW}{dt}=-\left(\left(D(p)-S\left(p\right)\right)\right)-\gamma D'\left(p\right)$$
$$+\left(D\left(p\right)-S\left(p\right)\right)+t\left(D'\left(p\right)-S'\left(p\right)\right)$$
$$=-\gamma D'\left(p\right)+t\left(D'\left(p\right)-S'\left(p\right)\right).$$

Setting $\frac{dW}{dt}=0$ we have the necessary condition

$$t=\frac{D'\left(p^w+t\right)}{D'\left(p^w+t\right)-S'\left(p^w+t\right)}\gamma.$$

For linear demand and supply, and $D'=-d$ and $S'=s$, we have

$$t=\frac{-d}{-d-s}\gamma=\frac{d}{d+s}\gamma<\gamma.$$

(7) The large importing country is analogous to a monopsonist. A monopolist can increase the price of the good it sells by reducing its supply; a monopsonist can reduce the price of a good that it buys by reducing its demand. Replace the perfectly elastic ROW excess supply function in Figure C.9 by an upward sloping ROW export supply curve. Draw the marginal to this curve. (This curve is known as the "marginal outlay" curve in industrial organization.) The optimal tariff for the large importing country equates the marginal outlay curve with the social marginal benefit of imports. Monopsony power increases the incentive to restrict imports and therefore leads to a larger tariff.

(8) This change decreases the optimal tariff, because now the tariff provides less of a "cure" for the environmental externality. Decreased domestic consumption, resulting from the tariff, causes a fall in world price and an increase in consumption abroad, which results in a domestic environmental cost to home. Finding the optimal tariff in this setting using graphical methods would

be challenging, but it remains straightforward using calculus. To proceed, you need to add (to the welfare function W above) a cost that measures damages to Home resulting from ROW consumption.

C.6 Problem Set 6

Some of the figures that are needed to provide the graphical arguments look complicated, making the arguments appear difficult. This complication is a disadvantage of graphical arguments, relative to mathematical arguments. For the latter, the sequential nature of the proof is apparent: one thing comes before another. In contrast, with a graph, "everything appears at the same time". One way to overcome this difficulty is to use lots of graphs, so that the reader can see the development of the argument. But there is no substitute for "thinking with a pencil". As students read the explanation, they should follow along by drawing the figure being described.

The answer key first addresses all five questions for Case I (the constraint on food consumption) and then for Case II (the import constraint).

Case I (Constraint on food consumption)

(1) Use the PPF, the BOP constraint, and the IEP to represent an unregulated equilibrium with trade, and then choose a level of F^* lower than the equilibrium unregulated consumption level.

(2) The optimal policy is a consumption tax/subsidy. The production point remains fixed at the level shown in your figure from Question 1. The consumption tax/subsidy causes the IEP to move toward the cloth axis. The optimal policy causes the IEP to intersect the BOP constraint at the level F^*. Denote this intersection point as A. Draw an indifference curve through A. The absolute value of the tangent of this indifference curve, p^d, equals the relative consumer price under the tax/subsidy. The *ad valorem* consumption tax on food, t, solves

$$p^d = \frac{p^w}{1+t}.$$

Imposition of the constraint leads to a lower level of utility compared to free trade: there are points on the balance of payments constraint, above point A, that result in higher utility. Note that the consumption tax does not alter the production point nor the BOP constraint.

(3) and (4) First consider the production policy. If a production tax/subsidy is used, the consumer price equals the world price, so consumption must be on the original $IEP(p^w)$ from your figure in question 1. Denote as point B the intersection of $IEP(p^w)$ and the horizontal line at the constraint F^*. Point B is the consumption point when the constraint is achieved using a production policy. The only way to use the production policy to reduce consumption to F^* is by reducing income sufficiently. Draw a BOP (with slope give by p^w, because this is a small country) that intersects point B. There are two possibilities. (i) If this new BOP intersects the PPF, it will do so nearer the food axis (compared to the unregulated production point). Denote this intersection as C. The tangent to the PPF at C is the relative producer price that leads to a sufficiently distorted production level and a correspondingly small level of income that consumption takes place at B. (ii) If the new BOP intersects the food axis below the PPF,[2] then a production tax/subsidy on its own is unable to reduce income by enough to support consumption at B. An additional policy, e.g. a tax on factors that induces the economy to become specialized in food at a point below the PPF would be needed. (A crazy policy indeed!)

Under the production tax/subsidy, the consumption point is fixed at B. Growth has no effect on this point, and therefore has no effect on welfare. Growth changes the level of the policy that supports consumption at B, but does not change welfare.

Now consider the trade policy. Figure C.10 shows the PPF and the optimal (constrained) production point at A'. The BOP constraint intersects the constraint line F^* at point A, the highest feasible level of consumption of cloth, subject to the constraint that consumption of food does not exceed F^*. Any point to the right of A on the horizontal line at F^* and on a BOP line (i.e. a line with slope p^w) lies strictly outside the production possibility frontier, and therefore is not feasible. Thus, a tariff that supports the constraint

---

[2]This outcome can occur if F^* lies below the food intercept of the PPF.

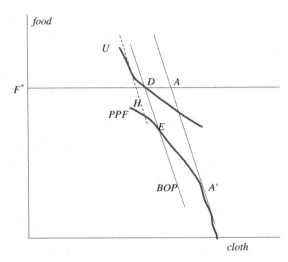

Figure C.10. If the target is achieved using the consumption tax, production remains at the (unconstrained) point A' and consumption occurs at point A. If the target is achieved using a tariff, production moves to point E and consumption to point D. If the target is achieved using a tariff, and growth lowers welfare, then consumption occurs to the left of point D, and production occurs along the BOP constraint but above the original PPF, e.g. at point H.

must result in consumption on the horizontal line at F^* at a point to the left of A, leading to a lower level of welfare than at point A. To avoid clutter, the figure does not show the IEPs corresponding to different domestic prices, but students should add these.

A tariff increases the consumer relative price of food (causing the IEP to move toward the cloth axis) and causes the production point to move up the PPF toward the food axis. Denote point D as the consumption point and E as the production point when the constraint is achieved by means of a tariff. Here is what you know about these points: Point D lies on the horizontal line through F^* to the left of point A; the tangent of the indifference curve through D has slope equal to the domestic relative price, $\frac{p^w}{1+\tau}$, where τ is the tariff; the BOP constraint through D, the line with slope p^w (because the small country's policy does not change the world price) intersects the PPF at point E; the tangent at E equals the domestic relative price, $\frac{p^w}{1+\tau}$. The tangent to the indifference curve at point D has the same slope as the tangent to the PPF at point E.

We know that the optimal way to satisfy the constraint is to change only consumer prices. The tariff changes both producer and consumer prices. It lowers food consumption (to achieve the constraint) by means of a substitution effect and an income effect. The income effect occurs because the tariff moves the production point away from the free trade level, thereby decreasing the value of national income. The optimal way to achieve the constraint is by changing consumer prices "a lot" and changing producer prices not at all. When we achieve the constraint by means of a tariff we change the consumer prices by less, (compared to the use of the optimal consumption tax/subsidy). Therefore, the IEP under the consumption tax lies below the IEP under the tariff. (These IEPs are not shown.) The tariff forces the income effect to do "too much work" in reducing food consumption, and forces the substitution effect to do "too little work" in reducing consumption.

Now construct an example where growth is immizerizing. A reduction in welfare, given that the constraint $F \leq F^*$ remains binding, requires that consumption move to the left on the horizontal line at F^*. Figure C.10 shows the (post-growth) dashed BOP that intersects this horizontal line at a point to the left of D. Given that there has been growth, the new production point must occur on this new BOP constraint, and (to reflect the fact that the growth shifts out the PPF) it must lie above the original PPF, e.g. at a point such as H. Point H lies to the left of point E, which lies to the left of the first-best level A'. In this example, growth exacerbates the production distortion that leads to too low a level of cloth production.

The IEP associated with the post-growth consumption level lies above the IEP associated with the pre-growth consumption level (D), so growth must have led to a *reduction* of the tariff. The tangent on the post-growth PPF at point H is flatter than the tangent at point E. In summary, I began with the observation that in order for growth to lower welfare under a tariff, given the constraint, consumption must move to the left from D. Then I recognized that in order for this to occur, the IEP must shift up, which means that growth must have caused the tariff to decrease. Despite this fact, growth has exacerbated the production distortion, causing cloth production to fall (from E to H).

(5) We have used a general equilibrium setting to examine the effects of growth under the different types of policies (given the same constraint). A partial equilibrium (PE) model ignores the fact that income changes (possibly it decreases) when the production possibility frontier shifts out. It is interesting to see how far you can get with a PE model. Draw a supply and demand curve with a consumption constraint that is violated under free trade. Show:

(i) Welfare (producer + consumer surplus plus tax or tariff revenue) is higher when the constraint is achieved using a consumer tax rather than a tariff. The two policies lead to the same level of consumption, but the tariff creates a production distortion, replacing relatively low-cost imports with the more expensive domestically produced good.

(ii) A production tax/subsidy is completely ineffective in reaching the target.

(iii) Growth can lead to lower welfare, but growth does not change the equilibrium tariff– which depends only on the demand function, the world price, and the constraint (none of which change with growth). Figure C.11 illustrates the last possibility. The initial supply and demand curves are D and S, and the tariff needed to achieve the constraint is shown as t. Suppose that growth causes the supply curve to shift to S', so that imports are eliminated in equilibrium. There is no change in consumer surplus since neither the level of consumption (F^*) nor the demand curve have changed. Producer surplus has increased by the small area aeb but tariff receipts have fallen by $abcd$, so social welfare (the sum of producer and consumer surplus and tax revenue) has fallen. Growth causes greater substitution away from low priced imports toward high cost domestic production.

Case II: Constraint of imports

(1) Once again, construct a free trade equilibrium, and identify the production and consumption levels and the level of imports, M. Choose the level of constraint so that $M > M^*$. Thus, the

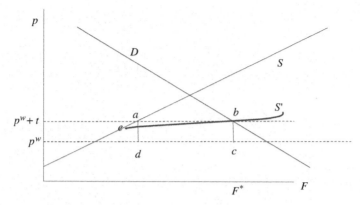

Figure C.11. The tariff t supports consumption at F*, satisfying the constraint, but also increasing domestic production, creating a production distortion. If growth causes domestic marginal costs to fall to S', domestic production satisfies all of domestic demand. Growth increases producer surplus by the small triangle abe, but it eliminates tariff revenue (formerly the rectangle abcd). Growth reduces welfare in this example, when the constraint is achieved using a tariff.

constraint is violated in the absence of regulation. Figure C.12 provides an example. Absent regulation, production occurs at A' and consumption at B'. The point C' completes the trade triangle, with imports equal to the length of the segment $B'C' > M^*$.

(2) With a tariff, production moves to A and consumption to B, with imports equal to the length of $BC = M^*$.

(3) Show that either a production or a consumption policy which satisfies the constraint $M \leq M^*$ leads to a lower level of utility (relative to the level under the tariff). I will sketch the argument for the case of a production policy. Without a consumption tax/subsidy, consumers continue to face price p^w, so they consume at a point on $IEP(p^w)$. We can slide the trade triangle ABC up the PPF, with point A remaining on the PPF. At some point, the vertex B of this (moving) triangle hits $IEP(p^w)$. Pick the producer tax/subsidy that causes producer relative price to equal the tangent to the PPF at the (new) vertex A of the shifted trade triangle. This tax leads to consumption on the original IEP, the same level of imports as under the tariff, and a lower level of income An analogous argument holds for the case of a consumption policy.

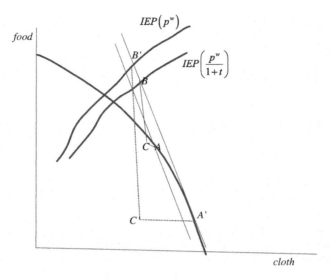

Figure C.12.

(4) If the constraint $M \leq M^*$ is achieved using a production policy, growth cannot be immizerizing. With a fixed consumer price, consumption occurs on $IEP(p^w)$. If growth were to reduce welfare, given that consumer prices remain constant and the level of imports remains fixed at M^*, the consumption point would have to move down $IEP(p^w)$. That would require that the vertex A of the trade triangle has moved southeast, i.e. that it lies below the pre-growth PPF. It would then lie below the post-growth PPF. However, the production policy, which changes only producer relative prices, cannot cause production to lie inside the PPF.

However, growth can be immizerizing if the import constraint is achieved using a consumption tax/subsidy. To achieve the import constraint given that production remains at point A' in Figure C.12, the IEP must shift toward the cloth axis. Here, the policy taxes food consumption. Students should modify Figure C.12 to illustrate this change. To construct an example where growth leads to lower welfare when the income constraint is achieved using a consumption policy, shift the trade triangle ABC southeast, so that the (shifted) vertex B lies below the pre-growth indifference curve, and the (shifted) vertex

A lies outside the pre-growth PPF. This configuration is consistent with the same (pre-growth) level of imports, a lower level of welfare, and production outside the pre-growth PPF (to reflect the fact that growth has shifted out the PPF).

Intuition: The "target" (or constraint) in this problem involves trade. Given that world price is fixed, and given the requirement that trade balance, constraining imports is equivalent to constraining exports. The Principle of Targeting says that we should use a trade policy to achieve a trade target. Imports involve both production and consumption. It is possible to alter imports by altering only production or consumption (i.e. using a consumption or a production policy) but it is optimal to meet the target by altering both production and consumption. It is optimal to achieve the constraint by "distorting" both consumption and production, rather than requiring one or the other to bear the entire brunt.

Why can growth be immizerizing with one type of policy but not the other? When the target is reached using a production policy, the reduction of imports is achieved by reducing income (measured at world prices). For growth to reduce welfare still further, it would be necessary for growth to reduce income (measured at world prices). However, such a reduction in income is not consistent with maintaining the same level of imports and also producing on the higher post-growth PPF. In contrast, when a consumption policy is used to achieve the target, national income (measured at world prices) is not changed, but a consumption distortion is introduced. Growth may require an increase in the consumption distortion in order to maintain the constraint. This increase in the distortion can lead to a fall in welfare, even though income (measure in world prices) rises.

(5) Figure C.13 shows a partial equilibrium model. With the world price p^w, imports equal the length of the line segment ae, which we assume violates the import constraint. The tariff t results in consumption at point f and production at c, with imports equal to the length of the line segment $cf = M^*$, the constrained level of imports. The reduction in consumption and the increase in

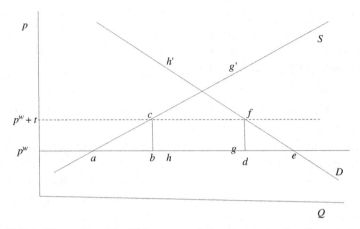

Figure C.13.   The optimal tariff increases domestic production from point a to c and reduces consumption from point e to f, satisfying the constraint on imports. This constraint can also be satisfied either by subsidizing domestic production or taxing domestic consumption, but at a higher welfare costs, compared to the tariff. However, in this partial equilibrium setting, growth is never immizerizing under either a production subsidy or a consumption tax, because there is no income effect in the partial equilibrium setting. Growth always increases welfare when the constraint is satisfied using a tariff.

production leads to a net loss in consumer + producer surplus of the area $aefc$. However, the tariff generates tariff revenue of $bdfc$, for a net welfare loss of the sum of the areas of the two triangles abc and def.

A consumption policy leaves production at point a. To reduce imports to M^* there must be a substantial reduction in consumption, e.g. to point h'. The reduction in consumer surplus minus the tax revenue generated by the consumption tax is the triangle heh'. If growth shifts down the supply = marginal cost curve only to the right of point a, it has no effect on the equilibrium under the consumption policy. However, if growth shifts down the supply curve to the left of point a, it shifts the consumption point to the right, increasing welfare. Growth is never immizerizing.

A production policy leaves consumption at point e. To increase domestic production by enough to satisfy the import constraint, the production point must increase to a point such as g'. Domestic production increases by the length of ag and imports decrease by an equal amount. This policy replaces cheap imports by expensive domestic production and results in a welfare loss (relative to the free trade level) of agg'. Growth (here, shifting down the supply $=$ marginal cost curve) reduces this welfare loss, so when the trade constraint is achieve using a production subsidy, growth is always beneficial; it cannot be immizerizing.

Index